REVISE AQA GCSE (9–1)
German
REVISION GUIDE

Series Consultant: Harry Smith

Author: Harriette Lanzer

Also available to support your revision:

Revise GCSE Study Skills Guide   9781447967071

The **Revise GCSE Study Skills Guide** is full of tried-and-trusted hints and tips for how to learn more effectively. It gives you techniques to help you achieve your best – throughout your GCSE studies and beyond!

Revise GCSE Revision Planner   9781447967828

The **Revise GCSE Revision Planner** helps you to plan and organise your time, step-by-step, throughout your GCSE revision. Use this book and wall chart to mastermind your revision.

Difficulty scale

The scale next to each exam-style question tells you how difficult it is.

Some questions cover a range of difficulties.   The more of the scale that is shaded, the harder the question is.

Some questions are Foundation level.

Some questions are Higher level.

Some questions are applicable to both levels.

For the full range of Pearson revision titles across KS2, KS3, GCSE, Functional Skills, AS/A Level and BTEC visit: www.pearsonschools.co.uk/revise

Contents

AUDIO

Audio files for the listening exercises in this book can be accessed by using the QR codes or hotlinks throughout the book, or going to www.pearsonschools.co.uk/mflrevisionaudio

Listen to the recording

A small bit of small print:
AQA publishes Sample Assessment Material and the Specification on its website. This is the official content and this book should be used in conjunction with it. The questions in Now try this have been written to help you practise every topic in the book. Remember: the real exam questions may not look like this.

Physical descriptions

You will need to describe people in the photo task of the Speaking exam, so make sure you have lots of this handy vocabulary at your fingertips!

Wie sieht er / sie aus?

Er / Sie hat ... Haare.   He / She has ... hair.

blonde   graue

braune   schwarze

dunkle / helle   dark / light
glatte / lockige   straight / curly
kurze / lange   short / long

Sie hat (blaue) Augen.   She has (blue) eyes.
Er trägt eine Brille.   He is wearing glasses.
Sie trägt große   She is wearing / wears
  Ohrringe.   big earrings.
Er hat einen Bart /   He has a beard /
  Schnurrbart.   moustache.
Sie hat ein rundes /   She has a round /
  hübsches Gesicht.   pretty face.
Er hat eine Glatze.   He is bald.

Comparing things

Grammar page 90

- For regular comparatives add -er to the adjective:

attraktiv ➡ attraktiver

dick(er)	fat(ter)
hässlich(er)	ugly (uglier)
hübsch(er)	pretty (prettier)
schlank(er)	slim(mer)
schön(er)	(more) beautiful

- These adjectives are irregular and many of them add an umlaut to their vowel:

alt ➡ älter (old / older)
groß ➡ größer (big / bigger)
gut ➡ besser (good / better)
hoch ➡ höher (high / higher)
jung ➡ jünger (young / younger)

- Use als to compare:

Ich bin älter als du. I am older than you.

Worked example

READING

Wanted

Read this article from a local German newspaper.

> Die Polizei sucht dringend einen gefährlichen Typ. Können Sie uns helfen, ihn zu finden? Der Jugendliche ist 17–18 Jahre alt mit langen, dunkelbraunen und ziemlich lockigen Haaren. Er hat nur wenige Zähne und hat eine bunte Tätowierung am rechten Arm. Er trägt eine blaue Jeans und ein schwarzes T-Shirt. Man hat ihn zum letzten Mal an der Bank in der Hauptstraße gesehen. Er hatte einen schwarzen Koffer in der Hand. Bitte rufen Sie sofort die Polizei an, falls Sie ihn sehen. Sprechen Sie ihn nicht an.

Gender gives you a clue here – the police are looking for **einen Typ** (masculine accusative) and **der Jugendliche** (masculine nominative) – so the answer cannot be **A**.

Which statement is true, **A** or **B**?

A	The suspect is female.
B	The suspect is male.

☐ B   **(1 mark)**

Exam alert

Check whether each statement is true or false, when compared against the text. Then write the letter of the correct statement in the grid. Repeat this process throughout the entire text and for every statement.

Now try this

READING

Look at the article in the worked example above. Which **three** other statements are true? Write the correct letters in the boxes.

☐ ☐ ☐   **(3 marks)**

C	The suspect hasn't got much hair.
D	The suspect hasn't got many teeth.
E	The suspect is in the bank now.
F	The suspect was last seen at a bank.
G	People shouldn't speak to the suspect.
H	The suspect wasn't carrying anything.

Character descriptions

To talk about character, you need to be confident with the verb sein and know plenty of adjectives to go with it!

Charakterbeschreibung

Ich bin ...	I am ...
altmodisch	old-fashioned
blöd	silly
böse	angry / cross
egoistisch	selfish
ehrlich	honest
ernst	serious
frech	cheeky
freundlich	friendly
gemein	mean / nasty
großartig	great
hilfsbereit	helpful
komisch	funny
lebhaft	lively
lieb	likeable / nice
nervig	annoying
nett	nice
schüchtern	shy
sympathisch	nice
vernünftig	reasonable

The verb sein (to be)

ich	bin	I am
du	bist	you are
er / sie / es	ist	he / she / it is
wir	sind	we are
ihr	seid	you are
Sie / sie	sind	you / they are

Imperfect tense
ich war (I was)
du warst (you were)
er / sie war (he / she was)
wir / sie waren (we / they were)

Eva ist intelligent, aber faul.
Eva is clever but lazy.

You may well need to distinguish between past and present characteristics:
Obwohl er heute frech ist, war er als Kind sehr schüchtern. Although he **is** cheeky today, he **was** very shy as a child.

Worked example

Characteristics
You are talking to your German exchange partner, Emil, and discussing friends.
Write in **English** Emil's opinion and the reason for it in the grid below.

Listen to the recording

Opinion	funny	(1 mark)
Reason	have a laugh with him	(1 mark)

– Thomas finde ich sehr lustig, denn mit ihm kann man immer gut lachen und das ist super.

Aiming higher

Give your work an edge by including one or two of these Higher-level adjectives in your writing-speaking.

angeberisch	pretentious
ausgeglichen	well-balanced
deprimiert	depressed
eingebildet	conceited
großzügig	generous
selbstbewusst	self-confident
verrückt	mad / crazy
zuverlässig	reliable

Listen for the key adjective – lustig. If you are not sure what it means, listen to the reason, which may help you identify the characteristic.

Now try this

Listen to the recording

Now listen to **three** more descriptions of friends and note the opinion and the reason given for each one.

1	Opinion	
	Reason	

(2 marks)

2	Opinion	
	Reason	

(2 marks)

3	Opinion	
	Reason	

(2 marks)

Childhood

Use different pronouns with the matching verb ending to add variety to your work.

Die Kindheit

Ich bin in (Wien) geboren.
I was born in (Vienna).
Er hatte oft Ärger in der Schule.
He was often in trouble at school.
Sie war ein stures Kind.
She was a stubborn child.
Wir durften nicht alleine zur Schule gehen.
We weren't allowed to go to school on our own.
Ich musste keine Hausaufgaben machen.
I didn't have to do any homework.
Mit acht Jahren konnte ich (schwimmen).
At eight years old I could (swim).
Er wollte (Feuerwehrmann) werden.
He wanted to be (a fireman).

Pronouns

Grammar page 91

Pronouns = he, him, their, her, your, our

nominative	accusative	dative
ich	mich	mir
du	dich	dir
er	ihn	ihm
sie	sie	ihr
es	es	ihm
wir	uns	uns
ihr	euch	euch
Sie / sie	Sie / sie	Ihnen / ihnen

Sie war immer gut gelaunt.
She was always in a good mood.
Hast du mich gesehen?   Did you see me?

Worked example

Look at the photo and be prepared to talk about it and topics related to **me**, **my family and friends**.

Read this student's response to one of the unprepared questions on this photo.

* Ist die Kindheit eine gute Zeit?

Die sechs Kinder im Foto sehen alle sehr glücklich aus, denn es gibt nichts, worüber sie sich Sorgen machen müssen! Sie stehen noch nicht unter Leistungsdruck an der Schule, denn der Schulalltag in der Grundschule ist entspannt und locker. Je älter man wird, desto stressiger wird das Leben, und das finde ich schade. In der neunten Klasse muss ich jeden Abend entweder Hausaufgaben machen oder für die Klassenarbeiten lernen, aber diese Kinder im Bild müssen das nicht machen. Sie spielen wahrscheinlich nach der Schule Fußball oder gehen ins Schwimmbad, stelle ich mir vor.

Picture-based task (Higher)

Use your preparation time well:

* Make sure you can **describe** the photo by recalling plenty of relevant adjectives as well as positional words: in der Mitte, links, etc.

* Consider the three **known** questions you will have to answer. Spend a few minutes on each one, noting the tenses you can use and any relevant vocabulary.

* Think about the two **unprepared** questions you might be asked. They won't be the same as the three questions on the sheet, so you need to think of further aspects you could be asked about.

Now try this

Now prepare answers to these questions you could be asked.

Aim to talk for 30 seconds on each one.

* Was für Probleme gibt es oft bei Kindern?
* Was hat dir an deiner Grundschule besonders gut gefallen?
* Wie könnte man deine Grundschule verbessern?
* Was werden die Kinder im Foto in Zukunft machen, meinst du?

Listen to the audio file in the answers section for ideas as to how you could answer these questions.

Family

Make sure you have a good supply of family-related vocabulary at your disposal!

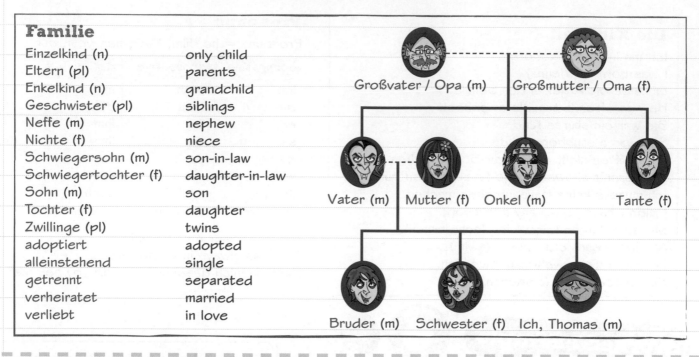

Familie

Einzelkind (n)	only child
Eltern (pl)	parents
Enkelkind (n)	grandchild
Geschwister (pl)	siblings
Neffe (m)	nephew
Nichte (f)	niece
Schwiegersohn (m)	son-in-law
Schwiegertochter (f)	daughter-in-law
Sohn (m)	son
Tochter (f)	daughter
Zwillinge (pl)	twins
adoptiert	adopted
alleinstehend	single
getrennt	separated
verheiratet	married
verliebt	in love

Großvater / Opa (m)   Großmutter / Oma (f)

Vater (m)   Mutter (f)   Onkel (m)   Tante (f)

Bruder (m)   Schwester (f)   Ich, Thomas (m)

Worked example SPEAKING

Your family

Answer the question.

- Wie ist deine Familie?

In meiner Familie gibt es meine Mutter und meinen jüngeren Bruder.

Aiming higher Als wir jünger waren, musste meine Mutter ab und zu auf Dienstreise fahren, also hat meine Großmutter auf uns aufgepasst. Das hat Spaß gemacht, weil wir immer viel Zeit beim Keksebacken in der Küche verbracht haben. Nächstes Jahr werden wir nach Amerika fliegen, um unsere Tante dort zu besuchen. Sie ist die Schwester meiner Mutter, und sie ist sehr lustig, also wird es mich freuen, sie zu sehen. Ich persönlich würde gern in Kanada wohnen, aber ich würde meine Familie kaum sehen, und das wäre schlecht.

Tenses

In the Speaking exam, include as many tenses as possible when discussing your family:

✓ who your family consists of – in the **present**

✓ description of an occasion with a family member – in the **past**

✓ your family plans – in the **future**

✓ something you would like to change about your family – in the **conditional**.

To show excellent knowledge of German, see if you can include the **pluperfect** tense!

Use a genitive to describe who's who in your family: **die Schwester meiner Mutter** – my mother's sister.

Improve your speaking by adding adverbs of time, such as **oft**, **ab und zu** and **immer**.

Now try this SPEAKING

Now prepare a description of your family, using the example above to help you. Can you talk about them for **one** minute?

Exam alert

You have to ask a question during the conversation. Can you think of something suitable to ask your teacher?

Friends

Are friends more important to you than family? What should your best friend be like?

Freunde

Freunde finde ich sehr wichtig.
I think friends are very important.
Wir kommen gut miteinander aus.
We get on well with each other.
Mit guten Freunden ist man nie einsam.
You are never lonely with good friends.
Ich kenne meine beste Freundin seit der Grundschule.
I have known my best friend since primary school.
Unsere Freundschaft ist sehr stark.
Our friendship is very strong.
Es ist mir egal, ob meine Freunde reich oder arm sind.
I don't care if my friends are rich or poor.
Die ideale Freundin / Der ideale Freund sollte meiner Meinung nach lieb und sportlich sein.
The ideal friend, in my opinion, should be kind and sporty.

Using sollen (should)
Grammar page 99

sollen + infinitive

ich sollte	wir sollten
du solltest	ihr solltet
er / sie sollte	Sie / sie sollten

Ein guter Freund sollte treu sein.
A good friend should be loyal.
Ein guter Freund sollte ...
A good (male) friend should ...
Eine gute Freundin sollte ...
A good (female) friend should ...
... geduldig sein.
... be patient.
... immer Zeit für mich haben.
... always have time for me.
... dieselben Interessen wie ich haben.
... have the same interests as me.
... nie schlechte Laune haben.
... never be in a bad mood.
... immer gute Laune haben.
... always be in a good mood.

Worked example

Translation
Translate the following sentence into **German**.

My best friend, Max, is quite sporty and happy.

Mein bester Freund, Max, ist ziemlich sportlich und glücklich.

In German you need to identify the gender of a 'friend': **der Freund** – male friend / boyfriend; **die Freundin** – female friend / girlfriend.

Translating into German

If you just can't think of the word for the translation, don't panic, but try one of these strategies:
- ☑ Do you know the German for the opposite word? If you have forgotten the German for 'happy', use the opposite, traurig (sad), instead, with the negative nie: nie traurig = never sad = happy.
- ☑ Can you change an adjective into a verbal phrase? For example, if your best friend is sporty and you can't remember the adjective, you could say er mag Sport or er treibt gern Sport.
- ☑ Can you perhaps use a word similar to English? 'Sporty' could equally be aktiv, a very similar word to one in English, which conveys the same meaning.

Now try this

Now translate the following sentences into German.
1 My friend, Carol, is clever and very funny.
2 I see my friends after school.
3 My brother doesn't have any friends.
4 My best friend lives with her family in Spain.
5 Last week my boyfriend played golf. **(10 marks)**

You need the German word for 'female friend' here, as it is a 'she'!

Peer group

Understanding question words is crucial to exam success – make sure you have the answers!

Die Altersgenossen

Alleinstehende (m/f)	single person
Bande / Gruppe (f)	gang / group
Bekannte (m/f)	acquaintance
Beziehung (f)	relationship
Diskriminierung (f)	discrimination
Feier / Party (f)	party
Freundschaft (f)	friendship
Jugend (f)	youth (i.e. time of life)
Jugendliche (m/f)	teenager / adolescent
Typ / Kerl (m)	guy
aussehen wie	to look like
gehören	to belong
mobben / schikanieren	to bully
minderjährig	underage
multikulturell (multikulti)	multicultural
rassistisch	racist
sexistisch	sexist
treu	loyal / faithful
unter Druck stehen	to be under pressure

> Make sure you don't confuse **wer?** (who?) with **wo?** (where?).

Question words

> Grammar page 108

Wann?	When?
Warum?	Why?
Was?	What?
Wer?	Who?
Wie?	How?
Wo?	Where?
Was für ...?	What sort of ...?
Wen? Wem?	Who(m)?
Wessen?	Whose?
Wie viele?	How many?

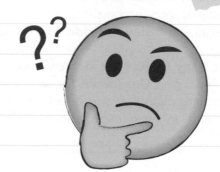

Worked example

Freunde

Du schreibst einen Artikel über Probleme im Freundschaftskreis für eine deutsche Jugendzeitschrift.

- Schreib über die Probleme und wie sie begonnen haben.
- Vergleich Probleme unter Freunden mit Problemen in der Familie.

Du musst ungefähr **150** Wörter auf **Deutsch** schreiben. Schreib etwas über beide Punkte der Aufgabe.

(32 marks)

Letztes Jahr musste ich an einer anderen Schule anfangen, wo ich glücklicherweise schnell neue Freunde in der Klasse kennengelernt habe. Ein Kerl in der Gruppe ist aber rassistisch, und da meine Familie aus der Türkei kommt, hat er ein Problem mit mir.

Justifying opinions

- Always **justify** your opinion by adding a weil or dass clause to give the reason.
- You can also use an um ... zu ... clause to give a reason: Man muss ehrlich sein, um Probleme unter Freunden zu vemeiden.
- Or start with a justification: Damit man eine gute Freundschaft bildet, muss man offen und treu sein.

> The second bullet point asks you to **compare** two relationships: friends and family. Make sure you mention both!

Now try this

Now prepare your own answers in **German** to the bullet points above. Try to write **150** words in total.

Marriage

Look at this page for ideas on the topic of marriage – what is your opinion on it?

Heirat

Braut (f)	bride
Bräutigam (m)	bridegroom
Ehe (f)	marriage
Frau (f)	wife
Hochzeit (f)	wedding
Kirche (f)	church
Mann (m)	husband
Trauung (f)	wedding ceremony
Verlobung (f)	engagement
heiraten	to get married
sich scheiden lassen	to get divorced
sich trennen	to separate
sich verloben	to get engaged
geschieden	divorced
getrennt	separated
ledig	single
verheiratet	married
verlobt	engaged

The verb haben (to have)

Present tense

ich	habe	I have
du	hast	you have
er / sie / es	hat	he / she / it has
wir	haben	we have
ihr	habt	you have
Sie / sie	haben	you / they have

Use the verb haben to add variety to your sentences: Ich habe keine Einladung zur Hochzeit, aber ich hätte gern eine. I don't have an invitation to the wedding, but I would like one.

Imperfect tense

ich hatte (I had)   wir hatten (we had)

Perfect tense

ich habe … gehabt (I have had …)
er hat … gehabt (he has had …)

Worked example

„Tipps vom Profi für die perfekte Hochzeitsfeier" by Thomas Sünder
Read this extract from a book about wedding plans.
Write **T** if the statement is **true**, **F** if it is **false** and **NT** if the information is **not in the text**.

> Don't confuse the adjectives **beliebt** = popular (i.e. well-loved) and **verliebt** = in love.

Ines (26) und Frank (25) scheinen sehr beliebt zu sein. Zumindest stehen auf ihrer Gästeliste verdammt viele Freunde. Stattliche 102 Personen sind geladen, um mit ihnen zu feiern. Wie sich ein Paar Mitte zwanzig das leisten kann, erfuhr ich beim Vorgespräch: Die beiden haben vor, das Essen mit 55 Gästen zu zelebrieren, während der Rest zur Party ab 22 Uhr dazustoßen soll.
Das Ganze findet in einem Landgut 40 Kilometer nordwestlich von Hamburg statt. Da der Hof ziemlich abgelegen ist, haben Ines und Frank für den Transfer der späteren Partygäste sogar einen eigenen Bus vom nächsten Bahnhof aus arrangiert. Die Heimfahrt soll jeder selbst per Taxi organisieren.

Ines and Frank appear to be a popular couple.   ☐ T   **(1 mark)**

Exam alert

Don't be distracted by plural forms of familiar words: der Gast = guest and Gäste = guests.
You will need to break down words in a reading text to get to the meaning: Heim + Fahrt = Heimfahrt (journey home).

Now try this

Now complete the activity.

1 The couple are in their thirties.   ☐   **(1 mark)**
2 The author has been invited to the party.   ☐   **(1 mark)**
3 Only some of the guests are invited for the food.   ☐   **(1 mark)**
4 Ines and Frank live in the countryside.   ☐   **(1 mark)**
5 They have arranged transport to and from the party.   ☐   **(1 mark)**

Partnerships

Talking about different people, you need to know the possessive adjectives 'my', 'his', 'your', etc.

Partnerschaften

Beziehung (f)	relationship
Geschlecht (n)	gender, sex
gleichgeschlechtliche Partnerschaft (f)	same-sex partnership
zivile Partnerschaft (f)	civil partnership
minderjährig	under legal age
volljährig	of age
zusammenleben	to live together
Wir streiten uns nie.	We never argue.

Meine Mutter kann (meinen Partner) nicht ausstehen. My mother can't stand (my partner).

Ich verstehe mich gut mit (deiner Partnerin). I get on well with (your partner).

Ich finde Partnerschaft besser als Heirat. I think partnership is better than marriage.

Ich kann mich auf (meinen Partner) verlassen. I can rely on (my partner).

(Meine Familie) unterstützt mich. (My family) supports me.

Possessive adjectives

Grammar page 88

These use the same endings as ein and kein.

mein	my	unser	our
dein	your	euer	your (plural familiar)
sein	his	Ihr	your (polite)
ihr	her	ihr	their

Masculine

Ich liebe meinen Hund.
I love my dog.

Feminine

Ihre Katze ist so süß.
Her cat is so sweet.

Neuter

Er mag sein Meerschweinchen sehr.
He likes his guinea pig a lot.

Plural

Wo sind eure Mäuse?
Where are your mice?

Worked example

LISTENING TRACK 3

Listen to the recording

Partnership tips

Hakan is preparing a talk about partnerships for his college in Austria. Write the correct letter in the box.

Hakan thinks the most important thing in a partnership is …

A	birthdays.
B	honesty.
C	love.

B	**(1 mark)**

– Das, was ich in einer Partnerschaft für wichtig halte, ist die Ehrlichkeit. Meine Partnerin muss immer offen sein, obwohl manchmal ein Geheimnis doch erlaubt ist. Zum Beispiel bei der Geburtstagsplanung!

Exam alert

Don't jump to the wrong conclusion! Just because you hear a word from the answer options, such as option A here: 'birthdays' (Geburtstagsplanung), it does not mean this must be the answer. Listen to the context of the entire extract to identify the correct answer.

The possessive pronoun **meine** tells you Hakan is talking about a female partner.

Now try this

LISTENING TRACK 4

Listen to the recording

Now listen to the rest of the recording and write the correct letters in the boxes.   **(3 marks)**

1 The second most important thing is shared …

A	hobbies.
B	finances.
C	goals.

2 One reason for relationships not lasting is …

A	different interests.
B	work commitments.
C	financial pressures.

3 Hakan thinks it is important within a partnership to …

A	socialise as a couple.
B	keep some independence.
C	argue occasionally.

Social media

Be aware of separable verbs in listening and reading passages – the verb is not complete until you have heard / read the **whole** sentence to see if there is a missing prefix at the end!

Soziale Netzwerke

Blog (m/n)	blog
Chatraum (m)	chatroom
Homepage (f)	homepage
Internetseite / Webseite (f)	website
soziales Netzwerk (n)	social network
brennen	to burn
chatten	to chat (online)
hochladen	to upload
laden	to load
löschen	to delete
mailen	to email
sichern / speichern	to save
teilen	to share
tippen	to type

Separable verbs

Grammar page 96

Separable verbs break into two parts:
- main verb = second in the sentence
- prefix = at the end.

Make sure you can use separable verbs in all tenses.

hochladen – to upload

Present	Ich lade Fotos hoch.
Past	Ich habe Fotos hochgeladen.
Future	Ich werde Fotos hochladen.
Modals	Ich kann Fotos hochladen.

More separable verbs

ausschalten	to turn off
einschalten	to turn on
herunterladen	to download

Worked example

LISTENING TRACK 5

Technology

Listen to this radio report from your German partner school.

Which statement is true, **A** or **B**?

Write the correct letter in the box.

Listen to the recording

Hilfe! Die Katze hat mein Profil gelöscht!
Help! The cat has deleted my profile!

A	The school is planning a study on social media.
B	89% of teenagers had a profile.

☐ B   **(1 mark)**

– Diese Woche diskutieren wir im Schulradio: Jugendliche und soziale Medien. Letztes Jahr hat eine Studie herausgefunden, dass 89 Prozent der Jugendlichen ein Profil haben.

Exam alert

Numbers are bound to come up somewhere in the exams, so make sure you are confident with them – see page 108 to brush up on them now.

The key time phrase **letztes Jahr** tells you this is something that has already taken place: last year.

Now try this

 LISTENING TRACK 6

Listen to the recording

Listen to Gerd as he continues the discussion from the worked example. Complete the activity by choosing **two** more statements that are true. Write the correct letters in the boxes.

C	All teenagers visit social media daily.
D	Gerd enjoys using social media regularly.
E	Gerd shares digital material online.
F	Gerd worries about other people accessing his material.

☐ ☐   **(2 marks)**

Listen carefully to **every** word – Gerd says **manche Jugendliche** (some teenagers). That is not statement **C** (all teenagers).

Mobile technology

In the Speaking exam, you could be asked about what technology you use and the effect it has on your life – be prepared with the vocabulary on this page!

Grammar page 105

Die mobile Technologie

Anschluss (m) / Verbindung (f)	connection
E-Mail (f)	email
Handy (n)	mobile phone
Klingelton (m)	ring tone
Passwort (n)	password
Platte (f)	disk
Schrägstrich (m)	forward slash
Smartphone (n)	smartphone
Software (f)	software
Tablet-PC (m)	tablet computer
Telefon (n)	telephone
Webcam / Netzkamera (f)	webcam
WLAN (n)	Wi-Fi
(be)nutzen	to use
digital	digital

Pluperfect tense

Pluperfect tense = **had** done something.
It is formed by using the imperfect form of haben / sein + past participle
Ich hatte es gedruckt.
I had printed it.
Sie war in den Urlaub gefahren.
She had gone on holiday.

Er hatte einen Computer gekauft, aber er wusste nicht, wie er funktionierte.
He had bought a computer but didn't know how it worked.

Worked example

 SPEAKING

A competent answer – starting both sentences with time phrases – makes this work flow nicely and the **um ... zu** clause shows good command of the German language. Note also the opinions used.

Technology
Answer the question.

- **Wie benutzt du Technologie zu Hause?**

Abends sehe ich gern meine Lieblingsserien auf meinem Tablet-PC. Im Moment spare ich mein Taschengeld, um ein Smartphone zu kaufen, weil ich das echt super finde.

Aiming higher

Zu Hause werden wir in Zukunft immer mehr Technologie haben, denke ich. Abends sitzen wir im Wohnzimmer zusammen und jeder schaut auf seinen eigenen Bildschirm. Das finde ich schade, weil wir uns nicht direkt miteinander unterhalten. Letzten Monat hat meine Mutter mir einen neuen Computer für die Hausaufgaben gekauft und ich finde ihn sehr nützlich.

This student uses:
- ✓ **wir** and **ich** parts of the verb
- ✓ **jeder** (everyone) + **schaut**
- ✓ an idiom: **schade** (pity)
- ✓ a reflexive verb: **sich unterhalten**
- ✓ present, past and future tenses

Adapting tenses

Prepare to speak in a variety of tenses by imagining that the question is in the past tense (Wie hast du letzte Woche Technologie zu Hause benutzt?) or in the future tense (Wie wirst du in Zukunft Technologie benutzen?).
You can use the same vocabulary, but you just need to change the tense each time to suit the question being asked.

Now try this

 SPEAKING

Now prepare to speak for about 30 seconds on the same subject.
Wie benutzt du Technologie zu Hause?

The length of time you speak for is crucial. Don't try to squeeze in too much content – you might run out of time. It is important that your conversation flows and that you speak clearly and don't gabble.

Online activities

Use time phrases – zu oft, fast täglich, kaum – to add interest when discussing your online life.

Aktivitäten online

Ich spiele online / Computerspiele.	I play online / computer games.
Ich lade Fotos hoch.	I upload photos.
Ich lade Musik herunter.	I download music.
Ich sehe mir Videoclips an.	I watch video clips.
Ich surfe im Internet.	I surf the internet.
Ich schreibe E-Mails / mein Blog.	I write emails / my blog.
Ich chatte online mit meinen Freunden.	I chat to my friends online.
Ich besuche Chatrooms.	I visit chatrooms.
Ich benutze soziale Netzwerke.	I use social networking sites.
Ich bleibe mit meinen Freunden in Kontakt.	I stay in contact with my friends.
Ich mache Einkäufe.	I do shopping.
Ich schicke eine Kurznachricht. / Ich simse.	I send a text.
Ich lese die Nachrichten am Computer.	I read the news on the computer.

Dürfen (to be allowed to)

Grammar page 98

Dürfen is a modal verb so it needs an infinitive.

Ich darf nicht nach 22:00 Uhr auf Facebook surfen.
I am not allowed to be on Facebook after ten o'clock.

Ich darf keine Musik herunterladen.
I am not allowed to download music.

Worked example

Technologie
Du hörst ein Podcast im Radio über Technologie.
Beantworte die Frage auf **Deutsch**.
Was macht Mia abends?   **(1 mark)**

(sie) ruht sich aus / chillt

Listen to the recording

– Mia freut sich immer auf den Abend, weil sie sich dann endlich einmal ausruhen kann.

Listening tips

✓ Don't worry about doing a simultaneous translation for yourself as you listen – read the questions in advance and then focus on the parts of the recording that are **relevant** to those questions.

✓ The more practice you have of **listening** to German, the easier you will find it. Make sure you listen to all the recorded material supplied with this Revision Guide to give your listening skills a boost.

Now try this

Listen to the recording

Now listen to the rest of the recording and answer these questions in **German**.

1 Mit wem sieht Mia die Nachrichten?   **(1 mark)**
2 Was macht Mia gern auf dem Handy?   **(1 mark)**
3 Was macht Mia am Computer?   **(1 mark)**

wem = dative case of **wer** (who) – whom

For and against technology

Be prepared to give positive and negative views on modern technology by using the phrases here.

Technologie: dafür und dagegen

Computerspiele sind kreativ.
Computer games are creative.
Man kann in Kontakt mit Leuten aus der ganzen Welt bleiben.
You can stay in contact with people from all over the world.
Die Spiele sind lehrreich.
The games are educational.
Man muss sich der Gefahren bewusst sein.
You must be aware of the dangers.
Computerspiele sind eine Geld- und Zeitverschwendung.
Computer games are a waste of money and time.
Bildschirme sind für die Augen schädlich.
Screens are damaging for the eyes.
Internet-Mobbing ist ein großes Problem für Jugendliche.
Cyberbullying is a big problem for teenagers.
Es gibt immer ein Risiko mit Online-Aktivitäten.
There is always a risk with online activities.
Für kleine Kinder ist das Internet zu gefährlich.
The internet is too dangerous for young children.

Using ob (whether)

Grammar page 93

Ob sends the verb to the end of the clause:
Ich weiß nicht, ob er online ist.
I don't know whether he is online.

These conjunctions all send the verb to the end of the clause too:
als	when (in the past)
dass	that
obwohl	although
wenn	if

Als ich ein Kind war, hat das Internet mich fasziniert.
When I was a child, the internet fascinated me.

Aiming higher

- ✓ Use meiner Meinung nach + imperfect modal.
- ✓ Expand a sentence by using obwohl (although), which sends the verb to the end of the clause.
- ✓ Use a modal + infinitive to show you understand this construction.
- ✓ Use Higher-level structures such as etwas anderes and sich vorstellen + dative pronoun.

Worked example

Technologie

Dein Schweizer Freund, Thomas, hat dich über deine Technologie zu Hause gefragt. Du schreibst Thomas eine E-Mail über Technologie. Schreib:

- etwas über deine Technologie als Kind
- wie Technologie dir geholfen hat
- über einen Nachteil der Technologie
- ob du in Zukunft Technologie benutzen willst.

Du musst ungefähr **90** Wörter auf **Deutsch** schreiben. Schreib etwas über alle Punkte der Aufgabe.   **(16 marks)**

- Als Kind habe ich Technologie sehr unterhaltsam gefunden, aber mit der Zeit habe ich das weniger interessant und eher nervig gefunden.

- In der Schule habe ich gern Informationen im Internet gesucht, um das abzuschreiben. Leider musste ich aber noch alles für die Prüfungen richtig lernen.

- Ich finde es schade, dass Kleinkinder mit dem Internet aufwachsen müssen. Es ist wichtig, dass sie nicht zu lange vor dem Bildschirm sitzen, weil das schädlich ist.

- In Zukunft werde ich mit Technologie arbeiten, aber ich würde nicht gern in der Technnologieindustrie arbeiten.

Once you have written your text, check that:

- **word order is correct** (verb second or sent to the end by a subordinating conjunction)
- **tenses are secure** and make sense (don't hop from past to present to future without time markers or sensible meaning)
- **spelling is accurate**, including adjective endings, genders and capital letters.

Now try this

Now prepare your own answers in **German** to the bullet points above. Try to write **90** words in total.

Everyday life

Get to grips with the 12-hour clock times on this page – and watch out for 'half past'!

Der Alltag

Wir wohnen in einer Wohnung. We live in a flat.
Ich stehe um sechs Uhr auf. I get up at six o'clock.
Ich fahre mit dem Rad zur Schule.
I go by bike to school.
Nachmittags habe ich (keine) Schule.
I (don't) have school in the afternoon.
Um vier Uhr gehe ich in den Sportverein.
I go to the sports club at four o'clock.
Abends bin ich oft online.
I am often online in the evenings.
Um zwei Uhr ist Ruhezeit im Wohnblock.
At two o'clock it is quiet time in the block of flats.
Man darf sonntags nicht Auto waschen.
You are not allowed to wash the car on a Sunday.
Die Geschäfte sind bis acht Uhr abends geöffnet.
The shops are open until eight o'clock in the evening.

 zwei Uhr
 fünf nach zwei

 Viertel nach zwei
 halb drei

Be careful! **halb drei** is half past two (literally, half to three).

 Viertel vor drei
 zehn vor drei

Worked example

Daily life

A German family friend, Frau Meier, is telling you about how young people's daily lives have changed.

Answer the question in **English**.

What effect has modern life had on young people?

Listen to the recording

(1 mark)

no longer able to concentrate

– Wie hat sich das Leben für Jugendliche verändert?

–Tja, ständig neue Handys, Nachrichten zu jeder Zeit und die ganze Welt im Internet: Kein Wunder, dass sich junge Leute heute nicht mehr konzentrieren können.

Answering questions in English

✓ Use the rubric to guide you into the passage you are going to hear. How many clues can you already pick up from the introductory sentence here?

✓ You may well be pleased that you understand all the items of technology mentioned, but that is **not** what the question is asking you for.

Make sure you learn time words such as **früher / vorher** (earlier), **später** (later) and **momentan** (at the moment) to help you answer questions precisely. Here, **nicht mehr** means 'no longer' or 'not any more', and that needs to be in your answer.

Now try this

Listen to the recording

Now listen to the rest of the recording and answer these questions in **English**.

1 What helps young people cope with the change in lifestyle? **(1 mark)**
2 What quality does Frau Meier say is important for young people? **(1 mark)**
3 What does Frau Meier dislike about modern life? **(1 mark)**

Hobbies

Use present tense verbs correctly to talk about your hobbies, as well as those of family and friends.

Hobbys

Ich sehe gern fern.

Ich spiele gern Computerspiele.

Ich höre gern Musik.

Ich koche gern.

Ich lese gern.

Ich spiele gern Schach.

Ich schicke gern SMS.

Ich gehe gern kegeln.

Ich treibe gern Sport.

Present tense (regular)

Grammar page 95

machen – **to do / to make**

ich	mache
du	machst
er / sie / es	macht
wir	machen
ihr	macht
Sie / sie	machen

infinitive

Sie trainiert.
She does training.

Wir gehen aus.
We are going out.

Worked example

LISTENING TRACK 11

Favourite hobbies

This person is talking about hobbies. What is his favourite hobby?
Write the correct letter in the box.

A

B

C

B

(1 mark)

Watch out for negatives, such as **nicht** (not) in passages like this – they are cruciall!

– Ich gehe gern einkaufen, aber am liebsten koche ich. Ich setze mich nicht gern vor den Fernseher.

Now try this

LISTENING TRACK 12

Now listen to two more people saying what their favourite hobby is and write the correct letter in each box.

1 A   B   C

2 A   B   C

☐ **(1 mark)**

☐ **(1 mark)**

Interests

Make sure you can say what you **do** and do **not** enjoy doing in your leisure time.

Interessen

Bergsteigen finde ich toll.	I find mountaineering great. / I really like mountaineering.
Als Hobby bevorzuge ich Bogenschießen.	As a hobby I prefer archery.
Meine Lieblingsfreizeitbeschäftigung ist Chillen.	My favourite leisure activity is chilling.
Ich sammle gern Karten.	I like collecting cards.
Ich gehe nachmittags in den Sportverein.	I go to the sports club in the afternoons.
Diese Unterhaltung finde ich prima.	I think this entertainment is great.
Ich gehe gern mit dem Hund spazieren.	I like going for a walk with the dog.
Ich gebe mein Taschengeld für Musik aus.	I spend my pocket money on music.
Ich gehe lieber ins Kino als ins Konzert.	I prefer going to the cinema than to a concert.
An Klettern habe ich wenig Interesse.	I have little interest in climbing.
Das macht mir keinen Spaß.	I don't enjoy that.
Ich interessiere mich nicht für Nachtklubs.	I am not interested in nightclubs.

Weil (because)

Grammar page 93

Weil **always** sends the verb to the **end**.

Ich kann nicht kommen, weil ...
I can't come because ...
  ich dann Sport mache.
  I do sport then.
  ich kein Geld habe.
  I haven't got any money.
  meine Eltern es nicht erlauben.
  my parents won't allow it.
  Verwandte zu Besuch sind.
  relatives are visiting.

Haben and sein in the perfect tense go after the past participle. Modal verbs go after the infinitive.

Ich kann nicht kommen, weil ...
I can't come because ...
  ich den Film schon gesehen habe.
  I have already seen the film.
  ich Hausaufgaben machen muss.
  I've got to do homework.

Worked example

Translation

Translate this description of your German exchange partner into **English**.

> Mein Freund spielt gern Fußball. Er trainiert oft und isst gesund.

Don't miss out **gern** – what does it tell you?

My friend likes playing football. He trains often and eats healthily.

Learning vocabulary

To be able to translate into English, you need to recognise lots of vocabulary, so learning plenty is crucial to success.

- ✓ **Look** at and learn the German words.
- ✓ **Cover** the English words.
- ✓ **Write** the English words.
- ✓ **Look** at all the words.
- ✓ **See** how many you have got right.

To help prepare for the translation into German, cover the **German** words and repeat the above stages.

Now try this

Now translate the rest of the description into **English**.

> Er hört besonders gern Musik. Er geht dreimal pro Woche schwimmen. Am liebsten mag er Radfahren. Am Wochenende geht er immer mit seiner Freundin ins Kino. Letzte Woche haben sie einen spannenden Film gesehen.

Watch out for the tense here – this last sentence is no longer in the present!

(9 marks)

Music

Whether you just love listening to music or prefer to play in a band or orchestra, music is a topic that may well come up in one of your exams.

Musik

Ich spiele ...   I play ...

> ich spiele + instrument – no need for 'a'

 Flöte (f)

 Geige (f)

 Gitarre (f)

 Klarinette (n)

 Klavier (n)

 Schlagzeug (n)

 Trompete (f)

Ich höre gern Popmusik / Rockmusik (f)   I like listening to pop / rock music

Worked example

WRITING

Musik

Du hörst mit deinen Freunden gern Musik und schickst dieses Foto an deinen Freund in Österreich.

Schreib **vier** Sätze auf **Deutsch** über das Foto.

1 Auf diesem Foto gibt es eine Gruppe.
2 Zwei Jungen spielen Gitarre.
3 Ich denke, die Musik ist laut.
4 Musik ist sehr wichtig für mich.

> You need to write **four** sentences about this photo, so decide what you feel confident with and use that in your writing. Do not be over-ambitious – you can stick to the present tense but try to write each of your sentences accurately.

Favourite things

Make one word with Lieblings + any noun (lower case) to talk about favourite things.

band / gruppe (f) group

sänger (m) sängerin (f) singer

melodie (f) tune

Lieblings favourite

lied (n) song

orchester (n) orchestra

Now try this

WRITING

Now write **four** of your own sentences about the photo in **German**.   **(8 marks)**

> Final check: Have you put a capital letter for each noun? Is the verb in second position in each sentence?

Films

Films, books and television programmes all require the same kind of vocabulary, so make sure you are secure with the basics, and then transfer them across these topics.

Kino

fantastisch	fantastic
komisch	funny (strange)
lustig	funny (humorous)
spannend	exciting
toll	great
traurig	sad

Ich habe ... im Kino / auf DVD gesehen.
I saw ... at the cinema / on DVD.
Es war ein Abenteuerfilm / Horrorfilm / Liebesfilm.
It was an adventure film / horror film / romantic film.
Das Hauptthema war Liebe / Familie.
The main theme was love / family.
Die Geschichte war kompliziert / romantisch.
The story was complicated / romantic.
Der Film spielte in Köln. The film was set in Cologne.

Time expressions

Add time expressions wherever you can.

ab und zu	now and again
dann und wann	now and then
immer	always
manchmal	sometimes
nie	never
oft	often
selten	rarely / seldom

These sentences both mean the same thing, but they have a different word order (verb in second place).
Ich gehe manchmal ins Kino.
Manchmal gehe ich ins Kino.
I sometimes go to the cinema.

Worked example

Filme

Du schreibst einen Artikel für deine Partnerschule über ein Filmfest in deiner Stadt.

- Schreib etwas über das Filmfest – deine Eindrücke und deine Meinung.
- Vergleich das Filmfest mit einem normalen Kinobesuch.

Du musst ungefähr **150** Wörter auf **Deutsch** schreiben. Schreib etwas über beide Punkte der Aufgabe.

(32 marks)

Ich möchte euch über ein Filmfest bei mir informieren, das unsere Gemeinde jeden Sommer in meiner Heimatstadt organisiert. Dieses Jahr heißt das Fest „Kino lebt" und es wird in der Woche vom 12. bis zum 19. Mai stattfinden.

This is just the first paragraph of this student's answer

Writing tips

✓ Make notes beside each bullet point to focus your mind before you start writing – do not go off message.
✓ Keep an eye on tenses – include a good variety for the two bullet points.
✓ Be decisive – plan an answer and stick to it!

Exam alert

- Plan a piece of writing of this length – your first paragraph should start with a short introduction, then move on to write about your impressions and opinions.
- Your second paragraph needs to be a comparison – here of a film festival and a normal visit to the cinema.

Now try this

Now prepare your own answers in **German** to the bullet points above. Try to write **150** words in total.

 Can you come in on target?

Television

When reading or listening to extracts, tense markers such as those below can all help you identify when the action is happening.

Fernsehsendungen

Ich sehe mir gern … an.	I like watching … .
Dokumentarfilm (m)	documentary
Fernsehstar (m)	TV celebrity
Kabelfernsehen (n)	cable TV
Lieblingsprogramm (n)	favourite programme
die Nachrichten (pl)	the news
Quizsendung (f)	quiz programme
Seifenoper (f)	soap opera
Sendung (f)	(TV) programme
Serie (f)	series
Show (f)	show
Zeichentrickfilme (mpl)	cartoons
Zuschauer/in (m/f)	viewer
einschalten	to switch on
ausschalten	to switch off

ZDF and ARD are TV channels.

Ich sehe mir gern Zeichentrickfilme an.

Tense markers

Past tense

als kleines Kind	as a small child
früher	previously, in the past
gestern	yesterday
letzte Woche	last week

Present tense

heute	today
heutzutage	these days
jetzt	now
momentan	at the moment

Future tense

in Zukunft	in future
morgen (früh)	tomorrow (morning)
nächste Woche	next week
übermorgen	the day after tomorrow

Worked example

LISTENING TRACK 13

Watching television

What does Anna say about television? Complete the following statement in **English**.

Listen to the recording

Anna used to watch ...cartoons...   **(1 mark)**

– Früher, als ich noch in der Grundschule war, habe ich mir immer Zeichentrickfilme im Wohnzimmer angesehen. Sie waren lustig, habe ich gedacht.

Filling gaps (listening)

Do some sleuthing work before you listen.

✓ Does the statement need a noun, an adjective, a time expression or a verb to complete it?

✓ What tense do you need to listen for?

✓ Which parts of the recording can you ignore?

You need a noun for the answer and it will probably be a type of television programme.

Now try this

LISTENING TRACK 14

Listen to the recording

Now listen to the rest of the recording and complete Anna's statements in **English**.

1 Anna's parents liked .... **(1 mark)**

2 Anna hasn't watched the family TV for .... **(1 mark)**

3 Last weekend Anna watched .... **(1 mark)**

Sport

You may want to refer to sports when talking about various topics. Make sure the **main verb** always comes in **second** position in a sentence.

Sportarten

ich …	I …
angle	go fishing
jogge	go jogging
reite	go riding
fahre Rad	go cycling
fahre Skateboard	go skateboarding
gehe schwimmen	go swimming
mache Gymnastik	do gymnastics
mache Leichtathletik	do athletics
laufe Rollschuh	go rollerskating
spiele Fußball	play football
spiele Tischtennis	play table tennis
treibe Sport	do sport

Ich bin Mitglied einer Hockeymannschaft.
I am a member of a hockey team.
Letzte Saison haben wir die Meisterschaft gewonnen.
We won the championship last season.

Verb in second place

Grammar page 92

1 Ich **2** spiele **3** Rugby.

1 Im Winter **2** spiele **3** ich **4** Rugby.

In the perfect tense, the part of haben or sein goes in second place.

1 Im Winter **2** habe **3** ich **4** Rugby **5** gespielt.

Im Sommer spiele ich Tennis.

Worked example

Sport
Answer the question.
• Wie sportlich bist du?

Ich bin sehr aktiv und treibe dreimal in der Woche Sport. Letztes Jahr war es ganz anders, weil ich mir das Bein gebrochen hatte und vier Monate lang keinen Sport treiben konnte. Das war eine Katastrophe für mich und ich musste dauernd Computerspiele spielen, die ich langweilig fand. Mein Traum ist es, eines Tages Profifußballer zu werden und ich würde am allerliebsten für Chelsea spielen.

Aiming higher

Including three tenses in your work is as easy as 1, 2, 3, if you can say which sports you:
☑ **do** now
☑ **did** previously
☑ **would like to do** or **will do**.

Use past tense 'markers' such as **letztes Jahr** (last year), **vier Monate lang** (for four months), **eines Tages** (one day).

Now try this

Now prepare to answer these questions as fully as you can. Aim to talk for 30 seconds on each one.
• Welche Sportarten treibst du gern?
• Wie viel Sport hast du letzte Woche gemacht?
• Was ist dein sportlicher Traum?
• Ist Sport als Pflichtfach in der Schule wichtig?

Here's a useful Higher-level phrase: **Mein Traum ist es, mein Land bei den Olympischen Spielen zu vertreten.** It is my dream to represent my country at the Olympic Games.

Listen to the audio file in the answers section for ideas as to how you could answer these questions.

Food and drink

What is your Lieblingsessen (favourite dish)? Make sure you know how to say it in German and look at page 40 for lots of Obst and Gemüse vocabulary.

Essen

Braten (m)	roast
Ente (f)	duck
Hackfleisch (n)	mince
Käse (m)	cheese
Lammfleisch (n)	lamb
Leberwurst (f)	liver sausage
Obsttorte (f)	fruit tart
Pizza (f)	pizza
Reis (m)	rice
Schweinefleisch (n)	pork
Soße (f)	sauce
Spiegelei (n)	fried egg
Steak (n)	steak
Thunfisch (m)	tuna

Trinken

Bier (n)	beer
Fruchtsaft (m)	fruit juice
Limonade (f)	lemonade
Milch (f)	milk
Mineralwasser (n)	mineral water
Wein (m)	wine

Quantities

Be careful not to use von (of) with quantities:

eine Dose + Erbsen =

a tin of peas

Here are a few more:

ein Dutzend	a dozen
ein Glas	a jar / glass of
eine Packung	a packet of
eine Scheibe	a slice of
eine Tafel	a bar of
eine Tüte	a bag of

Wir essen gern Kuchen!
We like eating cake!

Worked example

Das Essen zu Hause

Du schreibst an deinen deutschen Freund über das Essen bei dir. Schreib etwas über:

- Mahlzeiten
- Lieblingsessen
- Obst und Gemüse
- Geburtstagsessen.

Du musst ungefähr **40** Wörter auf **Deutsch** schreiben.

(16 marks)

Ich esse um acht Uhr Frühstück, weil ich das sehr wichtig finde.

Developing a sentence

Start small: Ich esse gern Kekse.

Expand with und: Ich esse gern Kekse und Torten.

Add a reason: Ich esse gern Kekse und Torten, weil sie mir so gut schmecken.

You need to write about 10 words for each bullet – keep it straightforward and accurate.

Expand your writing using **weil** (or **und** or **aber**), like in this answer to the first bullet point.

Now try this

Now prepare your own answers in **German** to the bullet points above. Try to write **40** words in total.

Meals

Learn a variety of words for food and drink so you can talk about meals, whatever the time of day!

Mahlzeit!

Abendessen / Abendbrot (n)	supper
Aufschnitt (m)	cold meat
Brötchen (n)	bread roll
Ei (n)	egg
Frühstück (n)	breakfast
Gebäck (n)	biscuits
Hähnchen (n)	chicken
Mahlzeit! / Guten Appetit!	Enjoy your meal!
Mittagessen (n)	lunch
Obst (n)	fruit
Suppe (f)	soup
Teigwaren / Nudeln (fpl)	pasta / noodles

Dative verb schmecken (to taste)

The dative verb schmecken works in the same way as gefallen (to like): es gefällt mir (I like it).

 Es schmeckt mir gut.   It tastes good.

 Es hat mir nicht gut geschmeckt.   It didn't taste good.

bitter	bitter
lecker / köstlich	tasty / delicious
sauer	sour
scharf	highly seasoned / hot
süß	sweet
würzig	spicy

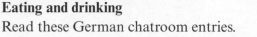

Worked example

READING

Eating and drinking

Read these German chatroom entries.

Write the **two** correct foods in the grid for Ben.

> **Ben:** Ich esse immer ein Brötchen, aber früher habe ich ein Stück Obst zum Frühstück gegessen. Nächste Woche werde ich viel Gemüse essen, weil ich trainiere.
>
> **Ines:** Gestern hat mein Vater zum Abendbrot Wurst gekocht, aber sie hat nicht gut geschmeckt. Nächste Woche werde ich einen Braten kochen. Bei uns gibt es immer Brot auf dem Tisch, damit niemand Hunger hat!
>
> **Alvin:** Meistens esse ich gern Hähnchen zu Abend. Gestern war das Wetter aber besonders kalt, also haben wir eine leckere Suppe gegessen. Hoffentlich werden wir morgen Nudeln essen, weil das mein Lieblingsessen ist.

	past	present	future
Ben	fruit	bread roll	vegetables

(2 marks)

Expanding your vocabulary

✓ While you are revising, use a dictionary to expand your vocabulary. All the words in this activity are ones which may crop up in an exam, so use an online dictionary to check their meanings and add them to your wordlists.

✓ Use the audio scripts from this book as well as the reading passages to find new words to learn – make a note of any you think are useful and revise them for your writing and speaking tasks.

Now try this

READING

Now write the **four** correct foods in the grid for Ines and Alvin.

	past	present	future
Ines	sausage		
Alvin			pasta

(4 marks)

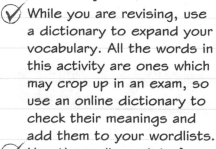

Eating in a café

Lots of these food words look very similar to the English words, so you should recognise them in a reading or listening passage.

Im Café essen

Bratwurst (f)	fried sausage
Erfrischungen (fpl)	refreshments
Frikadelle (f)	meatball
Fruchtsaft (m)	fruit juice
Hamburger (m)	hamburger
heiße Schokolade (f)	hot chocolate
Imbiss (m)	snack
Mineralwasser (n)	mineral water
Omelett (n)	omelette
Pommes (frites) (pl)	chips
Salat (m)	salad
Schinkenbrot (n)	ham sandwich
Schnellimbiss (m)	snack bar
Selbstbedienung (f)	self-service
Spiegelei (n)	fried egg
Einmal / Zweimal ... bitte.	One / Two portion(s) of ... please.

There is no need for 'of' in German when talking about quantities!
eine Tasse Tee – a cup of tea
ein Stück Torte – a piece of gateau
eine Portion Pommes – a portion of chips

Indefinite article (a, an)

Grammar page 86

Masculine nouns
- nominative – ein
  Ein Kaffee kostet 3 Euro.
  A coffee costs 3 euros.
- accusative – einen
  Ich hätte gern einen Kaffee.
  I'd like a coffee.

Feminine nouns
- nominative and accusative – eine
  Eine Limonade kostet 2,50 Euro.
  A lemonade costs 2.50 euros.
  Ich hätte gern eine Limonade.
  I'd like a lemonade.

Neuter nouns
- nominative and accusative – ein
  Ein Käsebrotchen kostet 4 Euro.
  A cheese roll costs 4 euros.
  Ich hätte gern ein Käsebrötchen.
  I'd like a cheese roll.

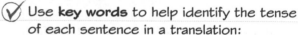

Identifying tenses

✓ Use **key words** to help identify the tense of each sentence in a translation:
  - jetzt (now) and im Moment (at the moment) tell you something is happening now, i.e. in the present tense
  - früher (earlier) and gestern (yesterday) indicate the past tense
  - nächste Woche (next week) is a future tense time marker.

✓ Use **grammar** to help identify tenses:
  - verbs ending in -e, -t, -st, etc. indicate the present tense: ich gehe, sie schläft
  - part of haben or sein and a participle starting with ge- at the end of a clause indicates the past tense
  - part of werden plus an infinitive at the end indicates the future tense.

Worked example

 READING

Translation
Translate this description of a café customer into **English**.

Er geht gern ins Café. Er sitzt oft alleine am Tisch.

Get the pronoun **er** correct here – who are you describing?

He likes going to the café. He often sits alone at the table.

Now try this

 READING

Now translate the rest of the description into **English**.

Er heißt Kai. Er wohnt mit seinem Sohn. Er bestellt oft eine Limonade und eine Portion Pommes. Im Sommer isst er gern Erdbeertorte mit Sahne. Gestern ist er nicht ins Café gekommen, aber morgen wird er wieder kommen.

Don't miss out **nicht** here – what does it tell you?

(9 marks)

Eating in a restaurant

Restaurant vocabulary might appear in various guises – a family celebration, a job interview, work experience or an instance where something goes wrong and help is required.

Im Restaurant

Auswahl (f)	selection / choice
Gabel (f)	fork
Geschirr (n)	crockery
Getränk (n)	drink
Hauptgericht (n)	main course
Löffel (m)	spoon
Menü (n)	set meal
Messer (n)	knife
Nachspeise (f)	dessert
Serviette (f)	serviette, napkin
Speisekarte (f)	menu
Speisesaal (m)	dining room
Spezialität (f)	speciality
Tagesgericht (n)	dish of the day
Teller (m)	plate
Vorspeise (f)	starter
gebraten	roast
gekocht	cooked
gemischt	mixed

Using wenn

Grammar page 93

Try to include a complex sentence using wenn to improve your work.

Wenn ich Hunger hätte, würde ich Frikadellen mit Pommes bestellen.
If I were hungry, I would order meatballs and chips.
Wenn ich Vegetarier wäre, würde ich meistens italienisch essen.
If I were a vegetarian, I would eat mostly Italian food.

Wenn ich viel Geld hätte, würde ich jeden Tag im Restaurant essen! If I had a lot of money, I would eat at the restaurant every day!

Worked example

 TRACK 15

Im Restaurant

Dein Austauschpartner, Lukas, will einen Restaurantabend organisieren und spricht mit einer Freundin darüber.
Beantworte die Frage auf **Deutsch**.
Welches Gebäude liegt in der Nähe vom Restaurant?

der Dom

Listen to the recording

(1 mark)

– Wo möchtest du heute Abend essen?
– Wenn es noch freie Tische gibt, möchte ich zum neuen Restaurant gegenüber dem Dom gehen.

Listening strategies

✓ When the questions are in German, zoom in on the key words, i.e. what you are listening for. Then focus your listening on that.
✓ Listening extracts will have a selection of vocabulary from across all the topics – just because this is titled Im Restaurant, it does not mean that what you hear will be exclusively restaurant-themed vocabulary.

Here you are listening for a **Gebäude** (building) – if you forget key words like this, listen to the recording and listen for anything which could be **in der Nähe** (near) the restaurant.

Now try this

 TRACK 16

There are **two** marks available here, so make sure you note two details.

 Listen to the recording

Now listen to the rest of the recording from the worked example and answer these questions in **German**.
1 Warum will Lukas, dass die Gruppe in dieses bestimmte Restaurant geht? **(2 marks)**
2 Was wird die Gruppe vielleicht später an diesem Abend machen? **(1 mark)**

Food opinions

If you are giving an opinion on food (or anything else), always justify it: 'I would recommend the restaurant because the staff are so friendly.'

Meinungen über das Essen

mein Lieblingsessen	my favourite food
lecker / schmackhaft	tasty
(un)gesund	(un)healthy
ekelhaft / eklig	disgusting
salzig	salty

Es hat mir (nicht) geschmeckt.
I liked (didn't like) it.
Ich würde das Restaurant (nicht) empfehlen.
I would (not) recommend the restaurant.
Es gab eine große / kleine Auswahl an Gerichten.
There was a big / small selection of dishes.
Meiner Meinung nach war es teuer / billig.
In my opinion it was expensive / cheap.
Ich fand die Vorspeise zu scharf.
I found the starter too spicy.
Das Hähnchen hat besonders gut geschmeckt.
The chicken was particularly tasty.
Ich kann Fastfood nicht ausstehen / leiden.
I can't stand fast food.

Imperfect tense

Es ist teuer.	It is expensive.
Es war teuer.	It was expensive.
Ich habe Hunger.	I'm hungry.
Ich hatte Hunger.	I was hungry.
Es gibt kein Besteck.	There's no cutlery.
Es gab kein Besteck.	There wasn't any cutlery.

Note how to refer to the plural:
Die Tischtücher waren schmutzig.
The tablecloths were dirty.
Meine Freunde hatten Hunger.
My friends were hungry.
Es gab viele Gläser.
There were a lot of glasses.

Grammar page 102

Worked example

LISTENING TRACK 17

Listen to the recording

Restaurants
You are chatting with Ralf, who is telling you about his sister, Helena. What is Helena's favourite food now and what is Ralf's opinion of it? Complete the table in **English**.

Helena's favourite food now	Ralf's opinion
eggs	disgusting

(2 marks)

– Meine Schwester ist total verrückt! Früher hat sie gern Hamburger und Pommes gegessen, aber jetzt lebt sie super gesund. Zum Abendbrot isst sie immer Eier. Ich finde Eier ekelhaft und jetzt muss ich sie oft essen!

Exam alert

You need to infer the favourite food here – as you won't hear the phrase for 'her favourite food is …'. Listen for something Helena does eat.

Just because you understand the food cognates, it does not mean that the first food item you hear is the answer you are after! Read the table headings carefully.

Now try this

LISTENING TRACK 18

Listen for the favourite drink here – not just any drink item mentioned.

Listen to the recording

Now listen to the rest of the recording from the worked example and complete this table in **English**.

Helena's favourite drink now	Ralf's opinion

(2 marks)

Shopping for clothes

Learn the words for clothes with their **gender**, so you can make sure your adjectives agree.

Einkäufe

Auswahl (f)	choice
Geld (n)	money
Größe (f)	size
Kunde (m) / Kundin (f)	customer
Marke (f)	brand
Quittung (f)	receipt
Umkleidekabine (f)	changing room
anprobieren	to try on
umtauschen	to exchange
das passt / steht dir	that fits / suits you

Kleider / Klamotten

Badeanzug (m)	swimming costume
Badehose (f)	trunks
Gürtel (m)	belt
Handschuh (m)	glove
Jeans (f)	jeans
Mütze (f)	cap
Schlafanzug (m)	pyjamas
Stiefel (m)	boot
altmodisch	old-fashioned
eng	tight
groß / weit	loose (i.e. too big)
mittelgroß	medium
schick / gepflegt / flott	smart

Adjective endings (der, die, das)

	nom	acc	dat	
Masculine nouns	der blaue	den blauen	dem blauen	Mantel Pullover
Feminine nouns	die blaue		der blauen	Hose Jacke
Neuter nouns	das blaue		dem blauen	Hemd Kleid
Plural nouns	die blauen		den blauen	Schuhen Socken

Leder leather 　Baumwolle cotton 　Wolle wool

gepunktel spotted 　gestreift striped 　gefärbt dyed

Exam alert

Speak clearly during the role play and use the correct register, which is given to you on the role play card: du for an informal role play and Sie for a formal one. When you see this – ! – you will have to respond to something you have not prepared. When you see this – ? – you will have to ask a question.

Worked example

 SPEAKING TRACK 19

Listen to the recording

Instructions to candidates

Your teacher will play the part of the shop assistant and will speak first.
You should address the shop assistant as Sie.

> Sie sind in der Modeboutique. Sie sprechen mit dem Verkäufer / der Verkäuferin.
> 1 Kleidungsstück gekauft – was.
> – Wie kann ich Ihnen helfen?
> – Ich habe dieses Hemd hier gekauft.
> 2 !
> – Oh, und gibt es ein Problem damit?
> – Ja, es ist zu klein.
> 3 Neues Stück – **zwei** Details.
> – Also, was möchten Sie dann kaufen?
> – Ich möchte eine blaue Hose kaufen, bitte.
> – Moment.

Be sure to communicate what the task card asks for. In number 1, it's the item that was bought.

A simple **ja** or **nein** will not answer the unexpected question in number 2. Listen carefully so you can respond appropriately.

Now try this

SPEAKING TRACK 20

Listen to the recording

Prepare your own answers to the prompts in the worked example and the final two prompts below.
Listen to the audio of the teacher part and speak your answers in the pauses.
4 Ihre Meinung zum neuen Stück – **ein** Detail.
5 ? Preis.

You can listen to another student's responses in the audio file in the answers section to give you more ideas.

Shopping

Make sure you are familiar with German numbers (see page 108) so you can deal with euro prices on purchases.

Einkaufen

Abteilung (f)	department
Andenken (n)	souvenir
Auswahl / Wahl (f)	choice
Bedienung (f)	service
Einkaufszentrum (n)	shopping centre
Ermäßigung (f)	reduction
Laden (m) / Geschäft (n)	shop
Notausgang (m)	emergency exit
Quittung (f)	receipt
Schaufenster (n)	shop window
kaufen	to buy
verkaufen	to sell
billig	cheap
preiswert	good value for money
an der Kasse zahlen	to pay at the till

Money

100 Cents = 1 Euro

 ein 10-Euro-Schein

 ein 2-Euro-Stück

Be careful with -zehn and -zig numbers in prices.

fünfzehn = 15　　　fünfzig = 50
siebzehn = 17　　　siebzig = 70

If you are noting down a price you hear, make sure you get the numbers the right way round:
vierunddreißig = 4 + 30 = 34

Worked example

READING

Zu Besuch in Berlin
Lies diese Geschichte aus dem Buch „Emil und die Detektive" von Erich Kästner.
Beantworte die Frage auf **Deutsch**.

> So ein Krach! Und die vielen Menschen auf den Fußsteigen! Und von allen Seiten Straßenbahnen, Fuhrwerke, zweistöckige Autobusse! Zeitungsverkäufer an allen Ecken. Wunderbare Schaufenster mit Blumen, Früchten, Büchern, goldenen Uhren, Kleidern und seidener Wäsche. Und hohe, hohe Häuser. Das war also Berlin.

Wie findet Emil Berlin?　　　**(1 mark)**
laut

Dealing with a literary text

- ✓ Don't be afraid of literary texts. They are no different from any other text in the Reading exam – and they give you an interesting insight into German culture.
- ✓ Use the same strategies as you would with any extract – cognates, context and reading the questions to see which words you really do need to focus on.
- ✓ The answers in German have to be precise, but there is often more than one way of relaying that answer. For example, the answer to the sample question could be lebhaft or hektisch, as well as laut.
- ✓ You will need to use your own words to answer these questions – read the extract through to get the gist first, so you can create a picture of the scene in your head.

Now try this

READING

Now answer these **two** further questions on the extract in **German**. You do not need to write in full sentences.

1　Welche öffentlichen Verkehrsmittel hat Emil in Berlin gesehen? Gib **zwei** Details.　**(2 marks)**
2　Was war an den Gebäuden beeindruckend?　**(1 mark)**

Customs

In German-speaking countries, a host parent and even your exchange partner might well shake your hand when they greet you, so be prepared.

Guten Tag!

Wie geht's dir / Ihnen?	How are you?
Entschuldigung	excuse me / sorry
wie bitte?	pardon?
bis später	see you later
bis bald	see you soon
guten Abend	good evening
auf Wiedersehen	goodbye
grüß Gott / Servus	hello
guten Tag	hello / good day
guten Appetit	enjoy your meal
hallo	hello
Mahlzeit!	enjoy your meal
gute Reise	have a good trip
danke schön	thank you
bitte sehr / schön	you're welcome
Ich bin satt.	I am full.
Bedien dich.	Help yourself.
Moment mal.	Wait a moment.
Was bedeutet das?	What does that mean?
Ich verstehe leider nicht.	Unfortunately, I don't understand.

Qualifiers

If you don't want to appear over-enthusiastic, add a qualifier to your adjectives:

gar nicht	not at all
nicht	not
ein bisschen	a bit
ganz	quite / completely
ziemlich	rather / quite
meistens	mostly
ein wenig	a bit
kaum	hardly
vielleicht	perhaps

Exam alert

When you read the instructions for the task, decide what you are going to say for each exchange. You do not have time to change your ideas once your preparation time is up, so stick to what you have prepared.

Worked example

Instructions to candidates

Your teacher will play the part of your Austrian friend and will speak first.
You should address your friend as du.

Listen to the recording

> Du kommst bei deiner Gastfamilie in Österreich an. Du sprichst mit deinem Freund / deiner Freundin.
> 1 Gruß.
> – Herzlich willkommen. Wie geht's?
> – Ich bin ein bisschen müde.
> 2 Etwas zu trinken – **ein** Detail.
> – Was möchtest du trinken?
> – Ein Glas Mineralwasser, bitte.
> 3 !
> – Wie findest du das Wetter bei uns?
> – Es ist sehr schön und warm.

You have one unexpected question to respond to somewhere in the dialogue. Make sure you listen to the entire question – then respond accordingly.

Look at the Exam alert on page 25 for further details on the role play.

Now try this

Now it's your turn. Prepare your own answers to the prompts, including the final two prompts below. Listen to the audio of the teacher part and speak your answers in the pauses.

Listen to the recording

1 Gruß.
2 Etwas zu trinken – **ein** Detail.
3 !
4 Meinung über das Haus – **ein** Detail.
5 ? Mahlzeit.

You can listen to another student's responses in the audio file in the answers section to give you more ideas.

Greetings

Widen your bank of verbs using the ideas on this page.

Grüße

Alles Gute!	All the best.
Schönes Wochenende!	Have a good weekend!
Schöne Ferien!	Have a good holiday!
Frohe Weihnachten!	Happy Christmas!
Entschuldigen Sie!	Excuse me. (to an adult)
Herzlich willkommen!	Welcome!
Herzlichen Glückwunsch!	Congratulations!
Prost!	Cheers!
Viel Glück!	Good luck!
Hals- und Beinbruch!	Break a leg!

Verbs

befehlen	to order / command
beschließen	to decide
erlauben	to allow
erreichen	to reach
erwarten	to expect
forschen	to research
helfen	to help
nennen	to call
raten	to advise
reden	to talk
schauen	to look
scheinen	to seem
stecken	to place / to put
vermeiden	to avoid
versprechen	to promise
wechseln	to change
zeigen	to show

Alles Gute zum Geburtstag!
Happy birthday!

Worked example

Good luck!

Read these messages by four young Austrian people on a social media site encouraging their teams.

Write the first letter of the correct name in the box.

Write **F** for **Fynn**.   Write **S** for **Sven**.
Write **I** for **Ilka**.   Write **Y** for **Yasmin**.

> **Fynn** Herzlichen Glückwunsch zum großen Erfolg beim Handballturnier! Unsere Mannschaft erreicht sicher das Finale. Schau dir das Spiel jetzt im Internet an!
>
> **Ilka** Viel Glück für die Mannschaft! Ich rate euch allen, früh ins Bett zu gehen und ruhig zu bleiben, wenn das möglich ist!
>
> **Sven** Hallo, Mannschaft! Ich verspreche euch jetzt, dass ich eine Party für alle Spieler in der Sporthalle machen werde. Hals- und Beinbruch!
>
> **Yasmin** Es scheint, ihr habt großen Erfolg! Zeigt der Welt, wie begabt ihr alle seid. Wir erwarten, dass ihr gewinnt!

Who offers advice to their team? | I | **(1 mark)**

Choosing the correct person

✓ Scan all four texts once you have read the accompanying statement to identify the relevant person – rule out any contributors who are obviously irrelevant.

✓ Look for key words – here, 'advice' is connected to raten (to advise) so this should set your alarm bells ringing!

✓ Concentrate when you write the letter of the contributor in the box – careless mistakes cost precious marks!

Scan for key words – Sven mentions a party, so read around the word to check the 'celebration' in question 3 relates to him.

Now try this

Now complete the activity by writing the correct letter in each box.

1 Who thinks their team is talented? ☐ **(1 mark)**

2 Who tells people how they can watch the game? ☐ **(1 mark)**

3 Who will organise a celebration for the team? ☐ **(1 mark)**

There is only one mark for each question so don't spend forever over this activity – there will be plenty more challenging questions coming up in the exam!

Celebrations

Prepare yourself to talk about parties and celebrations with the vocabulary on this page.

Feier

Ehe (f)	marriage
Feuerwerk (n)	fireworks
Herzlichen Glückwunsch zum Geburtstag!	Happy birthday!
Hochzeit (f)	wedding
Hochzeitsfeier (f)	wedding celebration
Sekt (m)	sparkling wine
Spezialität (f)	speciality
Torte (f)	gateau
Verlobung (f)	engagement
feiern	to celebrate
sich verkleiden	to dress up (costume)

Dative prepositions

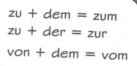
Grammar page 86

aus	from	nach	after
außer	except	seit	since
bei	at (the home of)	von	from
mit	with	zu	to

(m) der Freund ➡ bei dem Freund
at the friend's house

(f) die Party ➡ nach der Party
after the party

(n) das Zimmer ➡ aus dem Zimmer
out of the room

(pl) die Geschenke ➡ mit den Geschenken
with the gifts

zu + dem = zum
zu + der = zur
von + dem = vom

Add an **n** to the end of a noun in the dative plural.

Frohes Neues Jahr!
Happy New Year!

Worked example

 READING

Birthday celebrations
Read this blog by Alex about his birthday and complete the sentence in **English**.

> Wir feiern immer mit der ganzen Familie Geburtstag. Meine Schwester backt eine Schokoladentorte. Sie schmeckt immer lecker. Mein Bruder kauft immer noch Luftballons, obwohl ich schon achtzehn bin. Meine Oma schickt mir immer Geld und mein Opa trinkt ein Glas Sekt auf mich! Prost!

Alex's sister <u>bakes a cake</u>   **(1 mark)**

Exam alert

In this style of activity, you only need to write one or two words to complete each sentence. Concentrate on what would make sense to complete each sentence: a noun, an adjective or a verb? And then answer in English!

Read each word carefully! **Oma** (grandma) and **Opa** (grandpa) are different people!

Now try this

 READING

Now complete these sentences in **English** to show what each person does on Alex's birthday.

1 Alex's brother .... **(1 mark)**
2 Alex's grandad .... **(1 mark)**

Festivals

Festival vocabulary could come up in any part of your exams – make sure these words don't throw you!

Feste

Muttertag (m)

Ostern (n)

Silvester (n)

Weihnachten (n)

Fasching (m) / Karneval (m)

Dorffest (n)

Dreikönigsfest (n)	Epiphany (6 January)
Fastenzeit (f)	Lent
Heiligabend (m)	Christmas Eve
Karfreitag (m)	Good Friday
Ostermontag (m)	Easter Monday
Glühwein (m)	mulled wine
Imbissstube (f)	snack bar
Krapfen (m)	doughnut
Umzug (m)	procession
Volksmusik (f)	folk music

Accusative prepositions

Grammar page 86

The following prepositions are followed by the accusative case:

für	for
um	around
durch	through
gegen	against / towards
entlang	along (after the noun)
bis	until
ohne	without

(m) der Bruder ➡ für den Bruder
(der ➡ den) for the brother

(f) die Idee ➡ gegen die Idee
against the idea

(n) das Haus ➡ um das Haus
around the house

(pl) die Getränke ➡ ohne die Getränke
without the drinks

zu Weihnachten – at Christmas
an Neujahr – at New Year
auf der Neujahrsparty – at the New Year's party

Worked example

WRITING

Translation
Translate the following sentence into **German**.

> Every year at Christmas I go to the procession in the town.

Ich gehe jedes Jahr zu Weihnachten zum Umzug in der Stadt.

Aiming higher

✓ Get your word order right by reminding yourself of the rule: time – manner – place. Which is which in this first sentence?

✓ If you start with a time expression, make sure your verb is in second position.

✓ Make sure you learn words such as jeder (every), manche (some) and kein(e) (not a).

Now try this

WRITING

Now translate this passage into **German**.

> My family prefers to stay at home. Last year my class went to the fireworks but the weather was dreadful. This year I will go into the town centre on New Year's Eve and will go dancing. I would like to celebrate my birthday with friends, but we don't have any money.

Use gern (to like doing something), lieber (to prefer doing something) and am liebsten (what you like doing best of all). You can also use ich möchte to say 'I would like (to)'.

(12 marks)

Home

Use your knowledge of tenses to write about when something **is** happening, **has** happened or **will** happen in the future.

Three key tenses

To aim for the top grades, you need to recognise and use different tenses:

Present tense

- Make sure you know the present tense forms (page 95).

Er fährt gern Rad.   He likes cycling.

Wir essen zu Mittag.   We eat / are eating lunch.

Watch out for the present tense implying future meaning.

Morgen esse ich Pizza zu Mittag.

Tomorrow I am going to have pizza for lunch.

Das Zuhause

Badezimmer (n)	bathroom
Dusche (f)	shower
Esszimmer (n)	dining room
Küche (f)	kitchen
Schlafzimmer (n)	bedroom
Wohnzimmer (n)	sitting room
Garage (f)	garage
Garten (m)	garden
Haustier (n)	pet
Doppelhaus (n)	semi-detached house
Reihenhaus (n)	terraced house
Wohnung (f)	flat

Past tenses

- Use the correct form of haben and sein + past participle to form the **perfect** tense (pages 100–101):

Ich habe zu Mittag gegessen.

I ate lunch.

Er ist in die Küche gegangen.

He went into the kitchen.

- Use the **imperfect** tense war (was), hatte (had) and es gab (there was / were) for descriptions in the past (page 102):

- Use the correct form of haben and sein in the imperfect tense + past participle to form the **pluperfect** tense (page 105):

Ich hatte zu Mittag gegessen.

I had eaten lunch.

Er war in die Küche gegangen.

He had gone into the kitchen.

Future tense

- Use the correct form of werden (to become) + infinitive verb to form the future tense (page 103):

Ich werde zu Mittag essen.

I will eat lunch.

Er wird in die Küche gehen.

He will go into the kitchen.

Worked example

Translation

Translate this extract from your Swiss exchange partner's email into **English**.

> Zu Hause darf man nicht im Wohnzimmer essen, obwohl es dort so bequem ist.

At home you are not allowed to eat in the sitting room, although it is so comfortable there.

Remember that **darf** is part of the verb **dürfen** (to be allowed to).

Why is **ist** at the end of the sentence? It's because of **obwohl** (although) earlier on – read the entire sentence **before** you attempt to translate it.

Now try this

Now translate the rest of the email into **English**.

> Wir wohnen in einem mittelgroßen Einfamilienhaus am Stadtrand. Wir haben einen sonnigen Garten, wo ich oft Federball mit meinen Freunden spiele. Meine ältere Schwester ist vor einigen Monaten in ihre eigene Wohnung gezogen. Eines Tages möchte ich in die Vereinigten Staaten reisen, um dort an der Westküste zu wohnen.

(9 marks)

Places to see

When you talk or write about sights you have visited, try to include some comparatives or superlatives to improve your answer.

Grammar page 90

Sehenswürdigkeiten

Brücke (f)	bridge
Brunnen (m)	fountain
Denkmal (n)	monument
Dom (m)	cathedral
Fluss (m)	river
Hafen (m)	harbour / port
Kirche (f)	church
Kunstgalerie (f)	art gallery
Markt(platz) (m)	market(place)
Museum (n)	museum
Palast (m)	palace
Rathaus (n)	town hall
Schloss (n) / Burg (f)	castle
Stadion (n)	stadium
Theater (n)	theatre
Tiergarten (m) / Zoo (m)	zoo
Turm (m)	tower
historisch	historic
malerisch	picturesque
sehenswert	worth seeing

Comparisons

Make your writing more interesting by using **comparatives** and **superlatives**.

Meine Stadt ist … My town is …	interessant. interesting.
	interessanter als Hamburg. more interesting than Hamburg.
	am interessantesten. the most interesting.
	eine der interessantesten Städte in Deutschland. one of the most interesting towns in Germany.

Florenz ist die schönste Stadt, die ich je besucht habe. Florence is the most beautiful city that I have ever visited.

Worked example

Tourism

Read the leaflet about a popular German tourist destination.
Answer the question in **English**.

Entdecken Sie Rothenburg – die schönste Stadt Deutschlands

Rothenburg ist eines der beliebtesten Touristenziele in Deutschland. Die kleine Stadt hat viele historische Gebäude wie das Burgtor und das Rathaus, das zu den ältesten Gebäuden der Stadt zählt. Weitere Informationen findet man beim Verkehrsamt in der Innenstadt. Gehen Sie dorthin, um die günstigsten Theaterkarten zu reservieren.

Where can you book theatre tickets?

at the tourist office

➡ Stadtzentrum   hin – to
⬅ Stadtzentrum   her – from

Gehen Sie hin! – Go there!
Kommen Sie her! – Come here!

Now try this

Now answer these questions on the leaflet in **English**.

1 How do you know Rothenburg receives lots of visitors? **(1 mark)**
2 Why do you think it does not have a large population? **(1 mark)**
3 Why might tourists be especially interested in the town hall? **(1 mark)**
4 Where is the tourist office? **(1 mark)**

At the tourist office

Make sure you are familiar with the vocabulary for places in town from page 32 in case you have a role play situation at the tourist office.

Beim Verkehrsamt

Ausflug (m)	trip / outing
Ausstellung (f)	exhibition
Eintrittskarte (f)	entry ticket
Fahrradverleih (m)	bicycle hire
Hotelverzeichnis (n)	hotel list
Öffnungszeiten (fpl)	opening hours
Reservierung (f)	reservation
Rundgang (m)	tour (on foot)
Rundfahrt (f)	tour (by transport)
Veranstaltung (f)	event
geschlossen	closed
geöffnet	open
Guten Aufenthalt!	Enjoy your stay!
im Voraus	in advance

Using weil, dass, wo (because, that, where)

Grammar page 93

Don't be worried by conjunctions that send the verb to the end of the sentence. Learn a few key phrases and it will become natural.

Ich möchte ein Fahrrad mieten, weil die Fahrradwege hier sehr gut sind.
I would like to hire a bicycle, because the cycle paths are very good here.
Möchten Sie, dass ich die Eintrittskarten reserviere?
Would you like me to reserve the entry tickets?
Ist das die Ausstellung, wo es moderne Kunst gibt?
Is that the exhibition where there is modern art?

Worked example

 TRACK 23

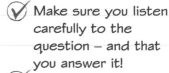
Listen to the recording

Instructions to candidates

Your teacher will play the part of the tourist information officer and will speak first.
You should address the tourist information officer as Sie.

Sie suchen Informationen beim Verkehrsamt in einer deutschen Stadt. Sie sprechen mit dem/der Angestellten im Verkehrsamt.
1 Ausflug – Tag.
– Guten Tag. Wie kann ich Ihnen helfen?
– Ich interessiere mich für einen Ausflug am Mittwoch.
2 !
– Warum wollen Sie das machen?
– Weil ich gern neue Orte besuche.
3 Meinung über die Stadt.
– Wie finden Sie unsere Stadt?
– Ich finde die alten Gebäude besonders schön.

Effective role play

☑ Make sure you listen carefully to the question – and that you answer it!
☑ Make sure you pronounce the German words accurately, and aim to use the correct articles and adjective endings.

A day of the week is needed here – make sure you have learned them.

An opinion is needed here. Stay focused to ensure you supply just that.

Now try this

 TRACK 24

Listen to the recording

Now it's your turn. Prepare your own answers to the prompts in the worked example and the final two prompts below. Listen to the audio of the teacher part and speak your answers in the pauses.
4 Pläne für heute – **ein** Detail.
5 ? Sehenswürdigkeit offen.

You can listen to another student's responses in the audio file in the answers section to give you more ideas.

Describing a town

Learn these words so you can write or speak about towns you have visited.

In der Stadt

Bäckerei (f)	bakery
Bahnhof (m)	station
Bank (f)	bank
Bowling (n)	tenpin bowling
Buchhandlung (f)	bookshop
Eishalle (f)	ice rink
Freizeitpark (m)	theme park
Freizeitzentrum (n)	leisure centre
Hallenbad (n)	indoor swimming pool
Kaufhaus (n)	department store
Kino (n)	cinema
Kneipe (f) / Lokal (n)	pub
Lebensmittelgeschäft (n)	grocery shop
Markt (m)	market
Polizeiwache (f)	police station
Tankstelle (f)	petrol / service station
Waschsalon (m)	launderette
Zeitungskiosk (m)	newspaper stall

Es gibt ... (there is / are ...)

Use es gibt + accusative (einen, eine, ein) in different tenses to help improve your speaking and writing.

Present: Es gibt ... There is ...

Imperfect: Als ich klein war, gab es ... When I was young, there was ...

Pluperfect: Vorher hatte es ... gegeben. Earlier there had been ...

Future: In Zukunft wird es ... geben. In future there will be ...

Conditional: In meiner idealen Stadt gäbe es ... In my ideal town there would be ...

... eine Eishalle
... an ice rink

Adjectives

Make sure you have a good supply of adjectives to express your opinion.

🙂			🙁		😐	
großartig	great	sauber	clean	dreckig / schmutzig	dirty	flach	flat
hübsch	pretty	malerisch	picturesque	industriell	industrial	ruhig	quiet

Worked example

Translation

Translate the following sentence into **German**.

> There is a leisure centre in my town.

In meiner Stadt gibt es ein Freizeitzentrum.

Translating into German

- ✓ Read the English sentence carefully and check you understand it properly: who or what is it talking about and when does the action take place?
- ✓ It doesn't matter if you start with In meiner Stadt or Es, but you **must** put the verb gibt next, so that it is in **second** position.

 Have you forgotten the German for 'leisure centre' (Freizeitzentrum)? Think of an alternative, such as Sportzentrum.

Now try this

 Check the tense – present, past or future?

Now translate the following sentences into **German**.

1 I live in a village and it is pretty.
2 Our church is very old.
3 There isn't a castle here.
4 I prefer to go shopping in town.
5 Yesterday I went to the cinema.   **(10 marks)**

Describing a region

Make sure you know the points of the compass, so you can be specific when describing where places are located.

Eine Gegend

Autobahn (f)	motorway	Land (n)	(German) state
Badeort (m)	seaside resort	Landschaft (f)	landscape
Berg (m)	mountain	Natur (f)	nature
Bundesstraße (f)	main road	Ort (m)	place
Bürgersteig (m)	pavement	See (f) / Meer (n)	sea
Dorf (n)	village	See (m)	lake
Einwohner (m)	inhabitant	Stadtrand (m)	outskirts (of town)
Feld (n)	field	Stadtviertel (n) / Stadtteil (m)	area of town
Gebiet (n)	area	Strand (m)	beach
Großstadt (f)	big city	Umgebung (f)	surrounding area
Hügel (m)	hill	Vorort (m)	suburb
Insel (f)	island	Wald (m)	forest, wood
Küste (f)	coast	sich befinden	to be situated

North, South, East, West

im Norden

im Westen   W — O   im Osten

im Süden

To say NE, NW, SE, SW:
in Südwestengland – in south-west England
in Nordostschottland – in north-east Scotland

Clues to listening

☑ Read the options first and see which words you might hear – then look at the compass to the left to help you with the first part of this recording.

☑ Even if you don't hear the full word Südwestdeutschland, did you catch the 'v' sound to alert you to the fact that it could have something to do with the 'west' of the country?

☑ Ignore the distractors! Peter lives in the north of Germany, but that is not where the Black Forest is.

Worked example

Listen to the recording

Travel and tourism

Listen to the comment about the Black Forest as a holiday destination.
Answer the question in **English**.
Where is the Black Forest?

A	In the north
B	In the east
C	In the southwest

C

– Peter wohnt in Hamburg in Norddeutschland und er besucht gern den Schwarzwald in Südwestdeutschland. Das ist ein wunderbares Gebiet, findet er.

Köln – Cologne
München – Munich
Wien – Vienna
die Donau – Danube
das Mittelmeer – Mediterranean
die Ostsee – Baltic Sea
der Rhein – Rhine

Now try this

Listen to the recording

Now listen to the rest of the recording and answer the question in **English**.

1 Why does Claudia visit the Black Forest?

(1 mark)

Volunteering

When talking about volunteering experiences, include time expressions with past tense modals: Zuerst musste ich ... (First I had to ...) or Danach sollte ich ... (Afterwards I was supposed to ...).

Freiwillig arbeiten

Ich habe ...   I ...

... freiwillige Arbeit geleistet.
... did voluntary work.
... eine Woche bei einem Wohltätigkeitsverein verbracht.
... spent a week at a charity.
... Aufgaben / Textverarbeitung gemacht.
... did tasks / word-processing.
... Akten abgeheftet.
... did filing.
... viele Anrufe gemacht.
... made lots of phone calls.
... neue Fähigkeiten gelernt.
... learned new skills.
... eine Spendenaktion organisiert.
... organised a charity event.
Das hat einen großen Eindruck gemacht.
That made a big impression.
Die Erfahrung war sehr lehrreich.
The experience was very educational.

Adverbs of time

Usually, the verb must come second:
Dann habe ich in der Klinik geholfen.
Then I helped in the clinic.

| danach | afterwards | vorher | beforehand |
| dann | then | zuerst | first of all |

With bevor and nachdem, the verb goes to the end:
Nachdem ich mit den Kindern gespielt hatte, war ich erschöpft.
After I'd played with the children, I was exhausted.

Ich habe Geld zu Gunsten einer Kindergruppe gesammelt.
I raised money in aid of a children's group.

Worked example

Wohltätigkeitsverein

Ein Radiomoderator berichtet über den Wohltätigkeitsverein „Hunger an der Tür".
Füll die Tabelle auf **Deutsch** aus.

Listen to the recording

Wie könnte man helfen?	Warum?
am Sonnabend protestieren	um Leute über Kinderarmut zu erzählen
(Ein Detail)	**(Ein Detail)**

– Der Wohltätigkeitsverein „Hunger an der Tür" sucht Leute, die am Sonnabend in Berlin protestieren könnten oder auch Poster und Flugblätter entwerfen könnten, um das Problem der Kinderarmut an die Öffentlichkeit zu bringen. Frau Kahn von der Vereinsleitung glaubt, dass wir alle Kinderarmut bekämpfen sollten.

(2 marks)

Exam alert

You have to give one detail and one reason for that detail here. Ask yourself Wie? and Warum? Then make sure you answer these two questions correctly.

You must complete the table in German – answers in English are not what are asked for here.

Now try this

Now listen to the rest of the recording and fill in the table in **German**.

Listen to the recording

Wie könnte man helfen?	Warum?
(Ein Detail)	**(Ein Detail)**

(2 marks)

Charity work

Make sure you know your way around a photo using the expressions on this page.

Wohltätigkeitsverein

Altenheim (n) / Altersheim (n)	old people's care home
Hilfe (f)	help
Tierheim (n)	animal shelter
Wohltätigkeit (f)	charity
Wohltätigkeitsveranstaltung (f)	charity event
freiwillig	voluntary / voluntarily
hilflos	helpless
menschlich	human(e)
sorgen (für)	to care (for)
spenden	to donate
sterben	to die
Briefe schreiben	to write letters
Geld sammeln	to raise money
Leuten helfen	to help people
Menschen unterstützen	to support people

Positions on a photo

When describing a photo, don't forget about your word order: verb second!
Man sieht ein Mädchen links. ➡
Links sieht man ein Mädchen.

im Hintergrund   oben
links   rechts
unten   im Vordergrund

Worked example

Freiwillig arbeiten

Du arbeitest freiwillig in einem Altenheim und schickst dieses Foto an deine Freundin in Deutschland.

Schreib **vier** Sätze auf **Deutsch** über das Foto.

1 Man feiert einen Geburtstag.
2 Diese Leute sind glücklich.
3 Der Mann im Hintergrund hat braune Haare.
4 Der Junge links hat Blumen in der Hand.

Photo writing task

✓ Describe the photo by choosing four elements of the image you feel comfortable with: hair, clothes, actions, emotions, positions of objects ... you decide!

✓ Do not repeat language – always think of a different way of expressing something to avoid this.

✓ Accuracy is key here – check your work at the end for spellings and capital letters and ensure that each sentence makes sense.

Use **diese** instead of **die** to emphasise 'these' people when writing or talking about a photo. You can adapt descriptions such as these to use in more detailed writing or speaking tasks on this topic.

Now try this

Now write **four** of your own sentences about the photo in **German**.   **(8 marks)**

You could describe the colours in the photo as well.
Der Stuhl ist blau / schwarz / weiß / rot ...
The chair is blue / black / white / red ...

Social problems

Use this page to help you discuss social problems, such as poverty, equality and racism.

Die Gesellschaft heute

Armut (f)	poverty
Ausländer (m/pl)	foreigner(s)
Bedürftige (m/f)	someone in need
Eingliederung (f)	integration
Einwanderer (m/pl)	immigrant(s)
Gleichheit (f)	equality
Hautfarbe (f)	skin colour
Rassismus (m)	racism
Rassist (m)	racist
Straftat (f)	criminal act
bedürftig	needy
benachteiligen	to disadvantage
rassistisch	racist
unglücklich	unfortunate / unhappy

How often/many

- Germans use a number + mal (all one word, lower case) when saying how often something happens:
  Er ist dreimal zum Arbeitsamt gegangen.
  He went to the job centre three times.
- Number + mal is also used to say how many of an item are required.
  Zweimal Pommes, bitte. Two (lots of) chips, please.

Gemeinsamkeit ist wichtig für ältere Leute.
Community is important for older people.

Worked example

LISTENING TRACK 29

Social issues

Karl is talking about his home town.
Which statement is true?
Write the correct letter in the box.

A	The car factory shut down last year.
B	Karl's father found a new job.
C	Karl had to go to the town hall.

☐ B

Listen to the recording

– Vor sechs Jahren hat die große Autofabrik in unserer Stadt zugemacht. Viele Leute haben ihren Job verloren, aber mein Vater hat eine neue Stelle im Rathaus gefunden. Er war sehr glücklich darüber.

Reading options carefully

- ✓ Check every word in multiple-choice questions – the first part might be correct, but is the whole sentence?
- ✓ Read carefully who or what each statement refers to – is it Karl or his father?
- ✓ Look for key words in the options – but don't let them distract you when you hear them. For example, you need to hear **when** the car factory shut down, not whether or not there is a car factory.

Now try this

LISTENING TRACK 30

Listen to the recording

Now listen to the rest of the recording and write the correct letter in the box.

A	Most immigrants could stay in their own country.
B	There is always racial tension in the playground.
C	Many immigrants have arrived in the town.

☐

(1 mark)

Key words in these options are 'many', 'could' and 'always'. Don't ignore them!

Healthy and unhealthy living

This page will help you to describe your lifestyle, be it healthy or unhealthy!

Gesundheit

Viele Leute sind fettleibig.	Many people are obese.
Ich esse (un)gesund.	I eat (un)healthily.
Ich habe 2 Kilo zugenommen.	I have put on 2 kilos.
Ich muss abnehmen.	I have to lose weight.
Man sollte aktiver sein.	You should be more active.
Ich will Schokolade aufgeben.	I want to give up chocolate.
Ich bin in guter / schlechter Form.	I am in good / bad shape.
Die Gesundheit ist mir wichtig.	Health is important to me.
Die Ernährung ist das Wichtigste.	Nutrition is the most important thing.
Wir essen immer Bio-Nahrungsmittel.	We always eat organic food.
Ich führe einen gesunden Lebensstil.	I follow a healthy lifestyle.

Saying 'when'

Grammar page 93

- Use **wenn** to mean 'when' in the present tense. It sends the verb to the end of the clause, and adds a comma before the next verb. Wenn ich ungesund esse, ist das schrecklich. When I eat unhealthily, that is dreadful.
- Use **als** to mean 'when' in the past tense. It also sends the verb to the end of the clause, and adds a comma before the next verb. Als ich jünger war, habe ich oft Sport gemacht. When I was younger I often did sport.

Wenn sie ins Restaurant geht, isst sie gesund.
When she goes to a restaurant, she eats healthily.

Worked example

Translation
Translate the following sentence into **German**.

> When I was at primary school I always ate lots of sweets.

Als ich in der Grundschule war, habe ich immer viele Süßigkeiten gegessen.

Making the translation suit you

It is unlikely that you will know **every** word or phrase in any given translation, so you need to work on strategies to adapt words to the knowledge you **do** have. Here are some examples:

Forgotten ...		Why not use ... ?
'mostly'	➡	fast immer (nearly always)
'gesund'	➡	gut or nicht schlecht
'sweets'	➡	Schokolade or Kaugummi
'ate'	➡	gehabt, genommen, gekauft

Now try this

Now translate this passage into **German**.

> I must give up crisps. When I went on holiday, I put on three kilos. Next week I will go to the gym every day to get fitter. I would never want to be obese, so I am trying now to follow a healthy lifestyle.

(12 marks)

Healthy eating

To buy fruit and vegetables, add a quantity first: ein Kilo (Äpfel) or 400 Gramm (Pilze), bitte! Note that there is no word for 'of' in this context in German.

Auf dem Markt

Obst	Fruit	Gemüse	Vegetables
Ananas(-) (f)	pineapple	Blumenkohl(-e) (m)	cauliflower
Apfel(") (m)	apple	Bohne(-n) (f)	bean
Apfelsine(-n) (f) / Orange(-n) (f)	orange	Erbse(-n) (f)	pea
		Gurke(-n) (f)	cucumber
Aprikose(-n) (f)	apricot	Karotte(-n) (f)	carrot
Banane(-n) (f)	banana	Kartoffel(-n) (f)	potato
Birne(-n) (f)	pear	Knoblauch (m)	garlic
Erdbeere(-n) (f)	strawberry	Kohl(-e) (m)	cabbage
Himbeere(-n) (f)	raspberry	Kopfsalat(-e) (m)	lettuce
Kirsche(-n) (f)	cherry	Pilz(-e) (m)	mushroom
Pfirsich(-e) (m)	peach	Rosenkohl (m)	Brussels sprout
Pflaume(-n) (f)	plum		
Tomate(-n) (f)	tomato	Spinat (m)	spinach
Traube(-n) (f)	grape	Zwiebel(-n) (f)	onion

Plurals

German nouns all have different plurals. You can look in a dictionary if you are unsure.
An online search for 'Kartoffel plural' gives you the answer instantly:

> Kartoffel (f) (genitive **der Kartoffel**, plural **die Kartoffeln**) – potato

The nominative plural word for 'the' is always **die**.

Fruit and vegetables

What do these young Swiss people think about fruit and vegetables? Read these four entries on social media.
Write the first letter of the correct name in the box.

Write **A** for **Alex**.   Write **P** for **Petra**.

Write **K** for **Kai**.   Write **E** for **Edi**.

> **Alex** Ich kaufe immer Karotten und manchmal kaufe ich auch eine Gurke.
>
> **Kai** Im Sommer kaufe ich gern Erdbeeren und Himbeeren, aber im Winter kaufe ich kein Obst.
>
> **Petra** Ich kaufe oft online und ich klicke immer Erbsen und Bohnen an, denn sie sind lecker.
>
> **Edi** Ich kaufe jede Woche ein Kilo Kartoffeln, denn ich liebe Pommes. Ich kaufe auch immer Kirschen, denn das ist mein Lieblingsobst.

Who buys potatoes? [E]

Exam alert

Just because one person has already been the answer to a question, it does not mean they can't still be the answer to another question.

Reading tips

- ✓ Go through the text and underline the nouns that are fruit and vegetables – they start with a **capital letter**.
- ✓ Use cognates, such as: Karotten (carrots), and words with a link to an English word: Gurke (cucumber), from 'gherkin'.

Now complete the activity by writing the correct letter in each box.

1 Who finds peas tasty? ☐ **(1 mark)**

2 Who sometimes buys a cucumber? ☐ **(1 mark)**

3 Who says they don't buy fruit in winter? ☐ **(1 mark)**

4 Who loves chips? ☐ **(1 mark)**

5 Who uses the computer to buy vegetables? ☐ **(1 mark)**

Feeling ill

Naming a body part and adding -schmerzen (pain) is an easy way to express where it hurts: Ich habe Kopfschmerzen (I have a headache).

Krankheiten

Krankenhaus (n)	hospital
Krankenwagen (m)	ambulance
Medikament (n)	medicine
Schmerz (m)	pain
Verkehrsunfall (m)	traffic accident
Verletzung (f)	injury
erste Hilfe (f)	first aid
das Rote Kreuz	the Red Cross
krank	ill
Es geht mir gut / schlecht.	I feel well / ill.
Mir ist übel.	I feel ill / sick.
Ich habe Magenschmerzen.	I have stomach-ache.
Ich habe mir die Nase gebrochen.	
I have broken my nose.	
Ich habe mir den Arm verletzt.	
I have injured my arm.	

Saying something hurts

Mein(e) ... tut weh. My ... hurts.
Use tut (one thing) or tun (more than one thing) + weh.

↓

Mein Fuß tut weh. My foot hurts.

↓

Meine Füße tun weh. My feet hurt.

You can also talk about past pain:
Meine Hand tat weh. My hand hurt.

↓

Meine Arme taten weh. My arms hurt.

Bein (n)	leg	Knie (n)	knee
Finger (m)	finger	Schulter (f)	shoulder

Worked example

SPEAKING TRACK 31

Listen to the recording

Instructions to candidates

Your teacher will play the part of a ski instructor and will speak first. You should address the ski instructor as Sie.

> Sie sind im Skiurlaub in Österreich. Sie haben einen Unfall auf der Piste und sprechen mit dem Skilehrer / der Skilehrerin.
>
> 1 Problem – **zwei** Details.
> – Kann ich Ihnen helfen?
> – Mein linkes Bein tut schrecklich weh.
> 2 !
> – Oh je. Was ist passiert?
> – Ich bin auf der Piste hingefallen.
> 3 Problem – Lösung.
> – Das war Pech.
> – Ja, ich muss sofort ins Krankenhaus fahren, glaube ich.

Exam alert

Don't be over-ambitious in your role play. Communication is the key, so concentrate on getting the message across from your task card.

The two details given here are 'leg' and 'hurts'. Message communicated, along with a nice addition of the adjective 'left'.

This unexpected question is in the past tense, and the student replies in the past tense too.

Using a modal here is an effective way to suggest a solution (what must happen).

You can listen to another student's responses in the audio file in the answers section to give you more ideas.

Now try this

SPEAKING TRACK 32

Now it's your turn. Prepare your own answers to the prompts, including the final two prompts below. Listen to the audio of the teacher part and speak your answers in the pauses.

4 Deine Eltern – wo.
5 ? Hilfe – wann.

Listen to the recording

Health issues

Alcohol, smoking and drugs are the focus here.

Süchtig

Ader (f) / Vene (f)	vein	rauchen	to smoke
Alkohol (m)	alcohol	sterben	to die
Bewusstsein (n)	consciousness	ausprobieren	to try
Droge (f)	drug	abhängig	dependent
Drogenhändler (m)	drug dealer	alkoholfrei	alcohol-free
Drogensüchtige (m/f)	drug addict	alkoholisch	alcoholic
Herz (n)	heart	betrunken	drunk
Krebs (m)	cancer	bewusstlos	unconscious
Leber (f)	liver	schädlich	harmful
Spritze (f)	injection / syringe	süchtig	addicted
Sucht (f)	addiction	tot	dead

Etwas, nichts, wenig + adjective

Try to include some of these Higher-level phrases, which convert an adjective into a noun.

viel Interessantes	a lot of interesting things
etwas Gefährliches	something dangerous
wenig Gutes	not much / little good
nichts Besonderes	nothing special

Exam alert

You have to infer meaning from texts – in the extract below, none of the words given in the answer options is in the text. You need to understand the entire sentence to find out that the way young people feel is not how they expected to feel.

Worked example

Health threats

You read this article in an Austrian magazine about addiction among teenagers.

Key words such as **statt** (instead) tell you that option B is definitely not the correct choice here.

Statt Freude am Rauchen zu haben, wie sie es sich seit langem vorgestellt haben, werden viele Jugendliche eher deprimiert und ängstlich, wenn sie Zigaretten und Drogen ausprobieren. Daniel raucht seit drei Jahren. Es ist zu einer schlimmen Gewohnheit geworden und die Gefahren davon sind ihm klar. Obwohl er mehrmals versucht hat, Zigaretten aufzugeben, ist es ihm als Süchtigem nicht gelungen. Sobald jemand ihm eine Zigarette anbietet, fängt er wieder damit an. Neulich hat er gemerkt, dass er beim Fußballspielen nicht so schnell laufen kann, weil er an Atemnot leidet. Seine Freundin, Maria, will unbedingt, dass er mit dem Rauchen Schluss macht, bevor es zu spät ist. Sie möchte ihm dabei helfen und nächste Woche werden sie zusammen im Park trainieren: „Daniel muss das Rauchen aufgeben", sagt sie, „sonst werde ich mit ihm Schluss machen!"

According to the article, how do young people feel when they smoke?
Write the correct letter in the box.

A	Down
B	Happy
C	Excited

A

Now try this

1 Give **one** reason why Daniel cannot quit smoking. Answer in **English**. **(1 mark)**

2 Why is it important that Daniel gives up smoking?

A	He may become addicted.
B	He can no longer run at all.
C	His health is suffering.

(1 mark)

3 What will happen if Daniel doesn't stop smoking? **(1 mark)**

Weather

There are lots of cognates in weather vocabulary, so it shouldn't take you long to master these.

Das Wetter

 Es ist sonnig.

 Es ist kalt.

 Es ist neblig.

 Es ist windig.

 Es ist heiß.

 Es schneit.

Es ist bewölkt / wolkig.

Es regnet.

Es donnert und blitzt.

Es friert.	It's freezing.	im Frühling	in spring
Es hagelt.	It's hailing.	im Sommer	in summer
Jahreszeit (f)	season	im Herbst	in autumn
		im Winter	in winter

Weather in different tenses

Add value to these weather expressions by adapting them to different tenses.

Present: Es regnet. It is raining.
Imperfect: Es war regnerisch / Es regnete.
It was rainy / raining.
Perfect: Es hat geregnet. It rained.
Pluperfect: Es hatte geregnet. It had rained.
Future: Es wird regnen. It will rain.

More expressions about weather in different tenses:

Es ist / war ...		It is / was ...	
Es wird ... sein.		It will be ...	
bedeckt	overcast	nass	wet
frostig	frosty	schlecht	bad
heiter	bright	trocken	dry

Worked example

 WRITING

Weather forecast

You read this weather forecast in a German newspaper.

> Nach Osten hin wird der Wind am Dienstag immer schwächer werden. Höchstwerte liegen bei –14 Grad am Alpenrand und bis –1 Grad an der Ostseeküste. Die Nacht über wird es stark schneien. Es bleibt weiterhin bedeckt.

Write the correct letter in the box.
What sort of weather is heading for this area?

A	Sunshine
B	Strong winds
C	Snow

C

Exam alert

Look out for the **detail**. 'Strong winds' is option **B**, but only weaker winds are mentioned in the text, so **B** can't be right.

- Read to the very end of the report to find the word **bedeckt** (cloudy), so you can rule out A (Sunshine).
- The minus temperatures and the verb **schneien** (to snow) in the future tense tell you that snow is on the way – answer C.

Now try this

 WRITING

Read the forecast again and write the correct letter in each box for these two questions.

1 What is the wind forecast?

A	Stronger
B	Weaker
C	Blowing from the north

☐   **(1 mark)**

2 What is the report for the edge of the Alps?

A	Colder than the coast
B	As cold as the coast
C	Rain

☐   **(1 mark)**

Being green

Make sure you can say what you do and do **not** do in respect of the environment.

Grünes Leben

Energie sparen	to save energy
weniger Strom / Gas verbrauchen	to use less electricity / gas
Wasser nicht verschwenden	to not waste water
Lichter ausschalten	to turn off lights
Fenster und Türen zumachen	to close windows and doors
sich wärmer anziehen	to dress more warmly
die richtige Mülltonne benutzen	to use the correct rubbish bin
den Müll trennen	to separate the rubbish
Dosen / Flaschen recyceln	to recycle cans / bottles
Speisereste kompostieren	to compost leftover food
mit dem Rad fahren	to go by bike
mit den öffentlichen Verkehrsmitteln fahren	to travel by public transport
eine Fahrradwoche organisieren	to organise a cycling week
an einer Umweltaktion teilnehmen	to take part in an environmental campaign

Negatives

If you want to say what you do **not** do to help the environment, use kein (not a / no) or nicht with a verb.

Unser Haus hat keine Solarenergie.
Our house has no solar energy.
Er recycelt nicht gern.
He does **not** like recycling.

Worked example

Environment

Listen to the podcast from your Swiss friend talking about his school.
What **two** negative aspects does he mention?
Complete the table in **English**.

Listen to the recording

Negative	Aspect 1	Aspect 2
	feels ill as they have to close windows	no public transport direct to school

– An unserer Schule muss man immer die Fenster zumachen, um Energie zu sparen. Das finde ich gut, aber die Klassenzimmer werden schrecklich warm und es wird mir oft schlecht. Es ist auch ärgerlich, dass keine öffentlichen Verkehrsmittel direkt zur Schule fahren.

Watch out for **keine** here! This indicates a negative aspect.

Listening tips

✓ The listening passages are not very long, so concentrate hard on **every word** to find the answers.

✓ If you do not understand every word, try to pick up on key words, cognates and parts of words, which may lead you to the answer.

Now try this

Now listen to the rest of the recording and complete the activity from the worked example.
What **two** positive aspects does he mention?
Complete the table in **English**.

Listen to the recording

Positive	Aspect 1	Aspect 2

(2 marks)

Protecting the environment

Idioms will add interest across the topics, so learn a few from this page to have up your sleeve.

Umweltschutz

Brennstoff (m)	fuel
FCKWs	CFCs
Klimawandel (m)	climate change
Luft (f)	air
Luftverschmutzung (f)	air pollution
Ozonschicht (f)	ozone layer
Ozonloch (n)	hole in the ozone layer
Sauerstoff (m)	oxygen
saurer Regen (m)	acid rain
Treibhauseffekt (m)	greenhouse effect
Verpackung (f)	packaging
aussterben	to die out
retten	to save
schützen	to protect
zerstören	to destroy

Idioms

Ich habe keine Ahnung. I haven't got a clue.
Ich habe die Nase voll. I am fed up.
Ich habe es satt. I have had enough.
Viel Glück! Good luck!
Es ist mir egal. I don't mind / care.
Es kommt darauf an. It depends.
Es macht nichts. It doesn't matter.
Es lohnt sich (nicht). It is (not) worth it.

Hals- und Beinbruch! Break a leg!

Worked example

Die Umwelt

Lies diesen Text aus dem Buch „50 einfache Dinge, die Sie tun können, um die Welt zu retten" geschrieben von Andreas Schlumberger. Beantworte die Frage auf **Deutsch**.

Mit Energie gegen den Klimakollaps

Der Klimawandel – da sind sich die Experten weltweit einig – kommt, ja, ist schon im Gange. Wir stehen mittlerweile nicht mehr vor der Aufgabe, ihn zu vermeiden, sondern vielmehr, seinen Effekt zu begrenzen und Strategien zu entwickeln, um uns daran anzupassen.

Jeder weiß, dass der Mensch einen großen Anteil an der Klimaerwärmung hat und dass deren Folgen sich negativ auf die Menschheit auswirken werden. Für Mitteleuropa sind zunehmend extreme Wetterereignisse wie Stürme oder Starkregen und auch extremes Wetter, wie zum Beispiel Dürren oder Überschwemmungen zu erwarten. Hitzewellen werden zur Norm. Besonders stark könnten auch die Alpenregionen unter dem Klimawandel leiden.

Wer glaubt fest an den Klimawandel?

jeder Experte in der Welt / alle Experten in der Welt

Prepositions

Make sure less common prepositions don't catch you out! Here are some you may come across:

außer + dative	except for
bei + dative	at, at the home of
gegen + accusative	against
ohne + accusative	without
trotz + genitive	in spite of
wegen + genitive	because of

Now try this

Now read the text again and answer the questions in **German**.

gelingen is a dative verb meaning 'to succeed'.

1 Was ist uns nicht gelungen? **(1 mark)**
2 Was ist das Einzige, was wir dagegen machen können? **(1 mark)**
3 Warum sind wir daran schuld? **(1 mark)**
4 Was wird die größte Auswirkung des Klimawandels sein? **(1 mark)**
5 Welches Gebiet wird besonders unter dem Klimawandel leiden? **(1 mark)**

Natural resources

When you are discussing or writing about certain topics, the **man** form is extremely useful to express what people in general do.

Naturschätze

  Kohle (f)

 Benzin (n)

 Öl (n)

 Tiere (pl)

 Solarzelle (f)

 Pflanzen (pl)

 Erde (f)

alternative Energiequelle (f)	alternative source of energy
Kraftwerk (n)	power station
Sonnenenergie (f)	solar energy
Wasserkraft (f)	hydroelectric power

Der Bauer muss immer auf die Natur auf seinen Feldern aufpassen.
The farmer always has to look after nature in his fields.
Der Klimawandel bedroht unsere Inseln und Meere.
Climate change threatens our islands and oceans.
Man sollte immer Obst und Gemüse aus der Gegend kaufen.
You should always buy fruit and vegetables from the area.
Wir müssen unsere Umwelt retten.
We have to save our environment.

Using man

- Man is used in German much more than 'one / you' is used in English.
- Use man to mean 'one / you / they / we / somebody / people'.
- Man takes the er / sie part of the verb (man hat).

Present tense

Man hilft bei Problemen.
They help with problems.

Past tense

Man hat einen Brief geschrieben.
One wrote a letter.

Future tense

Man wird das verbessern.
We will improve that.

> Don't confuse **man** with der Mann (the man).

Worked example

Translation

Translate this passage about the environment into **English**.

> Man soll alle Pflanzenarten schützen. Wenn man weniger Gas und Strom zu Hause verbraucht, hilft das der Umwelt.

You should protect all plant species. If you use less gas and electricity at home, that helps the environment.

Learning vocabulary

Look at the 'word family' for Umwelt.

Umweltschutz (m) environmental protection

umweltschädlich harmful to the environment

Umwelt (f) environment

umweltfreundlich environmentally friendly

umweltfeindlich environmentally unfriendly

> Aim to be precise in your translations – Pflanzenarten are 'plant species', not just 'plants'.

> 'One' or 'we' would also be acceptable in this translation.

Now try this

Now translate the rest of the passage into **English**.

> Ich interessiere mich sehr für Umweltschutz. Auf unserem Schuldach haben wir Solarzellen, die ich prima finde. Die Supermärkte sollten weniger Obst und Gemüse aus fernen Ländern importieren, weil das umweltschädlich ist. In der Zukunft möchte ich bei einer Umweltorganisation arbeiten, um unserem Planeten zu helfen.

(9 marks)

Poverty

Use this page to help you discuss poverty issues, whether in your own country or overseas.

Armut

Bettler (m)	beggar
Heizung (f)	heating
Not (f)	need
Obdachlosenheim (n)	homeless hostel
Sozialhilfe (f)	income support
Sozialwohnung (f)	social housing
Suppenküche (f)	soup kitchen
Unterstützung (f)	support
Zuhause (n)	home
erfrieren	to freeze to death
im Freien schlafen	to sleep rough
keinen festen Wohnsitz haben	to have no fixed abode
arbeitslos	unemployed
arm	poor
einsam	lonely
obdachlos	homeless

Qualifiers

Qualifier + adjective =

gar nicht	not at all
nicht	not
ein bisschen	a bit
ganz	quite
ziemlich	quite
meistens	mostly
sehr	very
besonders	especially

Einmal Suppe, bitte.
One soup, please.

Worked example

Living in poverty

Listen to your German exchange partner, Nina, talking about poverty. Which **two** statements are true? Write the correct letter in each box.

Listen to the recording

Make notes in English or German while you listen – you can then refer to them when you come to choose the two correct statements.

A	Nina volunteers in her town.
B	Nina's town has no housing problems.
C	Nina supports people with drug problems.
D	Nina preferred her previous voluntary work.
E	Nina thinks it is dull visiting old people.

☐ A ☐ D

– Ich habe neulich angefangen, freiwillig bei der Suppenküche in der Stadt zu helfen. Bei uns, so wie in allen Städten, gibt es Menschen, die obdachlos sind: Manche wegen der Arbeitslosigkeit und andere wegen Problemen in der Familie. Früher habe ich freiwillige Arbeit in einem Altenheim geleistet und das hat mir besser gefallen, obwohl ich es auch ziemlich traurig fand. Einige Bewohner hatten nie Gäste und sie waren sehr einsam. Ich werde meine Großeltern immer besuchen, weil das so wichtig ist.

Now try this

Now listen to Gustav and choose **two** sentences that are **true**. Write the correct letters in the boxes.

Listen to the recording

A	Gustav cannot cook.
B	Gustav helps with the laundry.
C	Many of the visitors stay with relatives in winter.
D	Gustav works for a housing company.
E	Gustav would like to work in social housing.

☐ ☐   **(2 marks)**

Global problems

Use this page to prepare for the topic of global issues, which could come up in any of your exams.

Globale Probleme

Diskriminierung (f)	discrimination
Flüchtling (m)	refugee
Gewalt (f)	violence
Krieg (m)	war
Opfer (n)	victim
Verbrechen (n)	crime
Verbrecher (m)	criminal
bedrohen	to threaten
fliehen	to flee
vertreiben	to drive out
gefährlich	dangerous
gewalttätig	violent
überbevölkert	over-populated

Expressing opinions

Use a range of opinion / reaction expressions in your Speaking exam.

Das ist traurig.	That's sad.
Das ist besser.	That's better.
Das geht.	That's OK.
Das finde ich unfair.	I think that's unfair.
Das ist schrecklich!	That's dreadful!
Ich habe Angst davor.	I'm afraid of that.
Meiner Meinung nach …	In my opinion …
Ich bin (nicht) damit einverstanden.	I (don't) agree with that.

Es ist schrecklich, dass so viele Kinder unter Kriegsfolgen leiden. It is dreadful that so many children suffer as a result of war.

Worked example

Charity action
You hear a radio report about the organisation 'Kind International'.

Listen to the recording

– Bei 'Kind International' kämpfen wir jetzt seit zehn Jahren gegen Krieg in vielen Ländern der Welt.

Answer the question in **English**.
What does 'Kind International' fight against? **(1 mark)**
war in many countries

Exam alert

Read the questions very carefully – even though they are in English. If you misread the question word, for example, you won't be able to give the correct answer.

If a question has one mark, you only need to write one piece of information, even if you hear a choice of more than that.

Now try this

Listen to the recording

Now listen to the rest of the recording and answer the questions in **English**.

1 What is absent for a lot of girls? **(1 mark)**
2 What happens to boys? **(1 mark)**
3 How does 'Kind International' help? **(1 mark)**

Travel

Whether it is by car, train or plane, travelling is part of life, so make sure you are secure with the vocabulary on this page.

Unterwegs

Autobahn (f)	motorway
Benzin (n)	petrol
Fahrt (f)	journey
Hubschrauber (m)	helicopter
Motor (m)	engine
Passagier (m)	passenger
Raststätte (f)	motorway services
Stau (m)	traffic jam
Stoßzeit (f)	rush hour
Tankstelle (f)	petrol station
Umleitung (f)	diversion
öffentliche Verkehrsmittel (npl)	public transport
Verspätung haben	to be delayed

24-hour clock

The 24-hour clock is easy if you know your numbers. It is used for opening times, train times or to say when an event is taking place.

 neun Uhr dreißig

 zwölf Uhr fünfundvierzig

 sechzehn Uhr fünfzehn

 zwanzig Uhr vierzig

dreiundzwanzig Uhr

Worked example

Travelling
You read this blog entry on the web.

Meiner Meinung nach sollte jeder versuchen, öfter mit der Bahn oder mit dem Rad zu fahren, weil die Umweltverschmutzung das Autofahren immer unakzeptabler macht. Ich finde es aber schade, dass die öffentlichen Verkehrsmittel hier auf dem Land so ungenügend sind. Wir müssen mit dem Auto fahren, weil uns andere Möglichkeiten nicht zur Verfügung stehen. Wenn die Politiker mehr Geld in Regionalzüge und -busse investieren würden, könnten wir vielleicht endlich stolz auf unser Verkehrsnetz sein! **Dana**

Answer the question in **English**.
Why should people travel by train more?
to reduce pollution

schade – a pity
stolz auf – proud of

The first part of the sentence tells you that Dana thinks people should travel by train more – so it is the next part which will provide your answer. **Weil** gives you a clue that the answer to a 'why' question lurks here.

Now try this

Now read the blog entry again and answer the questions in **English**.

1 What does Dana think of the current transport situation? **(1 mark)**
2 What is lacking in the countryside? **(1 mark)**
3 What is Dana's solution to the issue? **(1 mark)**
4 How would she like to feel about transport in her area? **(1 mark)**

Countries

Learn countries and nationalities together. Many of them sound like English!

Länder

upper case

lower case

Country	der Deutsche / ein Deutscher (m)	die / eine Deutsche (f)	Adjective
Deutschland	der Deutsche / ein Deutscher	die / eine Deutsche	deutsch
England	Engländer	Engländerin	englisch
Frankreich	Franzose	Französin	französisch
Großbritannien	Brite	Britin	britisch
Irland	Ire	Irin	irisch
Italien	Italiener	Italienerin	italienisch
Österreich	Österreicher	Österreicherin	österreichisch
Schottland	Schotte	Schottin	schottisch
Spanien	Spanier	Spanierin	spanisch
Wales	Waliser	Waliserin	walisisch
die Schweiz	Schweizer	Schweizerin	schweizerisch
die Türkei	Türke	Türkin	türkisch
die Vereinigten Staaten	Amerikaner	Amerikanerin	amerikanisch

Worked example

WRITING

Urlaub

Deine Freundin Silvia aus der Schweiz reist gern. Schreib Silvia eine E-Mail über Urlaube.

- Schreib etwas über deinen letzten Urlaub.
- Vergleich Urlaub im Ausland mit Urlaub zu Hause.

Du musst ungefähr **150** Wörter auf **Deutsch** schreiben. Schreib etwas über beide Punkte der Aufgabe. **(32 marks)**

Letzten Sommer habe ich zwei Wochen Urlaub in Italien gemacht. Obwohl es dort schön ist, hat es mir nicht besonders gut gefallen, weil das Wetter sehr schlecht war.

This is the first part of this student's answer.

Exam alert

- In the Higher Writing paper, you have to choose **one** topic from a choice of **two** to write 150 words about. Make sure you take enough time to select the topic you will be able to write best about – you will not have time to change your mind halfway through the task.
- Divide the words by two so you write around 75 words for each bullet point.

Aiming higher

For a higher grade, try to include:
- ✓ a subordinating conjunction, such as obwohl (although)
- ✓ dative expressions, such as es hat mir gefallen.

Now try this

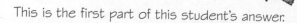

WRITING

Now prepare your own answers in **German** to the bullet points above. Try to write **150** words in total.

Transport

Don't forget the **time – manner – place** rule when you are writing and translating in German.

Verkehrsmittel

mit dem Auto / Wagen | mit der Bahn / mit dem Zug | mit dem Boot / Schiff | mit dem Bus

mit dem Rad (Fahrrad) | mit dem Flugzeug | mit dem Lastwagen | mit dem Mofa

mit dem Motorrad | mit der Straßenbahn | zu Fuß

DB = Deutsche Bahn
ICE = Intercityexpress

Time — Manner — Place

Grammar page 92

A detail of transport counts as manner (M), so put it **after** a time (T) expression, but **before** a place (P).

 gestern / heute / letzte Woche / in Zukunft

 mit dem Zug / zu Fuß / mit meiner Familie

 nach London / in die Stadt / über die Brücke

Heute fahre ich mit der U-Bahn in die Stadtmitte.
Ich bin letzte Woche mit der Straßenbahn gefahren.

Worked example

Verkehrsmittel

Deine Austauschpartnerin Maria schickt dir Fragen über die Verkehrsmittel in deiner Stadt. Du schreibst eine Antwort an Maria.
Schreib:
- wie du in die Stadt fährst
- wie du zur Schule fährst
- wie du letztes Jahr in den Urlaub gefahren bist
- welche Verkehrsmittel du am Wochenende benutzen wirst.

Du musst ungefähr **90** Wörter auf **Deutsch** schreiben. Schreib etwas über alle Punkte der Aufgabe.   **(16 marks)**

Wenn ich samstags mit meinen Freunden in die Stadt fahre, nehmen wir immer die U-Bahn.

Ich finde, dass die U-Bahn zuverlässiger und praktischer als der Bus ist.

Now try this

Now prepare your own answers in **German** to the bullet points in the worked example. Try to write **90** words in total.

Divide the number of words required by the number of bullet points you need to answer.   90÷4 = 22 to 23

Great use of singular **ich fahre** and plural **wir nehmen** structures.

Giving an opinion with **Ich denke / finde, dass ...** raises the level of your writing.

The use of a comparative adjective with **als** here shows a proficient command of German.

Directions

Practise your directions in German by giving yourself a running commentary in your head while you are out and about!

Richtungen

Gehen Sie ... Go ... (on foot)
Fahren Sie ... Drive

↑ geradeaus straight on

↰ links um die Ecke
left at the corner

← links left

→ rechts right

über die Brücke
over the bridge

über den Fluss
over the river

🚦↑ zur Ampel
to the traffic lights

↰ an der Kreuzung links
left at the crossroads

zum Kreisverkehr
to the roundabout

auf der linken Seite
on the left

Instructions using Sie

 Grammar page 97

Use the Sie form (-en) of the verb + Sie:
Überqueren Sie die Straße.   Cross the road.
Gehen Sie an der Ampel rechts.
Go right at the lights.

Instructions using du

Use the du form minus the final -st:
Geh die Einbahnstraße hinunter.
Go down the one-way street.

Learning vocabulary

✓ Make your own learning cards – German on one side, English on the other; or a picture on one side, German on the other.
✓ Use learning cards to help you revise. Write key words on them as well as structures you find tricky.

an der Kreuzung links

Worked example

 **LISTENING TRACK 39**

Listen to the recording

Directions in town
What directions do these people give? Complete the following statement in **English**.
To get to the marketplace, you have to cross
...the river... **OR** the bridge   **(1 mark)**

Sometimes there is more than one answer you could write to complete the statement – just choose one, as there is only one mark available.

– Zum Marktplatz gehen Sie hier gleich links und dann 100 Meter geradeaus. Sie kommen dann zum Fluss, wo es eine Fußgängerbrücke gibt. Gehen Sie hinüber und Sie sehen den Marktplatz auf der rechten Seite.

Now try this

 LISTENING TRACK 40

Listen to the recording

Now listen to three more directions and complete the statements in **English**.
1 This person is being directed to ....   **(1 mark)**
2 For the hospital you need to turn ....   **(1 mark)**
3 After eight kilometres the driver will see ....   **(1 mark)**

Had a look ☐   Nearly there ☐   Nailed it! ☐

Local, national,
international and global
areas of interest

Tourism

Look at page 32 for places in your nearest town which might be popular with tourists.

Die Touristik

Alpen	Alps
Anmeldung (f)	registration / booking in
Aufenthalt (m)	stay
im Ausland	abroad
Ausländer/in (m/f)	foreigner
Besuch (m)	visit
Flughafen (m)	airport
Gastfreundschaft (f)	hospitality
Grünanlage (f) / Park (m)	park
Informationsbüro (n)	information office
Parkplatz (m)	car park
Pauschalreise (f)	package holiday
Postkarte (f)	postcard
Reisebus (m)	coach
Tour (t)	tour
Tourist/in (m/f)	tourist
Verkehr (m)	traffic
Verkehrsamt (n)	tourist office

Definite article (the)

Grammar
page 85

Three genders and a plural make up the German words for 'the'.

der – masculine
die – feminine   die – all plurals
das – neuter

- **masculine** – Der Besuch war erfolgreich. The visit was successful.
- **feminine** – Die Grünanlage hat auch einen Spielplatz. The park also has a playground.
- **neuter** – Das Verkehrsamt ist montags geschlossen. The tourist office is closed on Mondays.
- **plural** – Die Alpen sind großartig. The Alps are magnificent.

Picture-based task

In your preparation time:
- ✓ make sure you can **describe** the picture by recalling plenty of relevant adjectives, such as rot, groß, schön, as well as positional words: in, auf der linken Seite, hier im Zentrum and so on.
- ✓ consider the **three** known questions that you will have to speak about. Spend a few minutes on each one, noting the tenses you can use and any useful phrases, but remember: you **must not** read out whole prepared sentences.

Worked example

 SPEAKING

Tourist transactions

Look at the photo and be prepared to talk about it and topics related to **travel and tourism.**

Read this student's response to the first prepared question on this photo.
- Was gibt es auf dem Foto?

Das Foto hat man in den Alpen gemacht, denke ich. Die Landschaft ist schön und ruhig, und hier gibt es Touristen draußen vor einem Café. Sie sitzen in der Sonne, um zu chillen. Meiner Meinung nach sind sie vorher Ski gefahren und jetzt wollen sie sich ausruhen. Skifahren muss anstrengend sein!

Now try this

 SPEAKING

Now prepare answers to these questions you could be asked.
Aim to talk for 30 seconds on each one.
- Findest du Skifahren gut oder nicht?
- Was hast du in den letzten Schulferien gemacht?
- Wohin fährst du in den Urlaub? ... Warum?
- Wie findest du Pauschalreisen?

Listen to the audio file in the answers section for ideas as to how you could answer these questions.

Holiday preferences

When talking about preferences in any topic, make sure you have plenty of positive and negative aspects, as well as examples from the past to back yourself up!

Vergangene Ferien

letzten Sommer	last summer
in den Winterferien	in the winter holidays
letztes Jahr	last year
vor zwei Jahren	two years ago
Ich habe eine Tour gemacht.	I went on a tour.
Er ist nach Rom geflogen.	He flew to Rome.
Wir haben gefaulenzt.	We lazed.

Ich bin Ski gefahren.
I went skiing.

Er ist Bergsteigen gegangen.
He went mountain climbing.

Sie ist schwimmen gegangen.
She went swimming.

Ich bin zelten gegangen.
I went camping.

The perfect tense

Grammar page 100

If you did something in the past, use the perfect tense.

ich habe	
du hast	gekauft (bought)
er / sie / man hat **+**	gemacht (did)
ihr habt	besucht (visited)
wir / Sie / sie haben	gesehen (saw)

ich bin	
du bist	gegangen (went)
er / sie / man ist **+**	geflogen (flew)
ihr seid	gefahren (went / drove)
wir / Sie / sie sind	gekommen (came)

To give your opinion in the past, use Es war + adjective:
Es war ...

spektakulär / schön   stinklangweilig / furchtbar

Ich bin nach Berlin gefahren. Es war prima!
I went to Berlin. It was great!

Worked example

WRITING

Mein Urlaub

Dein Freund Olaf aus Österreich hat dich über den Urlaub gefragt. Du schreibst Olaf eine E-Mail über deinen Urlaub. Schreib:

- wohin du gern in den Urlaub fährst
- was du im letzten Urlaub gemacht hast
- wie du das gefunden hast
- deine Pläne für den nächsten Urlaub.

Du musst ungefähr **90** Wörter auf **Deutsch** schreiben. Schreib etwas über alle Punkte der Aufgabe.   **(16 marks)**

> Ich fahre in den Ferien sehr gern ans Meer. Ich bin Wassersportfan. Ich windsurfe gern. Ich liebe Segeln.

Aiming higher

> In den Sommerferien fahre ich sehr gern ans Meer, da ich ein ziemlich großer Wassersportfan bin. Ich windsurfe äußerst gern, aber am liebsten segle ich. Segeln ist meine Leidenschaft.

These students have answered the first bullet point. Although the first student's answer is an accurate answer, it does little to show Higher skills because the sentences are very short and basic.

To improve your writing:
- Add more detail, which this student does by using **Sommer** + **ferien**.
- Add an adjective.
- Include a **da** (because, since) or **weil** clause – with verb moving to the end!
- Add **am liebsten** to express preference.
- Combine your sentences with the connective **aber**.

Now try this

WRITING

Now prepare your own answers in **German** to the bullet points above. Try to write **90** words in total.

Had a look ☐   Nearly there ☐   Nailed it! ☐

Local, national,
international and global
areas of interest

Hotels

Much of the hotel vocabulary on this page is also relevant for staying at a bed and breakfast or a youth hostel.

Im Hotel wohnen

Aufenthaltsraum (m)	recreation room
Aufzug / Fahrstuhl (m)	lift
Fenster (n)	window
Fitnessraum (m)	gym
Gast (m)	guest
Gepäck (n)	luggage
Klimaanlage (f)	air conditioning
Koffer (m)	suitcase
Reservierung (f)	reservation
Satellitenfernsehen (n)	satellite TV
Schwimmbad (n)	pool
auspacken	to unpack
funktionieren	to work
familienfreundlich	family friendly
mit Blick auf	with a view of

Compound words

Germans love long words! If you are joining words together in the Writing or Speaking exam to make a new word, the gender of the word is determined by the last word in the compound noun.

das Spiel + der Platz = der Spielplatz (playground)

der Preis + die Liste = die Preisliste (price list)

die Stadt + das Zentrum = das Stadtzentrum (town centre)

die Unterhaltung + die Möglichkeiten = die Unterhaltungsmöglichkeiten (things to do)

If you come across a long word in a reading extract, take it apart, as above, to work out what each part means individually.

Worked example

Ein Hotelbesuch

Lies Ninas Blogpost über eine Familienreise. Beantworte die Frage auf **Deutsch**.

Die Familienreise im Frühling macht uns allen immer viel Spaß. Das ist ein absoluter Höhepunkt für mich, finde ich immer! Wir wohnen in einem bequemen Drei-Sterne-Hotel. Das Hotel hat einen schönen Garten mit einem tollen Freibad, das wir zu jeder Zeit benutzen können. Glücklicherweise hat jedes Zimmer Anschluss an das Internet, damit mein jüngerer Bruder sich gut beschäftigen kann. Am Ende des Aufenthalts entscheiden wir uns, dieselben Zimmer für das folgende Jahr zu reservieren. Es ist immer ein einmaliger Urlaub!

Wie findet Nina die Reise im Frühling?

wunderbar / sehr gut

Unser Hotel bietet viele Unterhaltungsmöglichkeiten.

Exam alert

In this style of activity, you have to understand **both** the extract itself **and** the questions. Break down the long words to help you understand the extract **before** you tackle the questions, one by one.

Now try this

Now read the blog again and answer these questions in **German**.

1 Wo übernachtet Nina? **(1 mark)**
2 Was kann man im Garten machen? **(1 mark)**
3 Wer genießt die Technologie? **(1 mark)**
4 Was will Nina nächstes Jahr machen? **(1 mark)**

 Know your question words in German to make activities like this easier.

Campsites

Most of the vocabulary for this topic will also be useful for other types of holiday accommodation.

Auf dem Campingplatz

Badetuch (n)	towel
Bettwäsche (f)	bedlinen
Grill (m)	barbecue
Schlafsack (m)	sleeping bag
Wanderweg (m)	walk / trail
Zahnbürste (f)	toothbrush
Zahnpasta (f)	toothpaste
buchen	to book
reservieren	to reserve
wandern	to walk / hike
zelten	to camp
im Freien	in the open air
im Wohnwagen (m)	in a caravan
im Zelt (n)	in a tent

Giving location details

Here are some ways of letting someone know where you live or are staying.

am	at / on
dort	there
entfernt	away from
hier	here
in der Nähe	
von	near to / close to
neben	next to

Der Campingplatz ...	The campsite ...
liegt in der Nähe von Lindau.	is near to Lindau.
ist etwa 30 Gehminuten vom Stadtzentrum entfernt.	is about 30 minutes on foot from the town centre.
liegt am Bodensee.	is on Lake Constance.
befindet sich am Waldrand.	is situated on the edge of the wood.

Worked example

 LISTENING TRACK 41

Tourism

Listen to the local radio advert for a campsite.

Fill in the gap to complete the sentence in **English**.

Listen to the recording

At this campsite you can hire ....a boat....

– Herzlich willkommen auf dem Campingplatz Maria am Bodensee. Neu ist dieses Jahr unser Bootsverleih (Kajak und Kanu) vor Ort.

Unser Campingplatz befindet sich direkt am Meer.
Our campsite is right by the sea.

- Identify language which is not needed for the question. Here, the first couple of words are 'padding' and can be ignored. They don't offer any information about the campsite.
- Use all the clues provided. Don't be worried by **Bootsverleih** when you hear it mentioned. Break the word down and you may recognise the cognate **Boot**.

Now try this

 LISTENING TRACK 42

Listen to the recording

Now listen to the rest of the recording and fill in the gaps to complete the sentences in **English**.

1 The campsite welcomes caravans and .... **(1 mark)**

2 It is .... to book in advance. **(1 mark)**

3 The campsite is split into .... areas. **(1 mark)**

4 The drinking water is especially .... **(1 mark)**

5 The new wash facility will open .... **(1 mark)**

Had a look ☐ Nearly there ☐ Nailed it! ☐

Local, national,
international and global
areas of interest

Accommodation

Use this page to help you say what type of holiday accommodation you prefer.

Die Ferienunterkunft

Bauernhaus (n)	farmhouse
Bauernhof (m)	farm
Campingplatz (m)	campsite
Ferienwohnung (f)	holiday flat
Halbpension (f)	half board
Vollpension (f)	full board
Hotel (n)	hotel
Jugendherberge (f)	youth hostel
Mietwohnung (f)	rented flat
Pension (f)	bed and breakfast place
Übernachtung (f)	overnight stay
Unterkunft (f)	accommodation
Wohnwagen (m)	caravan / mobile home
mieten	to hire / to rent
übernachten	to stay the night
im Voraus	in advance
inbegriffen	included

Gern, lieber, am liebsten

A simple way of showing a preference is to use gern (like), lieber (prefer) and am liebsten (like most of all).

gern ♥
lieber ♥♥
am liebsten ♥♥♥

- Put gern and lieber after the verb:
  Ich schlafe gern im Freien.
  I like sleeping outdoors.
  Ich bleibe lieber im Hotel.
  I prefer staying in a hotel.
- Use am liebsten to start your sentence:
  Am liebsten zelte ich.
  Most of all I like camping.

Ich schlafe lieber im Freien.

Worked example SPEAKING

Holidays

Answer the question.

- Wo übernachtest du am liebsten im Urlaub?

  Letzten Sommer haben wir in einer Pension übernachtet, aber das war schrecklich, weil wir abends um neun Uhr ins Bett gehen mussten. Diesen Sommer werden wir eine Ferienwohnung mieten und ich freue mich darauf.
  Ich finde es ungemütlich, im Zelt zu schlafen, weil es oft so kalt und unbequem ist. Am liebsten übernachte ich in einem Hotel.

Aiming higher

Aiming higher

Include the following in your speaking and writing, to aim for a higher grade.

- ✓ **Adjectives** make your speaking and writing much more ... fascinating, exciting, amusing.
- ✓ Think PPF (past, present, future) **tenses** before you say anything and then figure out a way to incorporate all three into your answer.
- ✓ **Conjunctions** give lots of scope for great sentences, so make sure you are confident with weil, wenn and dass, and can also have a go with obwohl, bevor and wo.
- ✓ Be prepared for prompts from your teacher such as noch etwas? (anything else?) or warum (nicht)? (why (not)?) to encourage you to add extra detail.

Now try this  SPEAKING

Now prepare to answer these questions as fully as you can. Aim to talk for 30 seconds on each one.

- Übernachtest du lieber weg von zu Hause oder zu Hause? Warum?
- Was war deine beste Übernachtung weg von zu Hause?
- Wo willst du in Zukunft übernachten?

Listen to the audio file in the answers section for ideas as to how you could answer these questions.

Think:
- connectives
- adjectives
- tenses
- conjunctions

Throw each of these into the mix and you are well on the way to a very good answer.

Holiday destinations

Always check your translation carefully – does your English flow well and does your text really make sense?

Ferienziele

Am liebsten übernachte ich ...	I like staying most of all ...
in den Bergen	in the mountains
in einem Dorf	in a village
bei Freunden	with friends
zu Hause	at home
an der Küste	on the coast
auf dem Land	in the countryside
in einer Stadt	in a town

,weil man im See schwimmen kann.
because you can swim in the lake.

,weil es dort viel wärmer als in England ist.
because it is much warmer there than in England.

,weil meine Eltern gern in den Bergen wandern gehen.
because my parents like walking in the mountains.

Dative and accusative prepositions

Grammar page 87

an   on, to, at
auf on, to
in   in, into

These use the **dative** case when there is **no movement** towards anything involved.
Ich wohne im Ausland. I live abroad.
Das Haus liegt am See.   The house is on the lake.

But if there is **movement towards** something, this signals the **accusative** case.
Ich fahre ins Ausland.
I am going abroad.
Ich fahre an die Küste.
I am going to the coast.

Am liebsten übernachte ich an der Küste.

Worked example

Translation
Translate this passage about holidays into **English**.

> Am liebsten übernachte ich am Meer, vor allem wenn das Wetter dort schön ist.

Most of all I like to stay at the seaside, especially when the weather is lovely there.

If you can't remember what **Meer** means, carry on reading for further clues. It is somewhere this person likes to go when the weather is good. Where might it be?

There is often more than one word you can use to translate a word – here, **schön** can be translated as 'lovely', 'fine' or even 'very good'.

Now try this

Now translate the rest of the passage into **English**.

> Mit der Familie fahren wir jedes Jahr an die Ostsee, wo wir unseren ersten Tag immer im größten Naturpark Europas verbringen. Ich würde auch einen Tagesausflug in die malerischen Dörfer empfehlen, um die wunderbaren Märkte zu besuchen und viele preiswerte Andenken zu kaufen. Bevor wir diesen Ferienort entdeckt haben, hatten wir den Sommerurlaub immer in einer historischen Hauptstadt verbracht.

(9 marks)

Holiday experiences

What are your memories of holidays and trips out – positive, negative, or a bit of both?

Thinking positively

Ich mache gern Urlaub in (Europa).
I like going on holiday to (Europe).
Ich ziehe (Aktivurlaube) vor.
I prefer (active holidays).
Am liebsten (bleibe ich in einem Hotel).
Most of all I like (staying in a hotel).
Mein Lieblingsurlaub wäre (eine Woche in der Türkei).
My favourite holiday would be (a week in Turkey).

Urlaub mit Freunden finde ich …	I find holidays with friends …
ausgezeichnet.	excellent.
entspannend.	relaxing.
locker.	relaxed / chilled.
super / prima.	super.

Thinking negatively

Ich fahre nicht gern (ins Ausland).
I don't like travelling (abroad).
(Sporturlaube) kann ich nicht ausstehen.
I can't stand (sports holidays).
Ich würde nie (Skiurlaub machen).
I would never (go on a skiing holiday).
(Eine Woche in der Sonne) interessiert mich nicht.
(A week in the sun) doesn't interest me.
Es gefällt mir gar nicht, (die Sehenswürdigkeiten zu besuchen).
I don't like (visiting the sights) at all.

Familienurlaub finde ich …	I find family holidays …
ermüdend / anstrengend.	tiring.
schlecht.	bad.
schrecklich.	terrible.
stressig.	stressful.

Worked example

 LISTENING TRACK 43

Holidays

You hear a radio debate about people's holiday experiences. What is their opinion of the holidays?

Write **P** for a **positive** opinion.
Write **N** for a **negative** opinion.
Write **P+N** for a **positive and a negative** opinion.
Listen to Hedda speaking and choose the correct option.

Hedda | P+N |

Listen to the recording

– Letzten Sommer bin ich in den Schwarzwald gefahren. Die Landschaft und die Gegend rund herum waren wunderbar, aber der Campingplatz war ziemlich dreckig und sehr laut.

You have to listen to the whole of the recording here – a **P** opinion can soon become a **P+N** one, if an **N** element is added in.

Now try this

 LISTENING TRACK 44

Listen to the recording

Now listen to three more people and choose the correct option for each one.

1 Fynn [ ] **(1 mark)**   2 Linda [ ] **(1 mark)**   3 Rory [ ] **(1 mark)**

Holiday activities

For more things you might do on holiday, look at the leisure activities on page 15.

Urlaubsaktivitäten

Man kann ...

Bergsteigen gehen

segeln

eislaufen gehen

Ski fahren

faulenzen

spazieren gehen

Rad fahren

Tennis spielen

schwimmen gehen

Saying what you can do

The verbs on the left are in the infinitive form – you need to use this form after the expression **Man kann ...** (You can ...).

Man kann ...   ins Schwimmbad gehen.
            sich sonnen.
You can ...   go to the pool.
            sunbathe.

If you start your sentence with a time or place expression, **kann** and **man** swap places.

In den Alpen kann man ...
In the Alps you can ...
In den Ferien kann man reiten.
In the holidays you can go horse riding.

Im Schwarzwald kann man reiten.

Worked example

Holidays

Read the rules covering this holiday park in Switzerland.

> **Willkommen im Feriendorf Halle – wir wünschen Ihnen schöne Ferien bei uns!**
>
> Bitte achten Sie auf unsere Hausordnung:
>
> - Hier darf man nicht auf dem Campingplatz Fußball spielen. Ballspiele sind nur auf dem Spielplatz erlaubt.
> - Wir freuen uns, wenn Sie Ihr Haustier mit auf Urlaub bringen, aber Hunde dürfen hier nicht frei laufen und sie sind im Minimarkt nicht erlaubt.
> - Wenn Sie Fahrräder mitbringen, dürfen Sie nicht damit auf dem Spielplatz fahren. Es gibt viele Fahrradwege nah am Campingplatz.
> - Kinder unter acht Jahren dürfen das Freibad nicht alleine benutzen – es muss ein Erwachsener dabei sein.
> - Wir sind stolz auf unsere ruhige Lage und wir bitten Sie, keine Handys nach neun Uhr abends zu benutzen. Sie stören dabei die Natur und die Mitbewohner!

What is not allowed at the holiday park?
List the **first** thing mentioned.

no football on campsite

Dealing with unknown words

- ✓ Break words down to decode them: Ferien (holidays) + Dorf (village) = holiday village.
- ✓ Think around the words: Freibad means literally 'free bath', but in the context of a holiday, it means 'outdoor pool'.
- ✓ Use any other language clues, such as parts of words and nouns from familiar verbs: mit (with) + Bewohner (from wohnen 'to live') = 'other residents'.

Now try this

Now read the rules again and list **five** more things that are not allowed at the campsite. **(5 marks)**

 You are looking for activities **not** allowed at the campsite – don't just list any five activities mentioned.

Holiday plans

There's more than one way of expressing future actions: a time marker such as nächste Woche + present tense does the trick nicely.

Ferienpläne

Ich werde ...	I will ...
In den Ferien wird er ...	In the holidays he will ...
Hoffentlich werden sie ...	Hopefully they will ...
Eines Tages werden wir ...	One day we will ...
nach Australien fahren.	go to Australia.
zu einem Musikfest gehen.	go to a music festival.
meine Cousine besuchen.	visit my (female) cousin.
nächsten Sommer	next summer
nächsten Winter	next winter
nächstes Jahr	next year
in Zukunft	in future
in zwei Jahren	in two years
Ich freue mich (sehr) darauf.	I am (really) looking forward to it.
Wenn ich älter bin, werde ich einen Ferienjob machen.	When I am older, I will do a holiday job.

You can also use **hoffen + zu** (to hope to) and **möchten** (would like) to indicate future plans.

Ich hoffe, nächstes Jahr nach Amerika zu fahren.
Next year I hope to go to America.

Future tense

The future tense is formed using a part of werden (to become) + infinitive.

ich	werde
du	wirst
er / sie / man	wird
ihr	werdet
wir / Sie / sie	werden

Ich werde nach Ungarn fahren.
I will go to Hungary.
Sie wird Wasserski fahren.
She will go waterskiing.
If you start your sentence with a time expression, werde and ich swap places.
Nächstes Jahr werde ich zu Hause bleiben.
Next year I will stay at home.

Worked example

Translation

Translate the following sentence into **German**.

> Next year I will fly to Germany to visit my girlfriend in Munich.

Nächstes Jahr werde ich nach Deutschland fliegen, um meine Freundin in München zu besuchen.

Aiming higher

 Although the present tense + time marker indicates a future action, you can also use the correct form of werden + an infinitive at the end to express 'will do something'.

☑ Genders – 'girlfriend' is a feminine noun, so make sure the article or adjective with it is also feminine.

☑ Translate **accurately** – the verb here is 'fly' – don't use fahren!

☑ Munich is an English translation – make sure you use the German name.

Now try this

Now translate this passage into **German**.

> I like travelling and visiting new places. When I was in Munich, I got to know some really nice people. We will meet again in May to go on a day trip to the lake. I would like to go on holiday with friends afterwards because that is so much fun.

(12 marks)

Holiday problems

Watch out for verbs in the present tense that change their vowels!

Urlaubsprobleme

Ich habe ...	I have ...
meinen Reisepass verloren.	lost my passport.
einen Unfall gehabt.	had an accident.
Jemand hat meine Brieftasche genommen / gestohlen.	Somebody has taken / stolen my wallet.
Das Hotelzimmer ...	The hotel room ...
ist schmutzig / laut.	is dirty / loud.
hat keinen Anschluss an das Internet.	has no internet connection.
Der Fernseher ist kaputt.	The television is broken.
Der Kühlschrank funktioniert nicht.	The fridge does not work.
Es sind Haare im Waschbecken.	There is hair in the basin.
Es gibt keine Seife.	There is no soap.

Present tense irregular verbs

geben (to give)	nehmen (to take)
ich gebe	ich nehme
du gibst	du nimmst
er / sie / es gibt	er / sie / es nimmt
ihr gebt	ihr nehmt
wir / Sie / sie geben	wir / Sie / sie nehmen

Negative words

Signs with these words on are warnings **not** to do something!

nicht — not

kein — not a / no

verboten — forbidden

Achtung — Attention!

Bitte hier nicht rauchen

Schwimmen verboten

Worked example

 SPEAKING TRACK 45

Listen to the recording

> This dialogue is about a complaint, so make sure you have your best language ready on the subject of dealing with a problem.

Instructions to candidates

Your teacher will play the part of the hotel manager and will speak first.

You should address the hotel manager as Sie.

> Sie sind an der Hotelrezeption. Sie beschweren sich über ein Problem.
>
> 1 Problem – **ein** Detail.
> – Guten Tag. Wie kann ich Ihnen helfen?
> – Der Fernseher ist kaputt.
> 2 Zimmer – Nummer.
> – OK. Wir werden mal schauen. Was ist Ihre Zimmernummer?
> – Ich bin im Zimmer Nummer dreihundertacht.
> 3 !
> – Wie lange bleiben Sie bei uns?
> – Ich bleibe zwei Wochen.

> This student keeps things simple – and completes the task by giving one detail about a problem.

> If you don't catch this unexpected question first time, just ask politely: Wie bitte?

> Make sure you have learned your numbers – here, you can choose any one you like!

> Look at page 25 for further details on the role play.

Now try this

 SPEAKING TRACK 46

Listen to the recording

Now it's your turn. Prepare your own answers to the prompts, including the final two prompts below. Listen to the audio of the teacher part and speak your answers in the pauses.

1 Problem – **ein** Detail.
2 Zimmer – Nummer.
3 !

4 Urlaubsaktivität – **ein** Detail.
5 ? Abendprogramm.

> You can listen to another student's responses in the audio file in the answers section to give you more ideas.

School subjects

Know your school subjects, as they might crop up in any of your exam papers.

Schulfächer

Mathe	Biologie	Chemie
Physik	Deutsch	Englisch
Französisch	Spanisch	Erdkunde
Geschichte	Religion	Informatik
Kunst	Sport	Turnen

Seit + present tense ('for' / 'since')

To talk about how long you have been doing something, use seit + present tense.

Ich lerne seit vier Jahren Deutsch.
I have been learning German for four years.

Seit (since) is followed by the dative case.

seit vier Monaten
for four months

> Dative plurals add -n!

seit diesem Trimester
for this term

seit letztem Jahr   since last year
seit letzter Woche   since last week

Other useful vocabulary:
Pflichtfach (n) – compulsory subject
Theater (n)   drama
Wahlfach (n) – optional subject
Werken (n) – DT

Worked example

 LISTENING TRACK 47

Listen to the recording

Die Schule

Was wird Arvid an der Uni studieren?
Schreib den richtigen Buchstaben in das Kästchen.

A	Fremdsprachen
B	Naturwissenschaften
C	Medienstudien

B

– Im Moment lerne ich viele Fächer für das Abitur. An der Uni will ich mich aber nur auf Chemie konzentrieren, denn ich will in der Pharmaindustrie arbeiten.

Exam alert

Knowledge of vocabulary is essential for Listening exams. Arvid says he wants to study Chemie, but if you didn't know that Naturwissenschaften means 'science', you wouldn't go straight to the correct answer.

Look at the options and work out which sorts of words you might hear for each one – for example, for A you might hear a language such as **Englisch** or **Italienisch**, whereas for B it could well be one of the sciences named individually.

Now try this

 LISTENING TRACK 48

Listen to the recording

Now listen to the rest of the recording and answer the question in **German**.

Was möchte Arvid vor der Uni machen? Beantworte die Frage auf **Deutsch**.   **(1 mark)**

Some activities have more than one part to them, so make sure you read the entire question before you listen and note both the answers.

Opinions about school

You may be asked to express your opinion about school in at least one part of the Speaking exam – the role play, talking about a photo or general conversation.

Meinungen über die Schule

Meiner Meinung nach ist Chemie viel einfacher als Biologie.
In my opinion chemistry is much easier than biology.

Ich finde, dass Mathe sehr schwierig ist.
I think that maths is very difficult.

Ich bin stark / schwach in Deutsch.
I am good / weak in German.

Es ist gut, dass ich in der Schule oft erfolgreich bin.
It's good that I am often successful at school.

Die Lehrer sind echt streng / sympathisch.
The teachers are really strict / nice.

Es gefällt mir (nicht), in die Schule zu gehen.
I (don't) like going to school.

Ich mag es (nicht), wenn Stunden ausfallen.
I (don't) like it when lessons are cancelled.

Ich finde den Schultag sehr anstrengend / abwechslungsreich.
I find the school day very tiring / varied.

Intensifiers

Use intensifiers to reinforce your opinion.

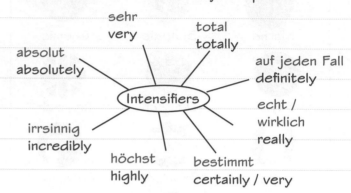

sehr — very
total — totally
absolut — absolutely
auf jeden Fall — definitely
echt / wirklich — really
irrsinnig — incredibly
höchst — highly
bestimmt — certainly / very

Ich finde Deutsch echt super.
I think German is really great.

Spanisch ist sehr schwierig.
Spanish is very difficult.

Mein Lieblingsfach ist auf jeden Fall Werken.
My favourite subject is definitely DT.

In Geschichte habe ich absolut keine Probleme.
In history I have absolutely no problems.

Worked example

School

Answer the question.

- Wie findest du deine Schule?

Meiner Meinung nach ist Mathe sehr schwierig, besonders wenn man kein fleißiger Schüler ist. Ich finde Sport viel besser, weil wir nie Klassenarbeiten schreiben müssen. Wie haben Sie die Schule gefunden?

Aiming higher

Es ist absolut fair, dass Rauchen auf dem Schulgelände streng verboten ist, weil Rauchen sowieso schlecht für die Gesundheit ist. Die Schule kann sehr stressig sein. Wenn ich schlechte Noten bekomme, werde ich auch ein schlechtes Zeugnis bekommen, und dann werden meine Eltern sehr böse sein. In der Grundschule hatte man keine Prüfungen, keinen Stress.

Exam alert

In the Speaking exam general conversation, you need to ask your teacher at least one question on the topic you are talking about. Use the polite Sie form for this.

Look at how this student uses a **variety** of elements and structures to give opinions about school:

- intensifiers
- present, future and past tenses
- modal verb
- **dass**, **weil** and **wenn** clauses.

Now try this

Listen to the audio file in the answers section for ideas as to how you could answer these questions.

Now prepare to answer these questions as fully as you can. Aim to talk for 30 seconds on each one.

- Wie findest du die Schulfächer?
- Was war der beste Tag an der Schule letztes Jahr?
- Findest du die Schule stressig?

Use the tip above to make sure you include plenty of variety in your speaking answers.

Types of schools

Make sure you are familiar with the German school system and types of schools, so you recognise a school if you hear or read about it!

Deutsche Schulen

Direktor (m) / Direktorin (f)	head teacher
Schulleiter (m) / Schulleiterin (f)	head teacher
Berufsschule (f)	vocational school
Gesamtschule (f)	comprehensive school
Grundschule (f)	primary school
Gymnasium (n)	grammar school
Hauptschule (f)	type of secondary school
Internat (n)	boarding school
Kindergarten (m)	pre-school / nursery school
Privatschule (f)	private school
Realschule (f)	type of secondary school
Trimester / Semester (n)	term / semester
lernen	to learn
lehren / unterrichten	to teach
gemischt	mixed
staatlich	state

sich freuen auf + accusative

To talk about something you are looking forward to, use the verb sich freuen auf + the accusative case. So, if talking about school-related topics, you might say:
Ich freue mich (nicht) auf ...
I am (not) looking forward to ...

den Druck (m)	the pressure
die Klassenfahrt (f)	the school trip
das Schuljahr (n)	the school year
die Prüfungen (fpl)	the exams

Ich freue mich auf die Klassenfahrt.
I'm looking forward to the school trip.

Worked example

Schule

Dein Freund Ben aus Deutschland hat dich über deine Schule gefragt. Du schreibst Ben eine E-Mail über deine Schule. Schreib:

- etwas über deine Schule
- welche Fächer du gern oder nicht gern machst
- was dir letztes Jahr an der Schule gefallen hat
- welche Pläne du für das Studium hast.

Du musst ungefähr **90 Wörter** auf **Deutsch** schreiben. Schreib etwas über alle Punkte der Aufgabe. **(16 marks)**

Ich besuche eine Gesamtschule mit etwa tausend Schülern. Als ich zum ersten Mal in diese Schule gegangen bin, war ich erstaunt, weil das Schulgebäude einfach so viel größer als meine Grundschule war, und es war sehr imposant.

This extract is a good piece of writing, as it includes:
- present and past tense
- **als** + opinion + **weil** clause
- an interesting adjective (**imposant**).

Think of some features you want to include in your writing tasks, such as:
- time expressions (**zum ersten Mal**)
- comparative adjectives (**größer**)
- qualifiers (**etwa, so, viel**).

Now try this

Now prepare your own answers in **German** to the bullet points above. Try to write **90** words in total.

Primary school

Talking about your primary school offers a great opportunity to use the imperfect tense.

School equipment

 Bleistift (m)   Etui (n)   Filzstift (m)

 Füller (m)   Heft (n)   Klebstoff (m)

 Kuli / Kugelschreiber (m)   Lineal (n)   Radiergummi (m)

Schere (f)   Schreibblock (m)   Spitzer (m)

 Taschenrechner (m)   Wörterbuch (n)

Modals in the imperfect tense

> Grammar page 99

kann – can	➡ konnte – could
muss – have to	➡ musste – had to
darf – am allowed	➡ durfte – was allowed
will – want	➡ wollte – wanted
soll – am supposed to	➡ sollte – should
mag – like	➡ mochte – liked

In der Grundschule … At primary school …	konnte ich kein Französisch sprechen. I couldn't speak French. musste ich mit meiner Mutter zur Schule gehen. I had to go to school with my mother. durfte ich kein Handy haben. I wasn't allowed a mobile.

Using an imperfect modal is a good indicator that you are aiming high.

Worked example

READING

An der Schule

Lies den Text über Schulerfahrungen. Beantworte die Frage auf **Deutsch**.

> Tim ist mein Zwillingsbruder und wir gingen zusammen zur Grundschule am Stadtrand. Die Schule lag neben dem Fluss und das war sehr schön. Schon an dieser Schule habe ich mich immer gut benommen und war brav. Im Gegenteil dazu wollte Tim nie machen, was die Lehrer von ihm verlangten. Unsere Lehrer sagten Tim, dass er mehr wie ich sein sollte. Wenn ich etwas Dummes machte, lachten meine Lehrer immer, aber mit Tim waren sie immer böse.

Wo war die Grundschule? Gib **zwei** Details.

1 am Stadtrand
2 neben dem Fluss

It doesn't matter what order you put these details in – just make sure you write **two** of them!

Exam alert

For this task, good comprehension skills are needed, as well as knowledge of the question words in German: wo, was, wer, wann are key across all the exam papers.

Now try this

READING

Now read the text again and answer these questions in **German**.

1 Wie war Tim?   (1 mark)
2 Wer fand Tim nicht lustig?   (1 mark)

Class trips

German, Swiss and Austrian schools all organise annual class trips, so you may come across one in your exams!

Die Klassenfahrt

einmal im Schuljahr	once in a school year
mit der Klasse wegfahren	to go away with the class
einander besser kennenlernen	to get to know each other better
miteinander gut / schlecht auskommen	to get on well / badly with each other
neue Sportarten ausprobieren	to try new sports
Erfahrungen sammeln	to gain experience
Wanderwoche (f)	walking week
Wochenprogramm (n)	week's agenda
im Freien	in the outdoors
im Wald	in the forest
in den Bergen	in the mountains
Heimweh haben	to be homesick
ein positives / negatives Erlebnis	a positive / negative experience

Giving your opinion

Make it clear when you are giving an opinion rather than stating a fact.

Ich	finde, denke, meine, glaube,	Klassenfahrten sind super. das Wochenprogramm ist interessant. das wird eine positive Erfahrung sein.

If you use these verbs with a dass clause (e.g. Ich finde, dass ...), remember that the verb goes to the end of the clause.

Ich meine, dass diese Klassenfahrt toll ist.
I think this class trip is great.

Worked example

School

Answer the question.

• Ist eine Klassenfahrt immer positiv?

Meiner Meinung nach machen Klassenfahrten immer viel Spaß, weil man eine Woche weg von der Schule und den Eltern verbringt.
Letztes Jahr bin ich auf Klassenfahrt nach Leipzig gefahren und das war ein wunderbares Erlebnis.

 Aiming higher Das Wochenprogramm war besonders interessant, weil wir jeden Tag etwas Neues unternommen haben. Am Ende des Tages waren wir so erschöpft, dass wir sofort eingeschlafen sind. Ich kann mir vorstellen, die Lehrer waren darüber besonders zufrieden.

This student has included the conjunctions **weil** and **dass**, as well as a complex verb construction: **ich kann mir vorstellen, ...**

Exam alert

Read every word on the exam card – words like immer (always) are important.

Give your opinion using a phrase such as **meiner Meinung nach** + verb next. A great way to start!

Don't hang around in the present tense for too long, but move your conversation along by talking about a related experience you **had** in the past.

Now try this

Now prepare to answer the question in the worked example as fully as you can. Try to speak for at least 30 seconds.

School exchange

You will have to ask a question in the role play and conversation sections of the Speaking exam – make sure you are confident with doing that.

Auf Austausch

Austauschpartner (m) / Austauschpartnerin (f)	exchange partner	Tagesausflüge machen	to go on day trips
Austauschschule (f)	exchange school	die Sehenswürdigkeiten besichtigen	to go sightseeing
Besuch (m)	visit	Die Tagesroutine hat mir (nicht) gefallen.	I liked (didn't like) the daily routine.
Brieffreund (m) / Brieffreundin (f)	penfriend	Das Essen hat mir (nicht) geschmeckt.	I liked (didn't like) the food.
Gastfamilie (f)	host family		
zu Besuch sein	to be visiting	Die Woche war ein großer Erfolg.	The week was a big success.
gut / schlecht miteinander auskommen	to get on well / badly with each other	Ich möchte wieder dorthin fahren.	I would like to go there again.

Worked example

 SPEAKING TRACK 49

Instructions to candidates

Your teacher will play the part of your exchange partner and will speak first. You should address your exchange partner as **du**.

Listen to the recording

> Du sprichst mit deinem Austauschpartner / deiner Austauschpartnerin in der Mittagspause in der deutschen Schule.
> 1 Schule – Meinung.
> – Hallo, wie findest du es hier in der Schule?
> – Es gefällt mir hier gut.
> 2 !
> – Wie findest du die Lehrer?
> – Sie sind meistens nett.
> 3 Meinung zum Schultag – **ein** Detail.
> – Wie findest du den Schultag bei uns?
> – Die Schule beginnt zu früh, denke ich.

Look at page 25 for further details on the role play.

Asking questions in two ways

1 With a question word – see page 6 for a longer list.

Wo?	Where?
Wer?	Who?
Was?	What?

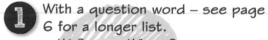

2 By inverting a sentence:

Wir treffen uns.	➡	Treffen wir uns?
Du fährst in den Austausch.	➡	Fährst du in den Austausch?

Question in the role play

✓ Decide how you are going to ask the question: using inversion or with a question word? There is always more than one way of communicating your message.

✓ The prompt ? Schulende could become: Wann endet die Schule? Endet die Schule um zwei Uhr? or Um wie viel Uhr endet die Schule?

You can listen to another student's responses in the audio file in the answers section to give you more ideas.

Now try this

 SPEAKING TRACK 50

Listen to the recording

Now it's your turn. Prepare your own answers to the prompts, including the final two prompts below. Listen to the audio of the teacher part and speak your answers in the pauses.

4 Pläne – nach der Schule – **ein** Detail.

5 ? Schulende.

School events

Make sure you know about lots of different activities that go on at school – competitions, productions, concerts, sport, festivals and so on.

Schulveranstaltungen

in der Theatergruppe sein
to be in the drama club
die Schülerzeitung produzieren
to produce the school newspaper
an einem Wettbewerb teilnehmen
to take part in a competition
beim Lesefest mitmachen
to take part in the reading festival
im Orchester mitspielen
to play in the orchestra
an einer Debatte teilnehmen
to take part in a debate
Mitglied in der Mannschaft sein
to be a member of the team
Die Veranstaltung wird in der Bibliothek
  stattfinden.
The event will take place in the library.
Interessierst du dich für den Kuchenverkauf?
Are you interested in the cake sale?

Verbs with prepositions

Some verbs are always followed by a preposition, so learn the parts together.

- Some take the accusative case:
  sich konzentrieren auf   to concentrate on
  sich interessieren für   to be interested in
  Ich muss mich auf die Kunstausstellung
   konzentrieren.
  I must concentrate on the art exhibition.

- And some take the dative case:
  Angst vor … haben   to be anxious about
  teilnehmen an   to take part in

Ich habe Angst vor dem Schulfußballspiel.
I am anxious about the school football match.

Worked example

School
Listen to an interview on your partner school radio about a competition.
Complete the following statement in **English**.
The drama competition took place in the
...........hall...........

Listen to the recording

– Gestern Abend hat der Theaterwettbewerb unter großem Applaus in der Aula stattgefunden.

Filling gaps

✓ You are listening for key words here – not the general gist of what is being said.
✓ Gap filling is all about precision, so give yourself a head start by reading the statements first and focusing on what sort of word you are listening for: noun, adjective, verb?
✓ Do not write a German word you hear – you have to translate it into English.
✓ If, at the end, you have not managed to catch an answer, try to guess what it might be, thinking about the rest of the passage.

Now try this

 Listen to the recording

Now listen to the rest of the recording and complete the statements in **English**.

1 The competition has been running for .... years.   **(1 mark)**
2 For the class 7 production nobody ....   **(1 mark)**
3 The dancers were very ....   **(1 mark)**
4 The piece received the .... applause of the evening.   **(1 mark)**

School day

To understand and talk about a typical school day, you need a secure knowledge of times and days of the week. Make sure you have learned them – see page 111.

Der Schultag

Die erste Stunde beginnt um zehn vor neun.
The first lesson starts at ten to nine.
Wir haben sechs Stunden pro Tag.
We have six lessons each day.
In der Pause gehen wir auf den Schulhof.
At break we go to the playground.
Wir essen zu Mittag in der Kantine.
We eat lunch in the canteen.
Man kann in der Bibliothek Hausaufgaben machen.
You can do homework in the library.
Nach der Schule gibt es ein gutes Angebot an AGs.
After school there is a good selection of clubs.
Sport haben wir immer als Doppelstunde.
We always have a double lesson for PE.

Linking words

Grammar page 92

These make your sentences longer and they **don't** change the word order!

aber	but
denn	because
	oder or
	und and

Man muss viel lernen und der Leistungsdruck ist enorm.
You have to learn a lot and the pressure to achieve is huge.

In der Pause plaudern wir oder wir machen Hausaufgaben.
At break we chat or we do homework.

Worked example

  READING

„Stundenplan" by Christine Nöstlinger
Read this extract about Anika's day at school.
Answer the question in **English**.

Anika geht aus der Klasse. Sie geht zum Waschraum, der am weitesten von der 4a entfernt ist. Sie geht an Türen vorbei, hinter denen es still ist, an Türen, hinter denen eine Stimme zu hören ist. Sie erkennt die Stimmen. Eine Stimme mag sie. Die erste Stimme sagt: »… trat in die Dienste des Prinzen Karl August von Sachsen-Weimar …«
Es ist eine langsame Mitschreibestimme. »Sachsen-Weimar«, sagt die Stimme noch einmal, »Sachsen-Weimar«. Vorne, dort wo der Gang zur Treppe biegt, sind Schritte. Schnelle Schritte, Lehrerschritte. Schüler, die während der Unterrichtsstunde auf den Gängen sind, gehen nie so schnell.
Anika verschwindet im Waschraum.

Why is Anika's choice of bathroom noteworthy?
it is the furthest away

Reading tips

✓ Answers to comprehension questions are short, but they do need to be **precise** and they do need to be in **English**, if the questions are in English.
✓ Read the whole text through once for gist, and then focus on a sentence-by-sentence reading, bearing the questions in mind.
✓ The questions follow the course of the passage, so don't waste precious time looking at the end of the text for the first answer.
✓ You need to infer meaning – not just translate. Here, the choice of bathroom is noteworthy because it is the one furthest away from the classroom.

Now try this

  READING

Now complete all parts of the task on the extract above.

1 Where can Anika hear noise coming from?
                               (1 mark)

2 What does she feel about the voices? **(1 mark)**

3 Why is the voice speaking slowly? **(1 mark)**

4 Whose footsteps does Anika hear?

A	a pupil's
B	a cleaner's
C	a teacher's

☐   **(1 mark)**

School facilities

Familiarise yourself with the rooms in a school so you can be specific in a description.

Das Schulgelände

Aula (f)	school hall
Bibliothek (f)	library
Computerraum (m)	computer room
Gang (m)	corridor
Kantine (f)	canteen
Klassenzimmer (n)	classroom
Labor (n)	laboratory
Lehrerzimmer (n)	staffroom
Schulhof (m)	playground
Sekretariat (n)	office
Sporthalle (f)	sports hall
Toiletten (fpl)	toilets
gut / schlecht ausgestattet	well / badly equipped
modern / altmodisch	modern / old-fashioned
neu gebaut	newly built

Relative pronouns

Relative pronouns translate as 'who', 'that', 'which'. They agree with the noun they are referring to and send the verb to the end of the clause.
Hier ist ein Schüler, der (m) auf den Bildschirm starrt.
Here is a pupil who is staring at the screen.
Hier ist eine Schülerin, die (f) einen Schal trägt.
Here is a pupil who is wearing a scarf.
Hier ist ein Klassenzimmer, das (n) altmodisch ist.
Here is a classroom that is old-fashioned.
Dort sind die Toiletten, die (pl) immer sauber sind.
There are the toilets, which are always clean.

Das ist die Bibliothek, die ganz neu gebaut ist.

Worked example

Look at the photo and be prepared to talk about it and topics related to **my studies**.
Read this student's response to the first prepared question on this photo.

- Was gibt es auf dem Foto?

Aiming higher Hier ist ein Foto von einer Schulklasse, die beim Unterricht im Computerraum ist. In dieser Reihe sitzen vier Schüler am Computer und schauen auf den Bildschirm. Im Hintergrund sehe ich einen Lehrer, der die Klasse beobachtet. In der Mitte gibt es einen Jungen, der ein rotes T-Shirt trägt und neben ihm bemerke ich einen anderen Jungen, der etwas auf der Tastatur tippt.

Describing a photo

✓ Give your opinion of the photo, saying what you think of the room pictured. Don't just identify it as a computer room.
✓ Compare the room to your school, saying whether you have lessons in a computer room and, if so, which ones and when.
✓ Try to use a different verb in each sentence to add variety to your work.

Describing a photo is a great opportunity to use relative pronouns to help your work flow better.

Now try this

Now prepare answers to these questions you could be asked. Aim to talk for 30 seconds on each one.

- Wie helfen moderne Schulen beim Lernen?
- Was war deine beste Schulstunde?
- Wie ist ein guter Lehrer oder eine gute Lehrerin? Warum?
- Wie willst du deine Schule verbessern?

 Listen to the audio file in the answers section for ideas as to how you could answer these questions.

School rules

Use modal verbs müssen (to have to) and dürfen (to be allowed to) with an infinitive verb when talking about rules at school – or at home.

Die Schulordnung

Die Regeln sind total ...
The rules are totally ...
(un)fair / (un)gerecht.   (un)fair.
dumm / blöd.   stupid.
nervig / ärgerlich.   annoying.
Strafarbeit (f)   lines (in detention)
nachsitzen   to have a detention
Man muss ...   You have to ...
  die Hausaufgaben
    machen.   do the homework.
  im Klassenzimmer
    ruhig sein.   be quiet in class.
  den Müll trennen.   sort the rubbish.

Man darf nicht rauchen.
  You are not allowed to smoke.
Man darf die Stunden nicht schwänzen.
  You are not allowed to skip lessons.
Man darf keine ...   You are not allowed to ...
  Kopfhörer im   wear headphones in
    Unterricht tragen.   lessons.
  Sportschuhe in der   wear trainers to school.
    Schule tragen.

Using müssen (to have to)

Grammar page 98

Müssen is a modal verb, so it needs an infinitive:
Man muss Hausaufgaben machen.
You have to do homework.

Man muss ... You have to ...	höflich sein. be polite.
	viel üben, um ein Instrument zu spielen.
	practise a lot to play an instrument.
	sich ordentlich anziehen.
	dress smartly.
	sitzen bleiben.
	repeat a school year.

Translating into English

✓ Make sure you have learned plenty of vocabulary across all the topics before the exam – that way translations like this will be much easier.

✓ Don't ignore qualifiers and words such as mindestens – they all need to be translated.

✓ Look for word families to help you understand unfamiliar vocabulary: mindestens is linked to Minderheit (minority).

✓ Use common sense – the two pencil case items are the basic equipment needed, so they are unlikely to be a fountain pen and a protractor.

✓ If you come across a conjunction, such as wo or weil, look to the end of the clause to find the accompanying verb(s).

Worked example

Translation
Translate this passage into **English**.

> Ich besuche eine Schule, wo die Schulordnung total dumm ist, weil man mindestens einen Bleistift und ein Lineal im Etui haben muss.

I go to a school where the rules are really stupid, because you have to have at least a pencil and a ruler in your pencil case.

Note how the English translation of die Schulordnung ... ist becomes 'the rules are'. Translating means using English terms, and not just doing a word-for-word translation: 'the school order ... is' does not make sense.

Now try this

Now translate the rest of the passage into **English**.

> Es ärgert mich besonders, dass wir keine Sportschuhe zur Schule tragen dürfen. Letztes Semester hat ein Schüler auf dem Schulhof geraucht, weil er das cool gefunden hat. Der Direktor war aber sehr böse und hat den Jungen sofort nach Hause geschickt. Ich würde an der Schule nie rauchen oder Alkohol trinken, weil ich keine Strafarbeit bekommen möchte.

(9 marks)

Pressures at school

Learn a few key phrases to talk about problems and pressures at school.

Der Schulstress

Elternabend (m)	parents' evening
Note (f)	grade
Zeugnis (n)	report
Angst vor den Noten haben	

to be anxious about the grades

das Jahr wiederholen	to repeat the year
sitzenbleiben	to repeat a year
durchfallen	to fail (an exam)

Die Prüfungen finde ich stressig.
I find exams stressful.
Wir stehen unter großem Leistungsdruck.
We are under a lot of pressure to achieve.
Viele Schüler leiden unter Schulstress.
Many pupils suffer from stress at school.
Ich bin oft abwesend, weil es mir schlecht geht.
I am often absent because I feel ill.
Die Lehrer fehlen oft, weil sie gestresst sind. The teachers are often absent because they are stressed.

Obwohl

Grammar page 93

Obwohl (although) is a subordinating conjunction which sends the verb to the end of the clause, like weil.
Obwohl es eine kleine Schule ist, gibt es hier viele AGs.
Although it is a small school, there are lots of clubs here.
Er ist zur Schule gegangen, obwohl er schreckliche Kopfschmerzen hatte.
He went to school, although he had a terrible headache.

Wir müssen zu viele Klassenarbeiten schreiben.
We have to do too many tests.

Worked example

Translation

Translate the following sentence into **German**.

Earlier you could go to school to play with your friends, and that was fun.

Früher konnte man zur Schule gehen, um mit Freunden zu spielen und das hat Spaß gemacht.

For the highest marks, you have to show you can use subordinating conjunctions, such as **weil**, **um ... zu** and **obwohl** with a variety of tenses.

Translating into German

☑ Grammar is the key to translations into German, so make sure you are confident with verbs and pronouns in the main tenses: present, past, future and conditional form.
☑ Get your word order right – unless there is a subordinating conjunction (e.g. dass), the verb has to come in second place.

Now try this

Now translate this passage into **German**.

I really like school. Although you frequently have to do tests, you can still look forward to class trips. Last year I studied hard to get good grades, and my parents were very pleased. I would like to go to university, because I want to be a vet.

(12 marks)

Future study

Talking about future plans enables you to say what you **want** to do over the next few years.

Sich weiterbilden

Ich möchte / werde ...	I would like to / will ...
in die Oberstufe gehen.	go into the sixth form.
einen Studienplatz bekommen.	get a college place.
auf die Uni(versität) gehen.	go to uni(versity).
die Prüfungen wiederholen.	retake the exams.
eine Weiterbildung machen.	do further education.
(Wirtschaftslehre) studieren.	study (economics).
Mittlere Reife (f)	GCSE equivalent
Abitur (Abi) (n)	A level equivalent
Abiturient (m) / Abiturientin (f)	person doing the 'Abitur'
Student (m) / Studentin (f)	student (uni)
Abschlussprüfung (f)	school leaving exam
Schulabschluss (m)	school leaving certificate
Hochschulabschluss (m)	degree
Hochschulbildung (f)	higher education
Berufsberater (m)	careers adviser
Kurs (m)	course
Resultat / Ergebnis (n)	result
Qualifikation (f)	qualification

Using wollen (to want to)

> Grammar page 98

Wollen is a modal verb, so it needs an infinitive.
Ich will in die Oberstufe gehen.
I want to go into the sixth form.

> Don't confuse the German will (meaning 'want to') with the English 'will' (future intent).

Ich will ... I want to ...	mich weiterbilden. carry on studying.
	auf die Universität gehen. go to university.
	eine Lehre machen. do an apprenticeship.
	an der Uni Englisch und Geschichte studieren. study English and history at university.

Worked example

Future plans
Answer the question.
• Was möchtest du nächstes Jahr machen?

Aiming higher

Gleich nach den Prüfungen will ich ein Wochenende mit meiner Clique an der Küste verbringen. Ich freue mich irrsinnig darauf, obwohl meine Eltern nicht so begeistert davon sind. Nächstes Trimester werde ich hoffentlich in die Oberstufe kommen, wenn ich die notwendigen Noten bekomme. Ich will Fremdsprachen und Mathe lernen, weil ich eines Tages gern im Ausland arbeiten möchte.

Aiming higher

✓ Go for **quality** not quantity. Allow plenty of time for interaction to show that you can understand and respond to what the teacher says.
✓ You will get no credit for repeating language from other parts of your Speaking exam or what your teacher says, so make sure you have a solid supply of **language** across **all topic areas**.

Now try this

Now prepare to answer the following questions and speak for one minute without **hesitating** or **repeating** yourself!
• Warum sind Pläne dir wichtig oder nicht wichtig?
• Welche Pläne hattest du in der Grundschule?
• Warum können sich Pläne oft ändern?

Listen to the audio file in the answers section for ideas as to how you could answer these questions.

Training

Practise the sounds of the alphabet to improve your German pronunciation for the Speaking exam.

Lehrlinge

Arbeitspraktikum (n)	work experience
Ausbildungszentrum (n)	training centre
Betriebspraktikum (n)	work experience
Lehrling (m)	apprentice
Praktikum (n)	internship
in die Berufsschule gehen	to go to vocational college
eine Ausbildung machen	to do training
eine Lehre machen	to do an apprenticeship
Man muss …	You have to …
Aufgaben ausführen.	do tasks.
Kaffee kochen.	make coffee.
Akten abheften.	do filing.
Telefonanrufe beantworten.	answer phone calls.
Kunden anrufen.	phone customers.
abends lernen.	study in the evenings.
einen Kurs besuchen.	do a course.

Man hat viel / wenig / keinen Kontakt mit Kunden.
You have a lot / little / no contact with customers.
Man ist sehr / nicht beschäftigt.
You are very / not busy.

The alphabet

Try to speak German words clearly and with a good accent. Use the listening passages from this book to help practise pronunciation.

LISTENING TRACK 53

Listen to the recording

A ah	B beh	C tseh	D deh	E eh	F eff
G geh	H hah	I ee	J yot	K kah	L ell
M emm	N enn	O oh	P peh	Q kuh	R err
S ess	T teh	U oo	V fow	W veh	X iks
Y upsilon	Z tsett	Ä ah umlaut	Ö oh umlaut	Ü oo umlaut	ß ess-tsett

Make sure you are familiar with the German alphabet, so that if a word is spelled out you know the letters.

Worked example 🗣 SPEAKING

Work

Look at the photo and be prepared to talk about it and questions related to **training and future plans**.

Read this student's response to the first prepared question on this photo.

• Was gibt es auf dem Foto?

Im Vordergrund sieht man ein Mädchen. Ich denke, sie ist ein Lehrling und sie arbeitet heute in einer Werkstatt. Ein älterer Mann erklärt, wie die Maschine funktioniert. Das Mädchen trägt eine blaue Arbeitshose, weil die Arbeit manchmal schmutzig ist. Vielleicht muss sie manchmal eine Brille tragen, weil die Arbeit gefährlich für die Augen sein kann.

Exam alert

The photo task lasts a maximum of two minutes. This covers a description of the photo: Was gibt es auf dem Foto? and then four further questions, two of which you will have prepared.

Describing a photo

☑ Don't worry if you don't know all the words for the items you can see – concentrate on those you **do** know how to say.

☑ German is great for inventing your own words. In the worked example you could use ein blauer Arbeitsanzug ('work suit') to describe the outfit the man is wearing.

Listen to the audio file in the answers section for ideas as to how you could answer these questions.

Record yourself and play it back to see if you hesitated!

Now try this  🗣 SPEAKING

Now prepare answers to these questions you could be asked.
Aim to talk for 30 seconds on each one.

• Willst du ein Arbeitspraktikum machen? … Warum (nicht)?

• Welche Arbeit hast du schon gemacht?

• Was würdest du nicht gern bei einem Arbeitspraktikum machen?

• Was findest du besser, trainieren oder studieren?

CV

Your CV information is all about the topic of **you**!

Der Lebenslauf

Arbeitserfahrung (f)	work experience
Berufsausbildung (f)	vocational / professional training
Durchschnittsnote (f)	average grade
Geburtsdatum (n)	date of birth
Geburtsort (m)	place of birth
persönliche Daten (pl)	personal details
Schulausbildung (f)	education
Zukunftspläne (pl)	future plans

Ich bin am (4. Juni) in (Hull) geboren.
  I was born on (4 June) in (Hull).
Ich habe Erfahrung als (Kellner).
  I have experience as (a waiter).
Ich interessiere mich für (Sport).
  I am interested in (sport).

This / that, these / those, every, which

Grammar page 88

These follow the pattern of der, die, das (see pages 85 and 86).

dieser	this / these
jener	that / those
jeder	every
welcher?	which?

	nom	acc	dat
masc	dieser	diesen	diesem
fem	diese	diese	dieser
neut	dieses	dieses	diesem
plural	diese	diese	diesen

(m acc) Welchen Job würdest du lieber machen?
Which job would you prefer to do?
(f acc) Ich finde jede Arbeit ermüdend.
I find every job tiring.
(n dat) Ich möchte in diesem Restaurant arbeiten.
I would like to work in this restaurant.

Ich möchte für diese Firma arbeiten.
I would like to work for this company.

Worked example

Du schreibst an deine deutsche Freundin über die Jobsuche. Schreib etwas über:

- Persönlichkeit
- Ausbildung
- Hobbys
- Arbeitserfahrung.

Du musst ungefähr **40** Wörter auf **Deutsch** schreiben.

(16 marks)

Ich bin freundlich, aber ich bin nicht sehr geduldig.

← This is just the first part of this student's answer.

Writing strategies

The best answers for a 40-word text are short and to the point.

- ✓ Don't overcomplicate your work – stick to structures you are familiar with and get them right.
- ✓ Don't overuse the same verbs – ist, hat and es gibt are great, but try to mix them up with other verbs too.
- ✓ Don't be afraid of including a negative, such as nicht or kein(e).
- ✓ Try to vary the word order – start with a time expression and then place the verb next: Im Moment arbeite ich ...
- ✓ Check you have used the correct word order – verb in second place in each sentence.

Now try this

Now prepare your own answers in German to the bullet points above. Try to write **40** words in total.

Jobs

Make sure you know both the male and female versions of the jobs listed below.

Arbeit

Angestellter (m) / Angestellte (f)	employee
Arbeitgeber/in	employer
Bäcker/in	baker
Bauarbeiter/in	builder
Bauer (m) / Bäuerin (f)	farmer
Elektriker/in	electrician
Fahrer/in	driver
Fleischer/in / Metzger/in	butcher
Flugbegleiter/in	cabin crew
Kassierer/in	cashier
Kellner/in	waiter / waitress
Klempner/in	plumber
Mechaniker/in	mechanic
Modeschöpfer/in	fashion designer
Techniker/in	technician
Tischler/in	carpenter / joiner
Vertreter/in	sales representative

Mein Bruder arbeitet in der Schneiderei.
My brother works in tailoring.

gut / schlecht bezahlt   well / badly paid

Saying 'somebody' and 'nobody'

jemand – somebody
Jemand arbeitet in der Metzgerei.
Somebody is working in the butcher's.

niemand – nobody
Niemand arbeitet auf dem Bauernhof.
Nobody is working at the farm.

accusative = für jemanden / niemanden
dative = mit jemandem / niemandem

Worked example

 LISTENING TRACK 54

Family and jobs

Your German penfriend, Leon, has sent you a podcast about his family.

Answer the question in **English**.

How many sisters does Leon have?

two sisters

Listen to the recording

– Ich stelle dir meine Familie vor. Meine ältere Schwester arbeitet als Vertreterin bei einer Techno-Firma und spielt gern Tennis in ihrer Freizeit. Meine andere Schwester heißt Carmen und sie ist nervig.

Listening tips

- ☑ Read the questions **before** you listen.
- ☑ Watch out for questions requiring **two** pieces of information.
- ☑ If the answers are supposed to be **in English**, jotting down words in German won't help you!

You have to wait some time to get the answer to this question. Don't jump to the conclusion that Leon only has one sister. Carry on listening and you will hear him mention **eine andere Schwester** (another sister).

Now try this

 LISTENING TRACK 55

Question 3 asks for **two** pieces of information – make sure you give both of them.

Listen to the recording

Now listen to the rest of the podcast and answer the following questions in **English**.

1 What are Carmen's job plans? Give **one** detail.   **(1 mark)**
2 How do you know that Leon's mother works hard?   **(1 mark)**
3 What is unusual about his father? Give **two** details.   **(2 marks)**

Professions

Use strategies to help you when translating into English – does the German word look like an English word?

Berufe

Apotheker/in	pharmacist
Architekt/in	architect
Arzt (m) / Ärztin (f)	doctor
Beamter (m) / Beamtin (f)	civil servant
Dichter/in	poet
Feuerwehrmann (m) / Feuerwehrfrau (f)	fire fighter
Informatiker/in	computer scientist
Ingenieur/in	engineer
Journalist/in	journalist
Krankenpfleger (m) / Krankenschwester (f)	nurse
Künstler/in	artist
Lehrer/in	teacher
Manager/in	manager
Mechaniker/in	mechanic
Polizist/in	police officer
Schauspieler/in	actor
Zahnarzt (m) / Zahnärztin (f)	dentist

Ich habe viel Ehrgeiz / Ich bin ehrgeizig.
  I am ambitious.
Man muss oft in Besprechungen sitzen.
  You have to sit in meetings a lot.

Imperfect subjunctive modals

Impress with these expressions in the Speaking exam. They are no more complicated than modals in the present tense, but they will improve your speaking and writing!

Ich möchte Tierärztin werden.
I would like to become a vet.

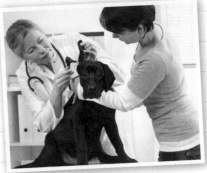

Du könntest viel Geld verdienen.
You could earn lots of money.
Du solltest versuchen, Arzt zu werden.
You should try to become a doctor.

Note that in German the word for 'a' is not needed before the job.

Worked example

Translation
Translate this description into **English**.

> Meine Mutter arbeitet als Ärztin. Um sechs Uhr fährt sie immer zum Krankenhaus.

My mother works as a doctor. At six o'clock she always drives to the hospital.

Translating into English

✓ Use words that look like their English equivalent to help with translations.
✓ Don't switch tenses when you are translating – arbeitet is present tense: 'works'.
✓ Krankenhaus is linked to krank (ill), so what do you think an 'ill house' is?
✓ Connect words – if you can't remember what Ärztin is, can you recall the male term Arzt? Think logically about where this person works, the Krankenhaus. Who works there?

Now try this

Now translate the rest of the description into **English**.

> Ihre Chefin heißt Angelika. Sie ist vierzig Jahre alt und sehr nett. Meine Mutter mag ihre Arbeit, aber sie findet die langen Stunden anstrengend. Abends sehen wir zusammen gern fern. Letzte Woche hat sie aber nachts gearbeitet.

(9 marks)

Job ambitions

Use this page to learn some Higher-level language about your ambitions for a future job.

Berufswünsche

Ich hoffe, …   I hope …

bei einer globalen Firma zu arbeiten.
to work for a global company.

ein hohes Gehalt zu verdienen.
to earn a high wage.

Chef/in zu werden.
to become the boss.

meine eigene Firma zu gründen.
to found my own company.

(nicht) in einer Fabrik zu arbeiten.
(not) to work in a factory.

(nicht) draußen / im Freien zu arbeiten.
(not) to work outside.

von zu Hause aus zu arbeiten.
to work from home.

gute Aufstiegsmöglichkeiten zu haben.
to have good chances of promotion.

im Ausland zu arbeiten. **to work abroad.**

Teilzeit zu arbeiten.   **to work part-time.**

im Sportbereich / Musikindustrie zu arbeiten.
to work in the sports sector / music industry.

Infinitive expressions

 Grammar page 94

Ich	hoffe, … (hope) versuche, … (try) habe vor, … (intend)	+ zu + infinitive.

Ich habe vor, ins Ausland zu reisen.
I intend to travel abroad.

Ich hoffe, viel Geld zu verdienen.
I hope to earn lots of money.
Ich fange an / beginne, an die Zukunft zu denken.
I am beginning to think about the future.
Ich versuche, einen Teilzeitjob zu finden.
I am trying to find a part-time job.

Worked example

 LISTENING TRACK 56

Jobs

Listen to the recording

– Routine ist nichts für mich. Ich suche etwas Spannendes. Am liebsten würde ich Feuerwehrmann werden, weil man jeden Tag etwas anderes macht.

1 Was möchte Lothar werden?
Beantworte die beiden Teile der Frage.

A   B   C

Schreib den richtigen Buchstaben in das Kästchen.

A

2 Warum? Beantworte die Frage auf **Deutsch**.

es ist immer anders

Don't forget: answering auf **Deutsch** means just that – English words are not allowed!

Look at the photos **before** you listen. Do you know the German words for the jobs pictured? What other words might give you a clue here? For example, photo **B** might mention **Krankenhaus** rather than **Arzt / Ärztin** as your clue.

For the second part, be prepared to come up with your own phrasing. Lothar says his reason is that he wants to do **etwas anderes** every day. Just writing **etwas anderes** is not enough – you need to give a verb as well for your answer to make sense.

Now try this

 LISTENING TRACK 57

Listen to the recording

Now listen to the rest of the recording and complete the activity.

1 Was ist Lothar unwichtig?
  Beantworte die beiden Teile der Frage.

A   B   C

Schreib den richtigen Buchstaben in das Kästchen. ☐ **(1 mark)**

2 Was ist ihm wichtig? Beantworte die Frage auf **Deutsch**.

………………   **(1 mark)**

Opinions about jobs

The opinions on this page can equally well be applied to other topic areas – holidays, school, visits.

Meinungen über die Arbeit

Arbeitsbedingungen (pl)	work conditions
Ich habe ein sehr positives Gefühl.	I have a very positive feeling.
Es war mein Traum, diesen Job zu bekommen.	It was my dream to get this job.
Ich fühle mich auf der Arbeit wohl.	I feel comfortable at work.
Der Job ist ein großer Erfolg.	The job is a big success.
Es ist das Beste für mich.	It is the best for me.
Das ist ein ausgezeichnetes Erlebnis.	That is an excellent experience.
Ich wäre gern noch länger geblieben.	I would have liked to stay longer.

Dieser Job würde mich ärgern.	This job would annoy me.
Das ist so ein Pech, kein Gehalt zu bekommen.	That is such bad luck not to get a salary.
Ich wünsche mir keine schlecht bezahlte Stelle.	I wouldn't wish for a badly paid position.
Es wäre eine große Enttäuschung.	It would be a big disappointment.
Ich würde es niemandem empfehlen.	I would not recommend it to anyone.
Ich würde das vermeiden.	I would avoid that.

Meiner Meinung nach

Use the expression Meiner Meinung nach + verb to express any opinion.

Meiner Meinung nach sind die Arbeitsbedingungen prima.

In my opinion the terms and conditions are excellent.

You can also use the verb meinen (to think) with a dass clause to give an opinion, but this time the verb goes to the end of the clause.

Ich meine, dass die Kantine auf der Arbeit sehr gut ist.

I think that the canteen at work is very good.

Worked example

 TRACK 58

Opinions practice

You may need to identify whether an opinion is **positive**, **negative** or both **positive and negative**, so practise with this activity.

	🙂	🙁	🙂 🙁
Example	X		

– Ich finde, die neue Stelle ist ein großer Erfolg, und macht mir besonders Spaß.

Understanding opinions

- ✓ Listening activities often rely on you understanding the **opinion** given, so always listen for clues, such as the speaker's **intonation**, to help you identify whether they are being **positive** or **negative**.
- ✓ Also listen out for the opinion words above to alert you to the fact it is an **opinion** and not a **fact**.
- ✓ You must listen to the opinion right to the end – a negative opinion might have a positive side to it, so don't miss this!

Now try this

 TRACK 59

 Listen to the recording

Now listen to ten more opinions.
Write **P** for a **positive** opinion.
Write **N** for a **negative** opinion.

Write **P+N** for a **positive and a negative** opinion.

(10 marks)

80

Job adverts

Make sure you're prepared with this vocabulary connected with job seeking.

Stellenangebote

Arbeitsstunden (pl)	hours of work
Aufstiegsmöglichkeiten (pl)	chances of promotion
Euro pro Stunde	euros per hour
Kollege (m) / Kollegin (f)	colleague
Mitarbeiter (m) / Mitarbeiterin (f)	co-worker
Stelle (f) / Job (m)	job
Stellenangebote (pl)	job vacancies
Stellenanzeige (f)	job advert
Termin (m)	appointment
ausgebildet	qualified, educated
erfahren	experienced
qualifiziert	qualified
teamfähig	good team worker
verantwortlich	responsible

Genitive prepositions

The following all take the genitive case:

außerhalb	outside, beyond
statt	instead of
trotz	despite
während	during
wegen	because of, owing to

(m) der Anruf – statt des Anrufs
(der ➡ des + -s) instead of the call
(f) die Pause – während der Pause
(die ➡ der) during the break
(n) das Gehalt – trotz des niedrigen Gehalts
(das ➡ des + -s) despite the low salary
(pl) die Arbeitsstunden – wegen der Arbeitsstunden
(die ➡ der) due to the working hours

To show possession, use the following:
der Job meines Vaters – my father's job
der Chef der Firma – the firm's boss
der Bruder meiner Tante – my aunt's brother
das Ziel der Kinder – the children's aim

Der Job eines Arbeitsuchenden ist schwierig!
The work of a job seeker is hard!

Worked example

Translation

Translate the following sentence into **German**.

I am looking for a job.

Ich suche eine Stelle.

You do not need a word for 'for' in this translation, as **suchen** means 'to look for'.

eine Stelle = ein Job / eine Arbeit

Translating into German

✓ German nouns need **capital** letters!

✓ Look at **who** you are writing about in each sentence – yourself? Another person? More than one person? You need to have the correct part of the verb to match.

✓ Look at **when** you are writing about – is it something happening now (present tense) or a past action (past tense)?

Now try this

Now translate the following sentences into **German**.
1 I want to be a teacher.
2 My aunt earns fifteen euros per hour.
3 She works in an office in the town centre.
4 I need a job because I have no money.
5 Last year I worked as a waiter. **(10 marks)**

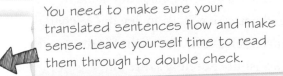

You need to make sure your translated sentences flow and make sense. Leave yourself time to read them through to double check.

If you can't recall a specific German word, work around it, making sure you convey the same meaning; for example, 'I worked' could equally well be expressed as 'I had a job'.

Applying for a job

Watch out for the imperfect tense in literary texts: arbeitete = 'worked' or 'was working'.

Sich um einen Job bewerben

einen Bewerbungsbrief schreiben
to write a letter of application
das Bewerbungsformular ausfüllen
to fill in the application form
Ich interessiere mich für den Job ...
I am interested in the job ...
  als Küchenhilfe. (f)   as kitchen staff.
  als Kellner/in.   as a waiter / waitress.
  am Schwimmbad.   at the swimming pool.
Ich habe ausgezeichnete Sprachkenntnisse.
I have excellent language skills.
Ich möchte von Juli bis September arbeiten.
I would like to work from July to September.
Anbei finden Sie meinen Lebenslauf.
Please find my CV enclosed.

Writing a formal letter

Sehr geehrter Herr X	Dear Mr X
Sehr geehrte Frau Y	Dear Mrs Y
zu Händen von Z	for the attention of Z
in Bezug auf	relating to / with regard to
Rufen Sie mich an.	Call me.
Vielen Dank im Voraus	Many thanks in advance
Mit bestem Gruß	With best wishes
Mit freundlichen Grüßen	Yours sincerely
Alles Gute	All the best

Reading tips

Don't expect to understand everything word for word, and be prepared for vocabulary from a variety of topics: jobs, clothes, shopping and personality all come up here.

Worked example

Wieder keine Arbeit

Lies diese Geschichte über Karl nach „Der Marder mit den Katzenpfoten" von Katja Lapp. Beantworte die Fragen.

Schreib **R**, wenn die Aussage **richtig** ist,

F, wenn die Aussage **falsch** ist,

NT, wenn die Aussage **nicht im Text** ist.

Ich muss heute zum Arbeitsamt gehen. Leider habe ich gestern schon wieder einmal meinen Job verloren. Das passiert mir leider häufig.

Es ist wie ein Spiel: ich finde einen Arbeitsplatz, den ich tolerieren kann. Ich suche aber immer noch etwas Interessanteres. Diese Stelle mache ich nur bis zu dem Tag, an dem etwas Besseres kommt.

Diesmal arbeitete ich in der Jackenabteilung eines berühmten Kaufhauses. Ich musste viel herumstehen, die Kunden begrüßen und viele, viele Jacken richtig aufhängen. Nach einigen Tagen langweilte ich mich so sehr, dass ich mir für meine Kollegen Spitznamen ausdachte. Ich weiß nicht, wie ich auf die Fix und Foxi Zeichentrickfilmcharaktere kam, doch ich teilte jedem Mitarbeiter je nach Charakter eine Figur aus diesem Comicheft zu.

Karl ging ins Kino. ☐ F

Now try this

Now complete the activity from the worked example.

1 Karl hat nie vorher einen Job gehabt. ☐ **(1 mark)**

2 Karl hatte eine Stelle in einem Geschäft. ☐ **(1 mark)**

3 Karl interessierte sich nicht für die Kleider. ☐ **(1 mark)**

4 Karl ist über dreißig Jahre alt. ☐ **(1 mark)**

5 Karl gab seinen Mitarbeitern Namen, um sich zu amüsieren. ☐ **(1 mark)**

6 Er weiß genau, warum er die Namen aus einer Sage gewählt hat. ☐ **(1 mark)**

7 Seine Mitarbeiter haben die Namen lustig gefunden. ☐ **(1 mark)**

8 Karl stellte sich ein fröhliches Fest mit den Charakteren vor. ☐ **(1 mark)**

Exam alert

Tasks like these can be deceptively tricky. If you didn't know the meaning of wieder einmal (once again), this first question would trip you up! Knowing vocabulary is essential.

Job interview

Have a go at this role play to showcase your communication skills in five exchanges.

Vorstellungsgespräch

Ich bin höflich und freundlich.
I am polite and friendly.
Ich habe keine Erfahrung, aber ich lerne schnell.
I don't have any experience, but I learn fast.
Ich babysitte / mache Babysitting.   I babysit.
Ich komme gut mit anderen Menschen aus.
I get on well with other people.
Ich arbeite gern in einem Team.
I like working in a team.
Ich habe einen Erste-Hilfe-Kurs besucht.
I have done a first aid course.
Letztes Jahr habe ich zwei Wochen bei einer Firma gearbeitet.
Last year I worked at a company for two weeks.
Möchten Sie meinen Lebenslauf sehen?
Would you like to see my CV?

Different words for 'you'

Familiar

du = 'you' to another young person, family member, friend or animal
ihr = 'you' plural of du

Sie   du

Formal

Sie = 'you' to adult(s), teacher(s), official(s)
Sie = singular and plural

Questions in a job interview

Wie sind die Arbeitsstunden?
What are the hours?
Gibt es gute Aufstiegsmöglichkeiten?
Are there good promotion prospects?
Wie viel Urlaub werde ich pro Jahr bekommen?
How much holiday will I get each year?

Worked example

  TRACK 60

Listen to the recording

Instructions to candidates

Your teacher will play the part of the hotel manager and will speak first.
You should address the manager as Sie.

> Sie bewerben sich am Telefon für einen Job als Kellner / Kellnerin in der Schweiz.
> 1 Der Job – welchen.
> – Wie kann ich Ihnen helfen?
> – Ich telefoniere wegen des Jobs als Kellner in Ihrem Restaurant.
> 2 !
> – Haben Sie schon Arbeitserfahrung?
> – Ja, ich habe im Café in der Stadt gearbeitet.
> 3 Grund für den Job – **ein** Detail.
> – Warum wollen Sie bei uns arbeiten?
> – Ich möchte meine Deutschkenntnisse verbessern.

Exam alert

Make sure you read on the task card which register – du or Sie –you need to use and keep it going for the entire role play.

- Look at page 25 for further details on the role play.
- See page 6 for question words.

Role play strategy

Don't try to show off complex language in the role play – your aim is to communicate, so use constructions you are secure with. You can use the other Speaking parts of the exam to impress with more complex language!

Now try this

   TRACK 61

Listen to the recording

Now it's your turn. Prepare your own answers to the prompts, including the final two prompts below. Listen to the audio of the teacher part and speak your answers in the pauses.
4 Charaktereigenschaften – **zwei** Details.
5 ? Arbeitsstunden

You can listen to another student's responses in the audio file in the answers section to give you more ideas.

Part-time jobs

When talking about part-time jobs, always use a range of vocabulary and structures, including weil, bevor and obwohl.

Der Teilzeitjob

Ich arbeite samstags als ...	I work on Saturdays as a ...
Kassierer/in	cashier
Kellner/in	waiter / waitress
Tellerwäscher/in	washer-up
Verkäufer/in	sales assistant

Ich trage Zeitungen aus.
I deliver newspapers.
Ich habe einen Ferienjob in einem Restaurant.
I've got a holiday job in a restaurant.
Ich habe einen Teilzeitjob in einer Autowerkstatt.
I've got a part-time job at a garage.
Ich verdiene 10 Euro pro Stunde.
I earn 10 euros an hour.
Mein Ziel ist es, einen Ferienjob zu finden.
It's my aim to find a summer job.
Ich bin ein erfahrener Babysitter / eine erfahrene Babysitterin.
I am an experienced babysitter.
Ich hefte gern Sachen ab.   I enjoy filing.

Dative verb gelingen (to succeed)

The dative verb gelingen works in the same way as gefallen (to like): es gefällt mir (I like it).

Es gelingt mir, einen Job zu bekommen. I succeed in getting a job.
Gestern ist es mir gelungen, einen Preis zu gewinnen.
Yesterday I succeeded in winning a prize.

Es gelingt ...

mir	(me)	uns	(us)
dir	(you)	euch	(you – pl)
ihm	(him)	ihnen / Ihnen	(them / you –
ihr	(her)		polite)

Es ist mir gelungen, das Abitur zu bestehen!
I succeeded in passing my A levels!

Worked example

Nebenjob

Du hast einen Nebenjob und du schreibst deinem deutschen Freund Jens darüber.

- Schreib etwas über den Nebenjob – deine Eindrücke und deine Meinung.
- Vergleich deinen Nebenjob mit einem früheren Job.

Du musst ungefähr **150** Wörter auf **Deutsch** schreiben. Schreib etwas über beide Punkte der Aufgabe. **(32 marks)**

Samstags arbeite ich jetzt seit zwei Monaten als Assistent im Sportverein und ich finde den Job abwechslungsreich und sehr interessant. Ich lerne viele neue Fähigkeiten und die Erfahrung ist sehr nützlich, denke ich.

Exam alert

Make sure you:
- write the requested number of words – here it is 150
- address both bullet points by writing more or less the same number of words for each
- link your sentences so that your writing reads naturally and flows well
- use a variety of constructions and sentence lengths to ensure variety in your work.

This uses the construction **seit** + present tense to say how long this student has been working for.

This is just the first paragraph of this student's answer.

Now try this

Now prepare your own answers in **German** to the bullet points above. Try to write **150** words in total.

Look at the advice in the Exam alert – have you followed this guidance in your answer?

Gender and plurals

When you are learning a German noun, always learn it with its word for 'the' (gender).
All German words are masculine, feminine or neuter.

Der, die, das (the)

Every German noun is masculine (m – der), feminine (f – die) or neuter (n – das).

Der Mann ist groß.
The man is tall.
Die Frau ist klug.
The woman is clever.
Das Kind ist nervig.
The child is annoying.
Die Katzen sind süß.
The cats are cute.

	masc	fem	neut	pl
nominative	der	die	das	die

If you don't know the gender of a word, you can look it up in a dictionary:

Frau *f* woman, wife

Der, die, das as the subject

The definite articles der, die, das, die are used when the noun is the **subject** of the sentence. That means it is doing the action of the verb:

Der Lehrer spielt Fußball.
The teacher is playing football.
'The teacher' is in the **nominative** case.

> Look at pages 86–87 for more details of the cases in German.

Der, die, das as the object

But if the teacher becomes the **object** of the verb, e.g. is seen by someone else, then **der** changes to **den**:

Ich sehe den Lehrer.   I see the teacher.
I = subject, as it is doing the seeing, and the teacher is the object, as he is being seen.
Here, 'the teacher' is in the **accusative** case – die and das stay the same when used in this way.

	masc	fem	neut	pl
accusative	den	die	das	die

Plurals

German nouns have different plurals. Not sure what they are? Check in a dictionary:

Mann (⸚er) *m* man

The part in brackets tells you what to add to make the word plural. The umlaut before the -er ending tells you that an umlaut is added to the vowel before the ending, so the plural of **Mann** is **Männer**.

Now try this

Which definite article – der, die or das? Use a dictionary to find the gender and plural of these nouns.

(a) Anmeldung   (d) Haltestelle
(b) Fahrer   (e) Fernseher
(c) Rührei   (f) Brötchen

> The gender is taken from the last word of compound nouns: **der Abend** + **das Brot** = **das Abendbrot**.

Cases and prepositions

Prepositions such as durch (through) and zu (to) trigger a change in der, die or das, as they have to be followed by a specific case – the accusative, dative or genitive.

Changes to 'the'

	masc	fem	neut	pl
nominative	der	die	das	die
accusative	den	die	das	die
dative	dem	der	dem	den
genitive	des	der	des	der

Changes to 'a'

	masc	fem	neut	pl
nominative	ein	eine	ein	keine
accusative	einen	eine	ein	keine
dative	einem	einer	einem	keinen
genitive	eines	einer	eines	keiner

The genitive is not used very often, but it looks impressive if you can use it correctly!

keine – not a / no

Prepositions + accusative

Prepositions that trigger a change to the **accusative** case:

für	for
um	around
durch	through
gegen	against / towards
entlang	along (after the noun)
bis	until
ohne	without

FUDGEBO = first letters of all accusative prepositions!

Ich kaufe ein Geschenk für einen Freund.
I am buying a present for a friend.
Geh um die Ecke.
Go round the corner.

Prepositions + dative

Prepositions that trigger a change to the **dative** case:

aus	from	nach	after
außer	except	seit	since
bei	at, at the home of	von	from
gegenüber	opposite	zu	to
mit	with		

nach einer Weile
after a while
Fahr mit dem Bus.
Go by bus.

zu + dem = zum
zu + der = zur
bei + dem = beim

You need to add -n to the end of a plural masculine or neuter noun in the dative case:
mit meinen Freunden = with my friends.

Prepositions + genitive

Prepositions that trigger a change to the **genitive** case:

trotz	in spite of / despite
wegen	because of

 See page 81 for more prepositions + genitive.

laut der Zeitung	according to the newspaper
wegen des Wetters	because of the weather
während	during

 You also need to add an -s to the end of a masculine or neuter noun in the genitive case.

Now try this

Translate these phrases into **German** by adding the preposition and changing the word for 'the' or 'a'.
(a) against the wall (die Mauer)
(b) except one child (ein Kind)
(c) despite the snow (der Schnee)
(d) after an hour (eine Stunde)
(e) to the shops (die Geschäfte – pl)
(f) without a word (ein Wort)
(g) during the summer (der Sommer)
(h) at the doctor's (der Arzt)

Prepositions with accusative or dative

Movement towards or not? That is the key question! Dual-case prepositions can be followed by either the accusative or the dative case.

Dual-case prepositions

an	at
auf	on
hinter	behind
in	in
neben	next to
über	over
unter	under
vor	in front of
zwischen	between

- If there is **movement towards** a place, these prepositions trigger a change to the **accusative** case:
  Ich gehe ins Haus. = I go into the house.
- If there is **no movement** towards a place, these prepositions trigger a change to the **dative** case:
  Ich bin im Haus. = I am in the house.

in + das = ins
in + dem = im

Verbs + accusative

Some verbs work with a preposition followed by the accusative case.

aufpassen auf	to look after	Ich muss auf den Hund aufpassen.
sich ärgern über	to be annoyed about	I have to look after the dog.
sich gewöhnen an	to get used to	
sich streiten über	to argue about	Ich freue mich auf den Sommer.
sich erinnern an	to remember	I am looking forward to the summer.
sich freuen auf	to look forward to	
warten auf	to wait for	Ich habe mich an die Arbeit gewöhnt.
		I have got used to the work.

Prepositional phrases

Die Katze springt auf den Tisch. (acc)	The cat jumps onto the table.
Die Katze sitzt auf dem Tisch. (dat)	The cat is sitting on the table.
Ich surfe gern im Internet. (dat)	I like surfing the net.
Sie wohnt auf dem Land. (dat)	She lives in the countryside.
auf der linken Seite (dat)	on the left-hand side

As you can see here, where there is no movement the dual-case preposition is generally followed by the dative case, and where there is a sense of movement it is followed by the accusative.

Now try this

Complete the sentences with the correct definite article ('the').

(a) Ich wohne an .... Küste (f).

(b) Sie streiten sich über .... Fernseher (m).

(c) Was gibt es hinter .... Haus (n)?

(d) Wie finden Sie die Geschichte über .... Jungen (pl)?

(e) Die Nacht vor .... Hochzeit (f).

(f) Man muss zwischen .... Zeilen (pl) lesen.

(g) Denke an .... Namen (m).

(h) Erinnerst du dich an .... Person (f)?

Dieser / jeder, kein / mein

Other groups of words, such as adjectives, also change according to case.

Words that follow the der, die, das pattern

These words follow the pattern of der, die, das:
dieser (this)   jeder (each / every)   jener (that)
mancher (some)   solcher (such)   welcher (which)

dieser Mann   this man
bei jeder Gelegenheit   at every opportunity
jedes Mal   every time

	masc	fem	neut	pl
nominative	dieser	diese	dieses	diese
accusative	diesen	diese	dieses	diese
dative	diesem	dieser	diesem	diesen

Ways to use these words

dieses und jenes	this and that
in dieser Hinsicht	in this respect
jeder Einzelne	every individual
jeder Zweite	every other
zu jener Zeit / Stunde	at that time / hour
mancher Besucher	many a visitor / some visitors
Mit solchen Leuten will ich nichts zu tun haben.	I don't want to have anything to do with such people.
Welche Größe haben Sie?	What size are you?

Words that follow the ein pattern

These words follow the pattern of ein:
kein (not a)
mein (my)   unser (our)
dein (your)   euer (your, plural)
sein (his)   Ihr (your, polite)
ihr (her)   ihr (their)

	masc	fem	neut	pl
nominative	kein	keine	kein	keine
accusative	keinen	keine	kein	keine
dative	keinem	keiner	keinem	keinen

ich habe keine Lust zu – I don't want to + infinitive
meiner Meinung nach (dat) – in my opinion

Ways to use these words

keine Ahnung	no idea
mein Fehler	my mistake
gib dein Bestes	do your best
sein ganzes Leben	his whole life
ihr Ziel ist es ...	it's her / their aim ...
als unser Vertreter	as our representative
auf euren Handys	on your mobiles
Ihr Zeichen	your reference
für ihre Schularbeit	for her / their schoolwork

Now try this

Translate the sentences **into English**.
(a) Ich habe keine Lust, einkaufen zu gehen.
(b) Sie hat ihr ganzes Taschengeld für Kleidung ausgegeben.
(c) Solche Leute werden schnell unhöflich.
(d) Ich finde mein Leben langweilig.
(e) Dieses Mal fahren wir mit dem Zug.
(f) Seine Eltern sind arbeitslos.
(g) Solche Regeln finde ich dumm.
(h) Welches Buch liest du?

Adjective endings

Refer to the tables on this page to check you are using adjective endings correctly in your exam preparation work.

Adjective endings with the definite article 'the'

You can also use these endings after dieser (this), jener (that), jeder (each), mancher (some), solcher (such) and welcher (which). The endings are either -e or -en!

	masc	fem	neut	pl
nominative	der kleine Hund	die kleine Maus	das kleine Haus	die kleinen Kinder
accusative	den kleinen Hund	die kleine Maus	das kleine Haus	die kleinen Kinder
dative	dem kleinen Hund	der kleinen Maus	dem kleinen Haus	den kleinen Kindern

Siehst du den kleinen Hund? Can you see the little dog?

Adjective endings with the indefinite article 'a'

You can also use these endings after kein (not a), mein (my), dein (your), sein (his), ihr (her / their), unser (our), euer (your, pl) and Ihr (your, polite).

	masc	fem	neut	pl
nominative	ein kleiner Hund	eine kleine Maus	ein kleines Haus	meine kleinen Kinder
accusative	einen kleinen Hund	eine kleine Maus	ein kleines Haus	meine kleinen Kinder
dative	einem kleinen Hund	einer kleinen Maus	einem kleinen Haus	meinen kleinen Kindern

Ich wohne in einem kleinen Haus. I live in a little house.

Adjective endings with no article

	masc	fem	neut	pl
nominative	kleiner Hund	kleine Maus	kleines Haus	kleine Kinder
accusative	kleinen Hund	kleine Maus	kleines Haus	kleine Kinder
dative	kleinem Hund	kleiner Maus	kleinem Haus	kleinen Kindern

Many of these are similar to the definite articles: das Haus ➡ kleines Haus, der Mann ➡ großer Mann.

Kleine Kinder sind oft süß. Little children are often cute.

Now try this

Complete the sentences using the adjectives in brackets with their correct endings.

(a) Ich habe .... Noten in Deutsch. (ausgezeichnet) (pl)

(b) Im Jugendklub kann ich .... Essen kaufen. (warm) (n)

(c) Ich suche ein .... Bett. (preisgünstig) (n)

(d) Die .... Lage war sehr praktisch. (zentral) (f)

(e) Spanien ist ein .... Urlaubsziel der Deutschen. (beliebt) (n)

(f) Das ist eines der .... Lieder des Jahres. (meistverkauft) (pl)

(g) Letztes Wochenende gab es einen .... Sonntag. (verkaufsoffen) (m)

(h) Stell keine .... Daten ins Netz. (persönlich) (pl)

Comparisons

To aim high, you will need to use comparatives and superlatives, so always think of a way to include them in your speaking and writing work.

Formation

Add -er for the comparative, as in English (loud ➡ louder).
Add -(e)ste for the superlative 'most'.

Ich bin laut.   I am loud.

Ich bin lauter als du.
I am louder than you.

Ich bin die lauteste Person.
I am the loudest person.

- Adjectives are the same as adverbs, so you can compare how somebody does something very easily.
  Ich schreie laut.   I shout loudly.
  Ich schreie lauter als du.   I shout more loudly than you.
  Ich schreie am lautesten.   I shout the loudest.
- Comparative and superlative adjectives have to agree with the noun they are describing.
  die schöneren Ohrringe   the prettier earrings
  der lustigste Junge   the funniest boy

Irregular comparatives

Some adjectives have small changes in the comparative and superlative forms.

alt ➡	älter ➡	älteste
old	older	oldest
jung ➡	jünger ➡	jüngste
young	younger	youngest
groß ➡	größer ➡	größte
big	bigger	biggest
gut ➡	besser ➡	beste
good	better	best
lang ➡	länger ➡	längste
long	longer	longest
hoch ➡	höher ➡	höchste
high	higher	highest

Gern, lieber, am liebsten

Use gern (like), lieber (prefer) and am liebsten (like most of all) to compare your likes and dislikes.

- gern and lieber go after the verb:
  Ich spiele gern Schach.
  I like playing chess.
  Ich schwimme lieber.
  I prefer swimming.
- Use am liebsten to start your sentence:
  Am liebsten fahre ich Ski.
  Most of all I like skiing.

Lieblingssport (m) – favourite sport
Lieblingsgruppe (f) – favourite group

Now try this

Complete the sentences with a comparative or superlative form.
(a) Mathe ist viel .... als Chemie. (einfach)
(b) Mein Bruder ist .... als meine Schwester. (jung)
(c) Dieses Lied ist doch .... als der letzte Schlager. (gut)
(d) Meiner Meinung nach ist Physik .... als Chemie. (nützlich)
(e) Ich habe das .... Zimmer im Haus. (winzig)
(f) Das .... Fach in der Schule ist Informatik. (langweilig)
(g) Meine Stadt ist das .... Urlaubsziel in Deutschland. (beliebt)
(h) Letztes Jahr hatte ich die .... Noten in der Klasse. (schlecht)

Look at page 89 to check your endings.

Personal pronouns

Just like der, die and das, pronouns change depending on which case they are in – the nominative, accusative or dative case.

Pronouns

Pronouns = he, him, their, her, she, etc.

nominative	accusative	dative
ich	mich	mir
du	dich	dir
er / sie / es	ihn / sie / es	ihm / ihr / ihm
wir	uns	uns
ihr	euch	euch
Sie / sie	Sie / sie	Ihnen / ihnen

- Use pronouns to avoid repeating nouns:
  Ich mag Dieter, weil er nett ist.
  I like Dieter because he is nice.
- When a noun is the **accusative object** of the sentence, you need to use the **accusative pronoun**:
  Ich sehe ihn.   I see him.
- Use the correct pronoun after a preposition, depending on whether the preposition takes the accusative or dative case:
  bei mir (dat)   at my house
  für ihn (acc) for him

Dative pronoun phrases

These expressions need a dative pronoun:

Es tut mir leid.	I am sorry.	Wie geht's dir / Ihnen?	How are you?
Es gefällt ihm.	He likes it.	Es geht uns gut.	We are well.
Es fällt mir schwer.	I find it difficult.	Es gelingt mir.	I succeed.
Es tut ihr weh.	It hurts her.	Es hilft ihnen.	It helps them.
Das schmeckt mir.	That tastes good / I like the taste.	Es scheint ihnen, dass ...	It seems to them that ...
Sport macht ihr Spaß.	She thinks sport is fun.	Das ist uns egal.	We don't mind about that.

Sie or du?

Familiar

du = 'you' to another young person, family member / friend, animal
ihr = 'you' plural of du (more than one young person, etc.)

Formal

Sie = 'you' to adult(s), teacher(s), official(s)
Sie = singular and plural

Sie   du

Now try this

Choose the correct pronoun to complete each sentence.

(a) Nina ist sympathisch, obwohl .... manchmal auch launisch ist.

(b) Es tut .... leid, aber ich kann nicht zur Party kommen.

(c) Seit wann geht es .... schlecht, Leon?

(d) Wir sind ins Theater gegangen, aber leider hat .... das Stück nicht gefallen.

(e) Mein Freund geht .... auf die Nerven, aber ich will nicht mit .... Schluss machen.

(f) Hast du Zeit, ... bei den Hausaufgaben zu helfen?

Word order

German word order follows rules – learn the rules and your sentences will be in the correct order.

Verb in second place

The **verb** never comes first – it is always in second place!

1 Ich   **2** fahre   **3** mit dem Auto.   **1** Jeden Tag   **2** fahre ich   **3** mit dem Auto.

Perfect tense

Form of haben / sein goes in second position:

1 Gestern   **2** bin ich   **3** mit dem Auto   **4** gefahren.

Future tense

Form of werden goes in second position:

1 Morgen   **2** werde ich   **3** mit dem Auto   **4** fahren.

Modals

Form of modal goes in second position:

1 Ich   **2** will   **3** mit dem Auto   **4** fahren.

Remember:
ich werde – I will / I am going to
ich will – I want to

Time – Manner – Place

A detail of transport counts as manner (M), so put it **after** a time (T) expression, but **before** a place (P).

T gestern / heute / letzte Woche / in Zukunft

M mit dem Zug / zu Fuß / mit meiner Familie

P nach London / in die Stadt / über die Brücke

T	**M**	**P**
Ich fahre heute	mit dem Zug	nach Bonn.
Today I am going	by train	to Bonn.

Linking words

No word order change here!

aber   but   oder   or
denn   because   und   and

Ich spiele gern Tennis und ich fahre gern Rad.
I like playing tennis and I like cycling.
Ich esse gern Pommes, aber ich esse nicht gern Bratkartoffeln.
I like eating chips but I don't like roast potatoes.

Now try this

Order the sentences following the above rules.

(a) fahre / ich / ins Ausland / gern
(b) Verkehrsamt / findet / Informationen / beim / man
(c) gesund / ich / normalerweise / esse
(d) sehen / manchmal / Filme / wir / im Jugendklub
(e) arbeiten / ich / im Sportzentrum / möchte / im Juli
(f) habe / gearbeitet / ich / in einem Büro / letztes Jahr
(g) gehen / ins Kino / werde / mit meiner Mutter / morgen / ich

Try to invert your sentences by starting with a time expression rather than **ich, du,** etc.

Conjunctions

You will be expected to use plenty of conjunctions, such as weil, wenn and als, in your speaking and writing work – and you will **have** to show that you can use them correctly.

Verb to the end

Weil (because) sends the verb to the **end** of the clause:

Ich rede über Adele, weil sie meine Lieblingssängerin ist.

I am talking about Adele because she is my favourite singer.

Ich gehe nicht gern ins Kino, weil das zu teuer ist.

I don't like going to the cinema because it is too expensive.

All these conjunctions send the verb to the end of the clause, just like weil:

als	when (one occasion, past tense)	ob	whether
		obwohl	although
		während	while
bevor	before	was	what
bis	until	wie	how
da	because / since	wenn	when / if (present or future)
damit	so that		
dass	that	wo	where
nachdem	after		

Perfect tense

• In the **perfect** tense, the form of haben / sein is **last** in a clause:

Ich kann nicht zur Party kommen, obwohl ich meine Hausaufgaben gemacht habe.

I can't come to the party although I have done my homework.

Form of haben / sein in the perfect tense ➡ end of a clause.

• Watch out for the **verb, comma, verb** structure:

Als ich klein war, habe ich viel im Garten gespielt.

When I was small I played in the garden a lot.

Future tense and modals

• In the **future** tense, it is the form of werden which goes last in a clause:

Da ich nach Afrika reisen werde, muss ich zum Arzt.

Because I am going to travel to Africa, I have to go to the doctor.

• With **modal** verbs, it is the modal itself which is last in the clause:

Ich bin immer glücklich, wenn ich ins Konzert gehen darf.

I am always happy when I am allowed to go to the concert.

Form of werden ➡ end of a clause.
Form of modal ➡ end of a clause.

Now try this

Join each pair of sentences using the subordinating conjunction in brackets.

(a) Ich habe bei meiner Großmutter gewohnt. Meine Mutter war im Krankenhaus. (während)

(b) Ich bin ins Café gegangen. Ich habe ein T-Shirt gekauft. (nachdem)

(c) Ich war in Spanien im Urlaub. Ich habe einen neuen Freund kennengelernt. (als)

(d) Er ist sehr beliebt. Er ist nicht sehr freundlich. (obwohl)

(e) Ich werde für eine neue Gitarre sparen. Ich finde einen Nebenjob. (wenn)

(f) Ich bin froh. Ich habe gute Noten in der Schule bekommen. (dass)

(g) Ich muss meine Eltern fragen. Ich darf ins Konzert gehen. (ob)

(h) Er hat mir gesagt. Er will mit mir ins Kino gehen. (dass)

More on word order

There are a few more structures here that you should try to fit into your work to improve your writing and speaking. They also affect word order, so be careful!

Using um ... zu ...

Um ... zu ... means 'in order to' and is used in German where English might just say 'to'. It requires an infinitive verb at the end of the clause.

Ich trage Zeitungen aus, um Geld zu verdienen.   *infinitive verb*

I deliver newspapers, (in order) to earn money.

- Only use um ... zu ... where you would say 'in order to' in English, even if you drop the 'in order' bit.
- The verb after um ... zu ... is always in the infinitive and at the **end**.
- Add a comma before um.

ohne ... zu ... means without. It works in the same way:
Ich bin in die Schule gegangen, ohne ihn zu sehen. I went to school without seeing him.

Infinitive expressions

These expressions with zu need an infinitive.

ich ... (I ...)	hoffe, ... (hope) versuche, ... (try) beginne / fange an, ... (begin) habe vor, ... (intend) nutze die Chance, ... (use the opportunity)	+ zu + infinitive

Ich hoffe, Deutsch zu studieren.
I hope to study German.
Ich versuche, einen guten Job zu bekommen.
I am trying to get a good job.

With separable verbs, zu goes after the prefix.
Ich habe vor, fernzusehen.   I intend to watch TV.

Relative pronouns

Relative pronouns send the verb to the end of the clause.
They are used to express **who** or **that** or **which**.

m Der Mann, der im Café sitzt, ist Millionär.
The man who is sitting in the café is a millionaire.

f Die Katze, die unter dem Tisch schläft, ist sehr süß.
The cat that is sleeping under the table is very sweet.

n Das Mädchen, das einen roten Rock trägt, singt in einer Band.
The girl who's wearing a red skirt sings in a band.

Now try this

1 Combine the sentences with **um ... zu ...** .
  (a) Ich fahre nach Italien. Ich besuche meine Verwandten.
  (b) Ich gehe zum Sportzentrum. Ich nehme 5 Kilo ab.
2 Combine the clauses with **zu**.
  (a) Ich versuche – ich helfe anderen.
  (b) Ich habe vor – ich gehe auf die Uni.
3 Combine the sentences with a relative pronoun.
  (a) Das ist das Geschäft. Das Geschäft verkauft tolle Kleidung.
  (b) Hier ist eine Kellnerin. Die Kellnerin ist sehr unhöflich.

The present tense

There are regular and irregular present tense verbs for you here, but look at page 100 for the super-irregular verbs haben (to have) and sein (to be).

Present tense regular

Verbs change according to who is doing the action, just like in English: I drink ➡ he drinks.
The present tense describes what is happening now and can be translated as 'drink' or 'am drinking'.

machen – to do / to make		infinitive verb ⬅
ich	mache	I do / make
du	machst	you do / make
er / sie / es	macht	he / she / it does / makes
wir	machen	we do / make
ihr	macht	you do / make
Sie / sie	machen	you / they do / make

wir / Sie / sie forms = same as infinitive

- The present tense is used to describe what you are **doing now** or what you **do** regularly.
- Present tense time expressions include:
  jetzt (now)　　　　heute (today)
  im Moment　　　　(at the moment)
  dienstags　　　　(on Tuesdays)
- You can use the present tense with a time phrase to indicate the **future**:
  Morgen fahre ich nach London.
  Tomorrow I am going to London.

Present tense vowel changes

Some verbs have a vowel change in the du and er / sie / es forms of the present tense, but they still have the same endings (-e, -st, -t, etc.).

geben – to give			infinitive verb ⬅
ich	gebe	wir	geben
du	gibst	ihr	gebt
er / sie /es	gibt	Sie / sie	geben

vowel change

nehmen – to take	
ich	nehme
du	nimmst
er / sie / es	nimmt

essen – to eat	
ich	esse
du	isst
er / sie / es	isst

schlafen – to sleep	
ich	schlafe
du	schläfst
er / sie / es	schläft

Sie schläft.

Now try this

Complete the sentences with the correct form of the present tense verb in brackets.

(a) Ich .... gern Musik. (hören)

(b) Meine Schwester .... in ihrem eigenen Zimmer. (schlafen)

(c) Ihr .... montags schwimmen, oder? (gehen)

(d) .... du gern Wurst mit Senf? (essen)

(e) Wir .... nie mit dem Auto. (fahren)

(f) Was .... Sie in den Sommerferien? (machen)

(g) .... es eine Ermäßigung für Senioren? (geben)

(h) Mein Bruder .... heute im Bett, weil er krank ist. (bleiben)

Separable and reflexive verbs

To aim for a higher grade, include separable and reflexive verbs in your speaking and writing work.

Separable verbs

These verbs have two parts: a prefix + the main verb. They go their separate ways when used in a sentence.

← →

Ich sehe oft fern. I often watch TV.
Ich mache immer die Türen zu.
I always close the doors.

aufwachen	to wake up
aussteigen	to get off
einsteigen	to get on
fernsehen	to watch TV
herunterladen	to download
hochladen	to upload
umsteigen	to change (trains, trams, buses)
zumachen	to close

Make sure you can use separable verbs in all the tenses.

Present: Ich steige in Ulm um.
I change in Ulm.

Perfect: Ich bin in Ulm umgestiegen.
I changed in Ulm.

Separable verbs form the past participle as one word with -ge- sandwiched in the middle: **zugemacht** (closed), **ferngesehen** (watched TV).

Future: Ich werde in Ulm umsteigen.
I will change in Ulm.

Modals: Ich muss in Ulm umsteigen.
I have to change in Ulm.

Reflexive verbs

Reflexive verbs need a reflexive pronoun – mich, dich, etc.

sich freuen – to be happy / pleased	
ich freue mich	wir freuen uns
du freust dich	ihr freut euch
er / sie / es freut sich	Sie / sie freuen sich

- Note that **sich** never has a capital letter.
- sich freuen auf ... (acc) – to look forward to ...

sich amüsieren	to enjoy oneself
sich befinden	to be located
sich entscheiden	to decide
sich erinnern an	to remember
sich langweilen	to be bored
sich interessieren für	to be interested in

Ich interessiere mich für Geschichte.
I am interested in history.

All reflexive verbs use **haben** in the perfect tense:
Er hat sich angezogen. He dressed.
Wir haben uns gelangweilt. We were bored.

Now try this

1 Translate the sentences **into German**.
  (a) I watch TV. I watched TV.
  (b) I change trains at six o'clock. I changed trains at six o'clock.
  (c) I download music. I will download music.
  (d) I got on. I have to get on.

2 Complete the sentences with the correct reflexive pronoun.
  (a) Ich erinnere .... kaum an meinen Vater.
  (b) Wir interessieren .... für Mode.
  (c) Habt ihr .... im Jugendklub gelangweilt?
  (d) Meine Schule befindet .... am Stadtrand.

Commands

Use this page to help you give commands and orders accurately.

Sie commands

Swap the present tense round so that the verb comes before the pronoun:
Sie hören (you listen) ➡ Hören Sie! Listen!
Schreiben Sie das auf Deutsch auf.
Write that down in German.
Gehen Sie hier links.   Go left here.
- Separable verbs separate and the prefix goes to the end of the sentence.
  Tauschen Sie nicht Ihre Telefonnummer aus.
  Don't swap your phone number.
- Sein (to be) is irregular.
  Seien Sie nicht aggressiv.
  Don't be aggressive.

Other Sie commands

Gas weg!	Reduce your speed!
Gefahr!	Danger!
Warnung!	Warning!
Achtung!	Attention! / Watch out!
Vorsicht!	Be careful!
Verboten!	Forbidden!
Kein Eintritt!	Keep off! / Keep out!
Nicht betreten!	No entry!
Ausfahrt freihalten!	Keep exit clear!
Lebensgefahr!	Danger of death!
Privatgrundstück	Private land

Du commands

Use the present tense du form of the verb minus the -st ending:
gehen ➡ du gehst ➡ du gehst ➡ Geh!
Bleib anonym. Stay anonymous.
Triff niemanden allein.
Don't meet anyone on your own.
Beleidige andere nicht.
Don't insult others.
Such dir einen Spitznamen aus.
Choose a nickname.

This is a separable verb so it splits.

Some verbs are irregular in the present tense, so make sure you get them right when giving commands.

haben – to have	➡	Hab (Spaß)! – Have (fun)!
sein – to be	➡	Sei (ruhig)! – Be (quiet)!
essen – to eat	➡	Iss! – Eat!
fahren – to drive	➡	Fahr! – Drive!
geben – to give	➡	Gib das her! – Give me that!
lassen – to leave	➡	Lass! – Leave!
nehmen – to take	➡	Nimm! – Take!

Now try this

What is this sign asking dog owners to do?

Liebe Hundehalter, bitte achten Sie auf Ihre Lieblinge und benutzen Sie Grünflächen und Wege nicht als Hundetoilette.

Vielen Dank!

Present tense modals

Modal verbs need another verb in the infinitive form, e.g. gehen (to go), kaufen (to buy).
The modal verb comes second in the sentence, while the infinitive is shifted to the very end.

Können (to be able to)

ich / er / sie / es	kann
du	kannst
ihr	könnt
wir / Sie / sie	können

Ich kann nicht schwimmen.
I can't swim.

Müssen (to have to / must)

ich / er / sie / es	muss
du	musst
ihr	müsst
wir / Sie / sie	müssen

Du musst deine Hausaufgaben machen.
You have to do your homework.

Wollen (to want to)

ich / er / sie / es	will
du	willst
ihr	wollt
wir / Sie / sie	wollen

Er will nicht umsteigen.
He doesn't want to change (trains).

Dürfen (to be allowed to)

ich / er / sie / es	darf
du	darfst
ihr	dürft
wir / Sie / sie	dürfen

Wir dürfen in die Disko gehen.
We are allowed to go to the disco.

Sollen (to be supposed to)

ich / er / sie / es	soll
du	sollst
ihr	sollt
wir / Sie / sie	sollen

Germans most often use the imperfect tense of sollen to express the sense of 'should' or 'ought':

Ich sollte meine Großeltern besuchen.
I should visit my grandparents.

Mögen (to like)

The present tense of mögen no longer tends to be used in the present tense with another verb to express liking. Instead, the subjunctive form is far more likely to be used in the sense of 'would like to'.

ich / er / sie / es	möchte
du	möchtest
ihr	möchtet
wir / Sie / sie	möchten

Sie möchte Rollschuhlaufen gehen.
She would like to go rollerblading.
Ich möchte nicht ins Kino gehen.
I would not like to go to the cinema.

Now try this

Write modal sentences using the verbs given in brackets.
(a) Ich gehe um einundzwanzig Uhr ins Bett. (müssen)
(b) In der Schule raucht man nicht. (dürfen)
(c) Du sparst Energie. (sollen)
(d) Hilfst du mir zu Hause? (können)
(e) Ich fahre in den Ferien Ski. (wollen)
(f) Ich sehe nicht fern. (mögen)
(g) Ich löse das Problem nicht. (können)

Note that separable verbs come together as infinitives: ich sehe fern = fernsehen.

Imperfect modals

Using modals and an infinitive in different tenses is a great way to incorporate a variety of tenses into your work.

Imperfect modals

Infinitive: können – to be able to
Present tense:
ich kann + infinitive at end – I can ...
Imperfect tense:
ich konnte + infinitive at end – I was able to ...
Ich konnte nicht mehr warten.
I couldn't wait any more.

The endings change, depending on the subject of the verb.

ich	konnte
du	konntest
er / sie / es / man	konnte
wir	konnten
ihr	konntet
Sie / sie	konnten

infinitive at the end

Other modals in the imperfect

- These modals work in the same way as konnte – just add the correct ending.
- There are no umlauts on imperfect tense modals.

müssen	➡ musste	had to
wollen	➡ wollte	wanted to
dürfen	➡ durfte	was allowed to
sollen	➡ sollte	was supposed to
mögen	➡ mochte	liked

Was musstet ihr gestern in Mathe machen?
What did you have to do in maths yesterday?
Er wollte doch nur helfen.
He only wanted to help.
Sie durfte ihn nicht heiraten.
She wasn't allowed to marry him.
Du solltest eine Tablette nehmen.
You should take a pill.

Subjunctive modals (Higher)

Add an umlaut to konnte and mochte and you have the subjunctive. This allows you to talk about things you **could / would** do.

imperfect	➡ subjunctive	
konnte	➡ könnte (could)	+ infinitive
mochte	➡ möchte (would like)	

The subjunctive has the same structure as imperfect modals with the infinitive at the end.

Möchtest du ins Kino gehen?
Would you like to go to the cinema?
Das Schwimmbad könnte geschlossen sein.
The swimming pool could be closed.

Now try this

1 Rewrite these sentences with an imperfect tense modal.
 (a) Ich mache Hausaufgaben. (müssen)
 (b) Sie helfen mir nicht. (können)
 (c) Er kauft eine neue Hose. (wollen)
 (d) Wir laden die Fotos hoch. (sollen)
 (e) In der Schule kaut man nie Kaugummi. (dürfen)
 (f) Alle Schüler bleiben bis sechzehn Uhr. (müssen)

2 Rewrite these with a subjunctive modal.
 (a) Es wird schwierig. (können)
 (b) Ich tausche die gelbe Jacke um. (mögen)

The perfect tense 1

The perfect tense is the tense most used to talk about the past in German – using it is a necessity at any level of your GCSE.

The perfect tense

- Use the perfect tense to talk about something you have done in the **past**.
- The perfect tense is made up of **two parts**:
  the correct form of haben or sein + past participle at the end.
  Ich habe Musik gehört.   I listened to music.

Past participles generally start with ge-.
spielen ➡ gespielt (played)
lachen ➡ gelacht (laughed)
fahren ➡ gefahren (drove)

Hast du den Film gesehen?
Have you seen the film?

The perfect tense – haben

Most verbs use haben (to have) in the perfect tense:

form of haben + sentence + past participle at the end.

ich habe	
du hast	gekauft (bought)
er / sie / es hat	gemacht (made)
wir haben	besucht (visited)
ihr habt	gesehen (saw)
Sie / sie haben	

Er hat im Reisebüro gearbeitet.
He worked at the travel agency.
Wir haben Frühstück gegessen.
We ate breakfast.

The perfect tense – sein

Some verbs of movement use sein (to be) to make the perfect tense:

form of sein + sentence + past participle at the end.

ich bin	
du bist	gegangen (went)
er / sie / es ist	geflogen (flew)
wir sind	gefahren (drove / went)
ihr seid	geblieben (stayed)
Sie / sie sind	

Sie ist zu Fuß gegangen.
She went on foot.
Ich bin nach Freiburg gefahren.
I went to Freiburg.

There are some verbs that use **sein** in the perfect tense where there is no apparent movement: **bleiben** (to stay) is an example.

Now try this

Write these sentences in the perfect tense.
(a) Ich kaufe eine Jacke.
(b) Wir fliegen nach Portugal.
(c) Ich sehe meinen Freund.
(d) Lena und Hannah gehen in die Stadt.
(e) Ich besuche meine Tante.
(f) Ich bleibe im Hotel.
(g) Was isst du zu Mittag?
(h) Am Samstag hört er Musik.

Put the form of **haben / sein** in **second** position and the past participle at the end of the sentence.

The perfect tense 2

Spotting past participles will help you to identify when a text is in the past tense – but watch out for the hidden ge- in separable verbs such as ferngesehen (watched TV).

Regular past participles

- Begin with ge-.
- End in -t.

Remove -en from the infinitive and replace with -t: machen ➡ macht ➡ gemacht
Das hat ihr Spaß gemacht.
That was fun for her.

Some exceptions

Verbs starting with be-, emp- or ver- do not add ge- to form the past participle.

Ich habe ...	I ...
besucht	visited
empfohlen	recommended
vergessen	forgot
verloren	lost

Separable verbs add **ge-** between the prefix and the main verb:
hochgeladen – uploaded   heruntergeladen – downloaded

Irregular past participles

There are no rules for forming irregular past participles – but here are some common ones to learn.

Ich habe ...	gegessen	I ate
	getrunken	I drank
	genommen	I took
	geschlafen	I slept
	geschrieben	I wrote
	gesungen	I sang
	getragen	I wore / carried
	getroffen	I met
	gestanden	I stood
Ich bin ...	gerannt	I ran
	geschwommen	I swam
	gewesen	I have been
	gestiegen	I climbed
	gestorben	I died
	geworden	I became

Word order

The past participle goes at the **end** of the sentence and the form of haben or sein is in **second** position:

1 Er   **2** ist   ins Kino   **3** gegangen.
He went to the cinema.

1 Am Montag   **2** habe ich Fußball   **3** gespielt.
I played football on Monday.

When the verb has already been sent to the end by a conjunction such as weil (because) or als (when), the part of haben or sein comes **after** the past participle:
Ich war dankbar, weil er mein Portemonnaie gefunden hat.
I was grateful because he found my purse.
Als er angekommen war, war er erschöpft.
When he arrived, he was exhausted.

Now try this

Complete the sentences with the correct past participle of the verb in brackets.

(a) Ich habe zu viele Kekse .... (essen)

(b) Haben Sie gut ....? (schlafen)

(c) Wir haben uns am Bahnhof .... (treffen)

(d) Ich war krank, weil ich den ganzen Tag .... habe. (stehen)

(e) Ich weiß, dass du .... bist. (umsteigen)

(f) Warum hast du die E-Mail ....? (schreiben)

(g) Ich habe ihr .... , dass sie nicht mitkommen sollte. (empfehlen)

(h) Ich war traurig, als er .... ist. (sterben)

The imperfect tense

If you are telling a story about the past or recounting a series of events in the past, use the imperfect tense.

Forming the imperfect tense

- Take the infinitive, e.g. hören (to hear).
- Take off the final -en ➡ hör~~en~~ = hör.
- Add these endings:

ich hörte	I heard / was hearing
du hörtest	you heard / were hearing
er / sie / es / man hörte	he / she / it / one heard / was hearing
wir hörten	we heard / were hearing
ihr hörtet	you heard / were hearing
Sie / sie hörten	you / they heard / were hearing

Ich hörte gar nichts.   I didn't hear a thing.

Sie spielten drei Jahre lang in der Gruppe.
They played for three years with the group.

Don't forget to use the imperfect modals – see page 99 for a reminder.

'To have' and 'to be' in the imperfect

haben (to have)

ich hatte	I had
du hattest	you had
er / sie / es / man hatte	he / she / it / one had
wir hatten	we had
ihr hattet	you had
Sie / sie hatten	you / they had

Ich hatte Glück.   I was lucky.

sein (to be)

ich war	I was
du warst	you were
er / sie / es / man war	he / she / it / one was
wir waren	we were
ihr wart	you were
Sie / sie waren	you / they were

Es war teuer.   It was expensive.

Irregular verbs

- Some verbs have irregular stems in the imperfect tense.
- Add the same basic endings as above to the irregular stems on the right:
  ich ging – wir gingen (I went – we went)
  ich fuhr – wir fuhren (I drove – we drove)

Im Stück ging es um eine Beziehung.
The play was about a relationship.
Die Kinder sahen blass aus.
The children looked pale.
Es fand in Hamburg statt.
It took place in Hamburg.

gehen ➡	ging	went
fahren ➡	fuhr	drove
finden ➡	fand	found
kommen ➡	kam	came
nehmen ➡	nahm	took
sehen ➡	sah	saw
sitzen ➡	saß	sat
stehen ➡	stand	stood
tut weh ➡	tat weh	hurt

Es gab is an impersonal verb and so does not change:
Es gab ein Haus.   There was a house.
Es gab zwei Häuser.   There were two houses.

Now try this

Put these sentences into the imperfect tense.

(a) Sie hat Angst.

(b) Es ist hoffnungslos.

(c) Es gibt Toiletten im Erdgeschoss.

(d) Hörst du das?

(e) Plötzlich kommt uns der Mann entgegen.

(f) Das ist eine Überraschung, nicht?

(g) Es ist niemand zu Hause.

(h) Sie spielen gern Tischtennis.

 Spielen is a regular verb like hören.

The future tense

As well as using the future tense, you can also express future intent using the present tense. Use this page to check you can do both!

The future tense

Use the future tense to talk about things you **will** do or things that **will** happen in the future:

form of werden (to become) + sentence + infinitive at the end.

ich werde	
du wirst	holen (collect)
er / sie / es / man wird	klopfen (knock)
wir werden	mieten (rent)
ihr werdet	zelten (camp)
Sie / sie werden	

Word order in the future tense

Form of werden in second position:

Nächste Woche werde ich in Urlaub fahren.
Next week I will go on holiday.

Ich werde erfolgreich sein.
I will be successful.
Wie groß wirst du werden?
How tall will you get?
Morgen wird es kalt sein.
It will be cold tomorrow.
Werden sie auf die Uni gehen?
Will they go to university?
Ich bin froh, dass du zu Besuch kommen wirst.
I am happy that you will come to visit.

Reflexive and separable verbs

- Reflexive verbs – add the pronoun after part of werden:
  Ich werde mich schnell rasieren.
  I will shave quickly.
- Separable verbs – stay together at the end of the sentence:
  Er wird das Lied herunterladen.
  He will download the song.

Present tense with future intent

You can use the present tense to express what you are **going to** do. Include a time marker to make it clear that the intent is based in the future.

morgen	tomorrow
übermorgen	the day after tomorrow
nächste Woche	next week

Nächsten Sommer fahren wir nach Amerika.
We are going to America next summer.

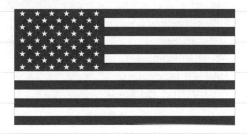

Now try this

Rewrite the sentences in the future tense with 'werden'.

(a) Ich gewinne das Spiel.
(b) Wir gehen in den Freizeitpark.
(c) Sie mieten eine große Wohnung.
(d) Ihr habt große Schwierigkeiten.
(e) Er besteht die Prüfung.
(f) Nächste Woche ziehen wir um.
(g) Trefft ihr euch später?
(h) Ich ziehe mich um sechs Uhr an.

The conditional

The conditional is very similar in structure to the future tense and using it will improve your writing and speaking.

Conditional

Use the conditional to talk about things you **would** do or things that **would** happen in the future:
part of würde (would) + sentence + infinitive at the end.

| ich würde
du würdest
er / sie / es / man würde
wir würden
ihr würdet
Sie / sie würden	+ infinitive

Ich würde gern nach Italien fahren.
I would like to go to Italy.
Würden Sie lieber Geschäftsmann oder Klempner werden?
Would you rather become a businessman or a plumber?
Würdest du je rauchen?
Would you ever smoke?
Man würde nie ein Auto kaufen.
We would never buy a car.

würde sein = wäre – would be
würde haben = hätte – would have
es würde geben = es gäbe – there would be

Using wenn

• You often use wenn (if) with the conditional.
• Remember: verb, comma, verb!
Wenn ich reich wäre, würde ich keine Designerkleidung kaufen.
If I were rich, I wouldn't buy designer clothes.

Wenn sie ein Vorstellungsgespräch hätte, würde sie rechtzeitig ankommen.
If she had an interview, she would arrive on time.

Making requests

Use the conditional to make a request for something you **would** like:
Ich möchte Pommes essen.
I would like to eat chips.

The plural form adds -n:
wir möchten   we would like
sie hätten gern   they would like to have

Sie hätte gern ein neues Handy.
She would like a new mobile.

Now try this

Rewrite these sentences using the conditional.
(a) Ich gehe gern ins Theater.
(b) Er kommt nie spät an.
(c) Wir trinken nie Bier.
(d) Helfen Sie mir bitte?
(e) Zum Geburtstag bekommt sie am liebsten Geld.
(f) Nächstes Jahr heiraten sie vielleicht.
(g) Wenn Latein Pflicht ist, gehe ich auf eine andere Schule.
(h) Wenn ich das mache, gibt es Krach mit meinen Eltern.

The pluperfect tense

The pluperfect tense is used to say you **had** done something. Use it to aim for a top grade!

Forming the pluperfect

- Use the pluperfect tense to talk about events which **had** happened.
- It is made from the **imperfect** of haben or sein + past participle.

ich hatte du hattest er / sie / es / man hatte wir hatten ihr hattet Sie / sie hatten	Pause gemacht (had had a break) Freunde gesehen (had seen friends)
ich war du warst er / sie / es / man war wir waren ihr wart Sie / sie waren	Ski gefahren (had been skiing) zu Hause geblieben (had stayed at home)

Haben or sein?

- Some participles take haben and some sein. The rules are the same as for the perfect tense.
  Sie hatte kein Wort gesagt.
  She had not said a word.

ich hatte (I had)	angefangen / begonnen (begun) gearbeitet (worked) gebracht (brought) eingeladen (invited) erreicht (reached) geholt (fetched) gelogen (lied)

Er war nicht gekommen.   He had not come.

ich war (I had)	geblieben (stayed) hineingegangen (entered) eingeschlafen (fallen asleep) vorbeigegangen (gone by)
es war	geschehen (it had happened)

The pluperfect and perfect tenses

Look how similar the pluperfect tense is to the perfect tense.

Ich habe Basketball gespielt.   ➡   Ich hatte Basketball gespielt.
I played basketball.   I had played basketball.
Es hat ihm Spaß gemacht.   ➡   Es hatte ihm Spaß gemacht.
It was fun for him.   It had been fun for him.
Wir sind zur Eishalle gegangen. ➡   Wir waren zur Eishalle gegangen.
We went to the ice rink.   We had gone to the ice rink.

Now try this

Write these sentences in the pluperfect tense.

(a) Ich habe zu Mittag gegessen.

(b) Sie haben als Stadtführer gearbeitet.

(c) Bist du schwimmen gegangen?

(d) Wir sind in Kontakt geblieben.

(e) Sie sind mit dem Rad in die Stadt gefahren.

(f) Ich habe sie vor einigen Monaten besucht, aber damals war sie schon krank.

(g) Bevor ich ins Haus gegangen bin, habe ich ein Gesicht am Fenster gesehen.

(h) Obwohl ich kaum mit ihm gesprochen habe, schien er sehr freundlich zu sein.

Questions

In the role play task, you will **have** to ask at least one question, so make sure you can do just that by studying this page carefully!

Asking questions

You can swap the pronoun and verb round to form a question:

Du hast einen Hund.   You have got a dog.

Hast du einen Hund?   Have you got a dog?

Make sure you use a variety of tenses when you ask questions about events at different times:

Sie sind nach Spanien geflogen.

You flew to Spain.

Sind Sie nach Spanien geflogen?

Did you fly to Spain?

Key question words

Wann?   When?

Warum?   Why?

Was?   What?

Wer?   Who?

Wie?   How?

Wo(hin)?   Where (to)?

Wohin werden Sie in Urlaub fahren?

Where will you go on holiday?

Wann sind Sie dorthin gefahren?

When did you go there?

Warum hat Ihnen der Film nicht gefallen?

Why didn't you like the film?

Other question words

Was für ...?   What sort of ...?

Was für Bücher lesen Sie gern?   What sort of books do you like reading?

Wie viele?   How many?

Wie viele Stunden pro Woche treiben Sie Sport?

How many hours a week do you do sport?

Wessen?   Whose?

Wessen Idee war das?   Whose idea was that?

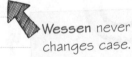

Wessen never changes case.

Welchen is in the accusative case.

Wen? Wem?   Who(m)?

Wen finden Sie besser?   Who do you find better?

Mit wem spielen Sie Squash?

Who do you play squash with?

Wem is in the dative case after mit.

Using welcher (which)

Welcher agrees with the noun it is asking about.

masc	Welcher Sport? Which sport?
fem	Welche Aufgabe? Which activity?
neut	Welches Fach? Which subject?
pl	Welche Fächer? Which subjects?

Welchen Sport finden Sie am einfachsten?

Which sport do you find the easiest?

Welches Fach machst du am liebsten?

Which subject do you like doing best?

Wen is in the accusative case.

Now try this

1 Turn the sentences into questions.
   (a) Sie lesen gern Science-Fiction-Bücher.
   (b) Sie finden Ihre Arbeit anstrengend.
   (c) Sie möchten nur teilzeit arbeiten.
   (d) Nächsten Sommer werden Sie nach Australien auswandern.

2 Write questions **in German** to ask in your role play.
   (a) Who could help me?
   (b) When does the restaurant open?
   (c) Why is there a bag here?
   (d) How can I get to the cathedral?
   (e) What can one do in the evenings?

Time markers

Here are some ideas to introduce a variety of time expressions into your work – remember to put the verb in **second** position if you are starting with one of these.

Present tense

aktuell	current(ly)
heute	today
heutzutage	these days
jetzt	now
seit	since / for

Jetzt, wo ich noch Schülerin bin, muss ich viel lernen.
Now, while I am still a pupil, I must work hard.

Past tenses

gestern	yesterday
vorgestern	the day before yesterday
vor drei Monaten	three months ago
letzte Woche	last week
letztes Wochenende	last weekend
früher	previously
als (kleines) Kind	as a (small) child
neulich	recently

Vor sechs Wochen habe ich mir das Bein gebrochen.
I broke my leg six weeks ago.

Future tense

bald	soon
in Zukunft	in future / in the future
morgen (früh)	tomorrow (morning)
übermorgen	the day after tomorrow
nächste Woche	next week
am nächsten Tag	on the next day

In Zukunft werde ich eine gute Stelle finden.
In the future, I will find a good job.

General

jeden Tag / täglich	every day / daily
wöchentlich	weekly
eines Tages	one day
immer	always
immer noch	still
schon immer	always
am Anfang	at the start / at first
von Zeit zu Zeit	from time to time
sofort	immediately
rechtzeitig	on time
regelmäßig	regularly

Ich habe schon immer in Wales gewohnt.
I have always lived in Wales.

Now try this

Rewrite these sentences with the time expressions provided in brackets.
(a) Ich spiele Klavier. (for three years)
(b) Er hat die Hausaufgaben nicht gemacht. (last week)
(c) Wir werden in den Bergen wandern gehen. (next summer)
(d) Wir wollten das Betriebspraktikum nicht machen. (at the start)
(e) Man wird alle Lebensmittel elektronisch kaufen. (in future)
(f) Ich hoffe, Disneyland zu besuchen. (one day)
(g) Ich hatte Halsschmerzen. (the day before yesterday)
(h) Sie spielen oft Tennis. (previously)

 Watch the tense!

Numbers

Numbers are really important in a variety of contexts so make sure you know them!

Numbers

1 eins	11 elf	21 einundzwanzig	100 hundert
2 zwei	12 zwölf	22 zweiundzwanzig	101 hunderteins
3 drei	13 dreizehn		200 zweihundert
4 vier	14 vierzehn		333 dreihundertdreiunddreißig
5 fünf	15 fünfzehn		
6 sechs	16 sechzehn		
7 sieben	17 siebzehn	30 dreißig	
8 acht	18 achtzehn	40 vierzig	
9 neun	19 neunzehn	50 fünfzig	1000 tausend
10 zehn	20 zwanzig	60 sechzig	
		70 siebzig	ein Tausend a thousand
		80 achtzig	eine Million a million
		90 neunzig	eine Milliarde a billion
			eine Billion a trillion

all one word – however long!

no und after hundert

Ordinal numbers

1st erste	11th elfte	am vierzehnten März	on 14 March
2nd zweite	12th zwölfte	ab dem achten Juni	from 8 June
3rd dritte	13th dreizehnte	vom ersten bis zum	from 1 to 13
4th vierte	14th vierzehnte	dreizehnten Dezember	December
5th fünfte		nach / vor dem zehnten April	after / before
6th sechste	20th zwanzigste		10 April
7th siebte	21st einundzwanzigste	seit dem dritten Februar	since 3 February
8th achte	30th dreißigste	**Years**	
9th neunte	31st einunddreißigste	(im Jahr)	
10th zehnte		neunzehnhundertachtundachtzig	in 1988
		(im Jahr)	
		zweitausendzwanzig	in 2020

In German you can write the number followed by a full stop. For example,
den 7. November = the 7th November
am 23. Januar = on the 23rd January

Now try this

 LISTENING TRACK 62

 Listen to the recording

Listen and fill in the numbers.

(a) ☐ . – ☐ . Mai

(b) ☐ | ☐

(c) € ☐ , ☐

(d) ☐ . Januar ☐

(e) € ☐ Millionen

(f) ☐ % Ermäßigung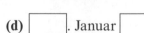

(g) ☐ | ☐

(h) ☐ Grad

108

Vocabulary

These pages cover key German vocabulary that you need to know. This section starts with general terms that are useful in a wide variety of situations and then divides into vocabulary for each of the three main topic areas:

1 General vocabulary **2** Identity and culture **3** Local, national, international and global areas of interest **4** Current and future study and employment

⊙ Sections to be learned by **all** students ⊙ Sections for **Higher** students only

Learning vocabulary is vital for success across all four papers. Don't try to learn too much at once – concentrate on learning and testing yourself on one small section at a time.

1 General vocabulary

Comparisons

ähnlich	similar
anders	different
Gegenteil (n)	opposite
gern – lieber – am liebsten	like – prefer – favourite
gleich	equal, same
gut – besser – am besten	good – better – best
hoch – höher – am höchsten	high – higher – highest
im Großen und Ganzen	on the whole
Mindest-...	the least ...
das ist so ... wie	that's as ... as
so viel ... wie	as much ... as
Unterschied (m)	difference
unterschiedlich	different
vergleichen	to compare
Vergleich (m)	comparison
verschieden	different
viel – mehr – am meisten	many – more – most

Conjunctions

bevor	before
bis	until
damit	so
dass	that
denn	because
entweder ... oder	either ... or
nachdem	after
ob	whether
seit(dem)	since
so dass	so that
sowohl ... als auch	both ... and
während	during
weder ... noch	neither ... nor

Connectives

abgesehen davon	apart from this
als ob	as if, like
also	therefore
angenommen	assumed
außer	except
außerdem	besides
danach	afterwards
dann	then
das heißt (d.h.)	that is (i.e.)
dennoch	nevertheless
deshalb / deswegen	therefore
doch	however, yet
drittens	thirdly
eigentlich	actually
erstens	firstly
jedoch	however
leider	unfortunately
natürlich	naturally
nicht nur ... sondern auch	not just ... but also
ohne Zweifel	doubtless
schließlich	finally
sonst	otherwise
trotzdem	despite
vorausgesetzt dass	given that
zuerst	first
zufällig	accidentally
zweitens	secondly

Prepositions

an	at
auf	on
aus	out of
bei	with, at (house)
durch	through
entlang	along
für	for
gegen	against
gegenüber	opposite
hinter	behind
in	in
mit	with
nach	after
neben	next to
ohne	without
über	over, above
um	around
unter	under
von	from
vor	in front of
vorbei	past
wegen	because of
zu	to
zwischen	between

Negatives

gar nicht	not at all
nicht	not
nicht einmal	not even
nicht mehr	no longer
nie	never
niemals	never
nirgend- nirgendwo	no- nowhere
noch nicht	not yet
überhaupt nicht	not at all

Money

Bargeld (n)	cash
Geldschein (m)	note
Geldstück (n)	coin
Kleingeld (n)	small change
Münze (f)	coin
Taschengeld (n)	pocket money
wechseln	to change
Zehn-Euro-Schein (m)	ten-euro note
Zwei-Euro-Stück (n)	two-euro coin

Now try this

Pick five words at random from each column and see if you can write a sentence using each word.

1 General vocabulary

Numbers

Million (f)	million
1. = erste/r	1st = first
2. = zweite/r	2nd = second
3. = dritte/r etc.	3rd = third
Dutzend (n)	dozen
Nummer (f)	number
Paar (n)	pair, couple
Zahl (f)	figure, number

zwo (regional)
  = zwei
	two (e.g.
	  phone no.)

Questions

Wann?   When?

Warum?   Why?

Was für?   What sort of?

Was?   What?

Wer?   Who?

Wessen?   Whose?

Wie viel(e)?   How much / many?

Wie?   How?

Wo?   Where?

Wieso?   Why?

Woher?   From where?

Wohin?   Where to?

Key verbs

haben	to have
sein	to be
werden	to become

Greetings and exclamations

Alles Gute!	All the best!
Auf Wiedersehen!	Goodbye!
Bis bald!	See you soon!
Bitte!	You're welcome!
Danke (schön)!	(Many) Thanks!
Entschuldigung!	Excuse me!
Es tut mir leid!	I am sorry!

Frohe
  Weihnachten!
	Happy
	  Christmas!

Gern geschehen!	My pleasure!
Grüß Gott!	Greetings!
Hallo!	Hello!
Herzlich willkommen!	Welcome!
Herzlichen Glückwunsch!	Congratulations!
Mit Vergnügen!	With pleasure!
Schöne Ferien!	Have a good holiday!
Tschüs!	Bye!
Verzeihung!	Pardon!
Viel Glück!	Good luck!
Wie geht's / geht es dir / Ihnen?	How are you?

Opinions

Ahnung (f)	inkling, clue
amüsant	amusing
angenehm	pleasant
ängstlich	afraid
ausgezeichnet	excellent
bequem	comfortable
bestimmt	certain(ly)
billig	cheap
dafür	therefore, for it
dagegen	against it
denken	to think
die Nase voll haben	to be fed up
doof	silly
dumm	stupid
ein bisschen	a little, bit
einfach	easy
entsetzlich	dreadful

es kommt darauf
  an, ob
	it depends
	  on whether

satt sein	to be full
fantastisch	fantastic
faszinierend	fascinating
froh	happy
furchtbar	dreadful
gefallen	to please, like
genießen	to enjoy

glauben	to believe
hassen	to hate
herrlich	superb
hervorragend	outstanding
Idee (f)	idea

interessieren
  (sich für)
	to be
	  interested (in)

klasse	great
kompliziert	complicated
können	to be able to
langweilen (sich)	to be bored
langweilig	boring
leicht	easy
lieb	dear, nice
lieben	to love

Colours

bunt	coloured
hell	light
dunkel	dark
blau	
braun	
gelb	
grau	
grün	
lila	
rosa	
rot	
schwarz	
weiß	

Now try this

Choose ten opinion phrases and write a sentence in German containing each of them.

① General vocabulary

lustig	funny
meinen	to think
Meinung (f)	opinion
mies	lousy
mögen	to like
mühsam	tedious
neu	new
nützlich	useful
nutzlos	useless
praktisch	practical
prima	great
sagen	to say
schade	shame
schlecht	bad
schlimm	bad
schrecklich	awful
schwierig	difficult
sensibel	sensitive
sicher	sure
sogar	even
spitze	awesome
stimmt	correct
teuer	expensive
toll	great
total	totally
typisch	typical
überrascht	surprised
unglaublich	unbelievable
unmöglich	impossible
unsicher	uncertain
vielleicht	perhaps
völlig	completely
vorziehen	to prefer
wahrscheinlich	probably
wichtig	important
wirklich	really
wollen	to want to
wunderbar	wonderful
wunderschön	wonderful
wünschen (sich)	to wish
ziemlich	quite
zustimmen	to agree

The seasons

Jahreszeit (f)	season
Frühling (m)	spring
Sommer (m)	summer
Herbst (m)	autumn
Winter (m)	winter

Days of the week

Woche (f)	week	Tag (m)	day

Montag	Dienstag	Mittwoch	Donnerstag	Freitag	Samstag / Sonnabend	Sonntag
Monday	Tuesday	Wednesday	Thursday	Friday	Saturday	Sunday

Months

 Januar  Februar März April

 Mai Juni Juli August

 September Oktober  November  Dezember

The clock

fünf nach halb	25 to
fünf vor halb	25 past
genau	exactly
Minute (f)	minute
Mittag (m)	midday
Mitternacht (f)	midnight
nachgehen	to be slow (clock)
pünktlich	punctual
Sekunde (f)	second
spät	late
Stunde (f)	hour
Uhr (f)	clock
Um wie viel Uhr?	What time?
Viertel (n)	quarter
vorgehen	to be fast (clock)
Wie spät ist es?	What's the time?
Zeit (f)	time

Other time expressions

ab	from
ab und zu	now and again
Abend (m)	evening
abends	in the evenings
als	when
Augenblick (m)	moment
bald	soon
damals	then
erst	first
Datum (n)	date
dauern	to last
ehemalig	former
einmal	once
endlich	finally
fast	almost
früh	early
Gegenwart (f)	present
gerade	just, currently
gestern	yesterday
gewöhnlich	usually
heute	today
heutzutage	today
im Voraus	in advance

Now try this

Practise the days of the week and the months of the year by translating the birthdays of ten family members and friends into German.

① General vocabulary

immer	always		
inzwischen	meanwhile		
Jahrhundert (n)	century		
jetzt	now		
kürzlich	recent		
langsam	slow		
letzter/e/es	last		
manchmal	sometimes		
Moment (m)	moment		
montags	on Mondays		
Morgen (m)	morning		
morgen früh	tomorrow morning		
morgens	in the mornings		
nachher	afterwards		
Nachmittag (m)	afternoon		
nächster/e/es	next		
Nacht (f)	night		
nachts	at night		
neulich	recently		
noch einmal	once more		
normalerweise	normally		
nun	now		
plötzlich	suddenly		
schnell	quick		
schon	already		
seit	since		
selten	rarely		
sofort	immediately		
täglich	daily		
übermorgen	day after tomorrow		
Vergangenheit (f)	past		
vor Kurzem	recently		
vorgestern	day before yesterday		
vorher	previously		
Vormittag (m)	morning		
wieder	again		
Wochenende (n)	weekend		
Zeitpunkt (m)	moment		
zu Ende	at an end		
Zukunft (f)	future		

Location and distance

außen	outside
außerhalb	beyond
bleiben	to stay
da (drüben)	(over) there
draußen	outside
drinnen	inside
Ecke (f)	corner
entfernt	away
her(aus)	out (of)
herein	in
herum	around
hin(aus)	out (of)
hinein	in
irgendwo	somewhere
liegen	to lie
Mitte (f)	middle
mitten	midway
nah	near
Nähe (f)	proximity
Norden (m)	north
nördlich	northern
oben	above
Ort (m)	place
Osten (m)	east
östlich	eastern
Stadtrand (m)	edge of town
Süden (m)	south
südlich	southern
überall	everywhere
unten	under
vorwärts	forwards
weit	far
Westen (m)	west
westlich	western
Zentimeter (m)	centimetre
zurück	back

auf der linken Seite
on the left

auf der rechten Seite
on the right

links
left

rechts
right

geradeaus
straight on

Weights and measures

alle	all
anderer/e/es	other
beide	both
breit	broad
dick	fat
Ding (n)	thing
Dose (f)	can, tin
Dreieck (n)	triangle
dünn	thin
ein paar	a couple
einige	some
einzeln	individual
enorm	huge
etwa	about
Flasche (f)	bottle
ganz	quite, whole
genug	enough
gewaltig	vast
Glas (n)	jar, glass
Gramm (n)	gram
groß	big
Größe (f)	size

ein Glas Marmelade

eine Tafel Schokolade

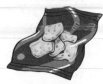

eine Packung Chips

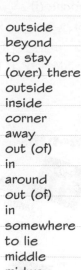

eine Flasche Medizin

eine Scheibe Toast

eine Dose Erbsen

Now try this

Cover the English words in the 'Location and distance' section and see how many of the German words you know. Write down the ones you did not know, in German and English, then test yourself again. Keep doing this until you know them all.

① General vocabulary

irgend ...	some ...
Karton (m)	carton
kaum	hardly
Kilometer (m)	kilometre
klein	small
Kreis (m)	circle
kurz	short
lang	long
leer	empty
Liter (m)	litre
Maß (n)	measure
mehrere	several
Meile (f)	mile
Menge (f)	quantity
messen	to measure
Meter (m)	metre
mindestens	at least
mittel-	medium
mittelgroß	medium
noch	still
nur	only
Quadrat (n)	square
Päckchen (n)	parcel
Packung (t)	package
Paket (n)	packet
Pfund (n)	pound
Rechteck (n)	rectangle
Schachtel (f)	box
Scheibe (f)	slice
Stück (n)	piece
Stückchen (n)	bit
Tube (f)	tube
Tüte (f)	bag
ungefähr	about
viele	many
viereckig	square
voll	full
wenigstens	at least
wiegen	to weigh
Zentimeter (m)	centimetre

Correctness

buchstabieren	to spell
falsch	wrong, false
Fehler (m)	mistake
Recht haben	to be right
richtig	right, correct
Unrecht haben	to be wrong
verbessern	to improve
Verbesserung (f)	correction

Weather

bedeckt	overcast
Blitz (m)	lightning
Donner (m)	thunder
es donnert	it's thundering
feucht	damp
frisch	fresh
Gewitter (n)	thunder storm
Grad (n)	degree
Hagel (m)	hail
heftig	fierce
heiß	hot
heiter	fair, fine and dry
Himmel (m)	sky
kalt	cold
Klima (n)	climate
kühl	cool
Mond (m)	moon
nass	wet
Niederschlag (m)	rainfall
Regen (m)	rain
Schatten (m)	shade
Schauer (m)	shower
Schnee (m)	snow
schneien	to snow
sonnig	sunny
Sturm (m)	storm
stürmisch	stormy
Temperatur (f)	temperature
trocken	dry
warm	warm
Wetter (n)	weather
Wetterbericht (m)	weather report
Wind (m)	wind
windig	windy
Wolke (f)	cloud
wolkig	cloudy

Materials

bestehen aus	to be made of
Baumwolle (f)	cotton
Eisen (n)	iron
Holz (n)	wood
Leder (n)	leather
Metall (n)	metal
Papier (n)	paper
Plastik (n)	plastic
Seide (f)	silk
Silber (n)	silver
Wolle (f)	wool

 die Sonne scheint

 es blitzt

 es regnet

 es friert

 es schneit

 es ist neblig

Abbreviations

AG Arbeitsgruppe (f) / Arbeitsgemeinschaft (f)	after-school group
d.h.	i.e.
GmbH	limited company
inkl.	inclusive
LKW	lorry
PLZ	postcode
usw.	etc.
z.B.	e.g.

Access

besetzt	engaged / occupied
Eintritt (m)	entrance
frei	free
geschlossen	closed
offen	open
öffnen	to open
schließen	to close
verboten	forbidden

Now try this

Learn the weather vocabulary above. Then write down in German what the weather has been each day during the past week. Remember to use the past tense.

2 Identity and culture

Relationships and choices

allein	alone
alt	old
Alter (n)	age
altmodisch	old fashioned
anonym	anonymous
ärgern (sich)	to get annoyed
attraktiv	attractive
auf die Nerven gehen	to get on your nerves
Auge (n)	eye
ausführen	to take for a walk
auskommen mit	to get on with
aussehen	to look
aussetzen	to abandon
Ausweis (m)	identification
Bart (m)	beard
beitragen zu	to contribute to
berühmt	famous
Besuch (m)	visit
besuchen	to visit
bevorzugen	to prefer
bitten	to ask
blöd	stupid
Blödsinn (m)	nonsense
böse	angry
Brieffreund (m)	penfriend
Brille (f)	glasses
bringen	to bring
Bruder (m)	brother
Cousin/e (m/f)	cousin
Dame (f)	lady
danken	to thank
dürfen	to be allowed to
egoistisch	egotistic
ehrlich	honest
einladen	to invite
Einladung (f)	invitation
einsam	lonely
einverstanden	agreed
Einzelkind (n)	only child
Eltern (pl)	parents
entschuldigen (sich)	to apologise
erfahren	experienced
erfüllen	to fulfil
erlauben	to allow
erleben	to experience
ernst	serious

Erwachsene (m/f)	adult
Familie (f)	family
Familienmitglied (n)	family member
Familienname (m)	surname
Frau (f)	woman, Mrs
frech	cheeky
Freund (m)	friend
Freundschaft (f)	friendship
füttern	to feed (animal)
Gast (m)	guest
Gastfreundschaft (f)	hospitality
Gastgeber (m)	host
geboren	born
Geburt (f)	birth
Geburtsdatum (n)	date of birth
Geburtsort (m)	place of birth
Geburtstag (m)	birthday
Gefühl (n)	feeling
gemein	mean
geschieden	divorced
Geschwister (pl)	siblings
Gesicht (n)	face
getrennt	separated
glatt	straight
großartig	great / magnificent
Großeltern (pl)	grandparents
gut / schlecht gelaunt	in a good / bad mood
gute / schlechte Laune haben	to be in a good / bad mood
Haar (n)	hair
Halb-	half-
hässlich	ugly
Hausnummer (f)	house number
Haustier (n)	pet
heiraten	to marry
heißen	to be called
herrisch	domineering
hilfsbereit	helpful
hoffen	to hope
hübsch	pretty
humorlos	humourless
humorvoll	humourous
jung	young
Käfig (m)	cage
Kind (n)	child
komisch	funny, curious
kritisieren	to criticise
kümmern (sich um)	to care (for)
Kuss (m)	kiss
küssen	to kiss
Laune (f)	mood
lebhaft	lively

ledig	unmarried
Leute (pl)	people
lockig	curly
Mädchen (n)	girl
Mann (m)	man
mitmachen	to join in
Mund (m)	mouth
Mutti / Mutter (f)	mum / mother
Nase (f)	nose
nennen	to name
nerven	to annoy
nett	nice
(nicht) leiden können	(cannot) can tolerate / stand
niemand	nobody
Ohr (n)	ear
Oma (f)	granny
Opa (m)	grandpa
Onkel (m)	uncle
optimistisch	optimistic
Persönlichkeit (f)	personality
pessimistisch	pessimistic
Postleitzahl (f)	postcode
reich	rich
Reisepass (m)	passport
Rentner (m)	pensioner
sauer	cross
schämen (sich)	to be ashamed

Goldfisch (m)	
Hund (m)	
Kaninchen (n)	
Katze (f)	
Pferd (n)	
Maus (f)	
Meerschweinchen (n)	
Vogel (m)	

Now try this

Highlight 10–15 adjectives on this page which describe people. Close the book and see how many you can write from memory. Check back to see how many you got right.

2 Identity and culture

scheiden (sich lassen)	to get divorced
Schnurrbart (m)	moustache
schön	lovely, beautiful
schüchtern	shy
Schwager (m)	brother-in-law
schwatzen	to chat
Schwester (f)	sister
Schwieger-	-in-law
selbst	(my / your)self
Sohn (m)	son
sorgen für	to care for
Stief-	step-
still	quiet
Straße (f)	street
Streit (m)	argument
streiten (sich)	to argue
Tante (f)	aunt
Tier (n)	animal
Tochter (f)	daughter
traurig	sad
Trauring (m)	wedding ring
trennen (sich)	to separate
Typ (m)	guy, bloke
(un)freundlich	(un)friendly
(un)geduldig	(im)patient
(un)höflich	(im)polite
(un)ordentlich	(un)tidy
(un)sympathisch	(un)likeable
unternehmungslustig	adventurous
unterstützen	to support
(un)zufrieden	(dis)satisfied
Vati / Vater (m)	dad / father
vergeben	to forgive
Verhältnis (n)	relationship
verheiratet	married
verloben (sich)	to get engaged
verlobt	engaged
verstehen (sich mit)	to get on (with)
Vogel (m)	bird
Vorliebe (f)	preference
Vorname (m)	first name
vorstellen (sich)	to introduce
wachsen	to grow
wegen	concerning
weinen	to cry
Wellensittich (m)	budgerigar

witzig	funny
Wohnort (m)	residence
Zahn (m)	tooth
Zeug (n)	stuff
Zuhause (n)	home
Zwillinge (pl)	twins
zivile Partnerschaft (f)	civil partnership

adoptiert	adopted
ähnlich	similar
Alleinerziehende	single parent
alleinstehend	single
angeberisch	pretentious
Anschrift (f)	address
auf Grund	due to
ausgeglichen	balanced
Begegnung (f)	encounter
Bekannte (m/f)	acquaintance
Beziehung (f)	relationship
Braut (f)	bride
Bräutigam (m)	groom
deprimiert	depressed
eifersüchtig	jealous
eingebildet	smug
Enkel (m)	grandson
Enkelin (f)	granddaughter
Geschlecht (n)	gender, sex
großzügig	generous
Humor (m)	humour
in Form sein	to be in shape
Junggeselle (m)	bachelor
Kanarienvogel (m)	canary
leiden	to suffer
minderjährig	under-age
miteinander	together
Neffe (m)	nephew
Nichte (f)	niece
Papagei (m)	parrot
Pensionär/in (m/f)	pensioner
Schildkröte (f)	tortoise
selbstständig	independent
selbstbewusst	self-confident
Trauung (f)	marriage
treu	true, faithful
Verlobte (m/f)	fiancé
vermeiden	to avoid
verrückt	crazy, mad
Verwandte (m/f)	relative
verzeihen	to forgive

Vetter (m)	cousin
volljährig	of legal age
Vorwahl (f)	code (phone)
zuverlässig	reliable

Technology in everyday life

Anrufbeantworter (m)	answer phone
anrufen	to phone, call
(aus)drucken	to print
benutzen / benützen	to use
Bindestrich (m)	dash, hyphen
Daten (pl)	data
Drucker (m)	printer
eingeben	to enter (data)
entwickeln	to develop
Entwicklung (f)	development
funktionieren	to work
Gefahr (f)	danger
herunterladen	to download
hochladen	to upload
Klingelton (m)	ring tone
lehrreich	informative
löschen	to delete
Medien (pl)	media
Missbrauch (m)	abuse
missbrauchen	to abuse
Nachrichten (pl)	messages
Netz (n)	net
Risiko (n)	risk
schicken	to send
Schrägstrich (m)	forward slash
Schutz (m)	protection
simsen	to text
soziale Medien (pl)	social media
speichern	to save (data)
Startseite (f)	homepage
teilen	to share
Unterstrich (m)	underscore
WLAN	Wi-Fi

Anwendungen (pl)	applications
Betriebssystem (n)	operating system
Einstellungen (pl)	settings
leistungsstark	powerful (battery, processor)
Sicherheit (f)	safety

Now try this

Make two lists in German – male and female – of all the words for family members you can think of, using this section to help you. Learn your words in pairs – male with female – and see how many you can remember after two minutes.

115

② Identity and culture

Free-time activities

Abenteuerfilm (m)	adventure film
amüsieren (sich)	to enjoy yourself
angeln	to go fishing
Apfelsine (f)	orange
Aprikose (f)	apricot
Badeanzug (m)	swimming costume
Badehose (f)	trunks
beschäftigen (sich)	to entertain/ amuse yourself
beschweren (sich)	to complain
bestellen	to order
bezahlen	to pay
Bildschirm (m)	screen
Blockflöte (f)	recorder
Bohne (f)	bean
Braten (m)	roast meat
Bratwurst (f)	fried sausage
Durst (m)	thirst
durstig	thirsty
Ei (n)	egg
Eintrittsgeld (n)	entry fee
Eintrittskarte (f)	entry ticket
Eisdiele (f)	ice cream parlour
Eislaufen (n)	ice skating
empfehlen	to recommend
Essig (m)	vinegar
fechten	to fence
Federball (m)	badminton
Freibad (n)	open air pool
Frikadelle (f)	meatball
Fruchtsaft (m)	fruit juice
Gurke (f)	cucumber
Haferflocken (pl)	oats
Hallenbad (n)	indoor pool
Hauptgericht (n)	main meal
Himbeere (f)	raspberry
Imbiss (m)	snack
Imbissbude (f)	snack bar
Interesse haben an	to be interested in
Jugendklub (m)	youth club
Kakao (m)	cocoa
Käse (m)	cheese
kegeln	to go bowling
Keks (m)	biscuit
klettern	to climb
Korbball (m)	netball
köstlich	tasty

 Zitrone (f)
 Ananas (f)
 Apfel (m)
Birne (f)

 Erdbeere (f)
 Kirsche (f)
 Pflaume (f)
Champignon / Pilz (m)

 Kartoffel (f)
 Erbsen (pl)
 Blumenkohl (m)
 Paprika (f)

Kotelett (n)	(meat) chop
Krimi (m)	thriller (film, book)
lecker	tasty
Leinwand (f)	big screen (cinema)
Liebesfilm (m)	romantic film
Lied (n)	song
Lust haben, etwas zu tun	to feel like doing something
Mitglied (n)	member
Nachrichten (pl)	news
Nachspeise (f)	dessert
Nachtisch (m)	dessert
Nudeln (pl)	pasta, noodles
Nuss (f)	nut
Obst (n)	fruit
Öl (n)	oil
Pfeffer (m)	pepper
Pfirsich (m)	peach
probieren	to try

Pute (f)	turkey
Rechnung (f)	bill
rennen	to run
riechen	to smell
ringen	to wrestle
rodeln	to sledge
roh	raw
Rollschuhlaufen	to go rollerskating
rudern	to row
Saft (m)	juice
Sahne (f)	cream
sammeln	to collect
satt sein	to be full
Schach (n)	chess
scharf	spicy, hot
Schaschlik (n)	kebab
schießen	to shoot
schmecken	to taste
Schnellimbiss (m)	snack bar
(Wiener) Schnitzel (n)	meat escalope (breaded)

Ich spiele ...
I play ...

 Geige (f)
 Trompete (f)
 Querflöte / Flöte (f)

 Schlagzeug (n)
 Klarinette (f)
 Klavier (n)
Blockflöte (f)

Now try this

Choose five compound nouns from this page and write them as their separate nouns. That way you can expand your vocabulary!

2 Identity and culture

Segelboot (n)	sailing boat
segeln	to sail
Seifenoper (f)	soap opera
Selbstbedienung (f)	self-service
Sendung (f)	programme
Senf (m)	mustard
Serie (f)	series
Sitz(platz) (m)	seat
spannend	exciting
Speisekarte (f)	menu
Speisesaal (m)	dining room
Spielzeug (n)	toy
Spinat (m)	spinach
Sportart (f)	type of sport
Stadion (n)	stadium
Stehcafé (n)	café (with tall tables, no chairs)
Stimme (f)	voice
stricken	to knit
Suppe (f)	soup
süß	sweet
Tagesgericht (n)	dish of the day
Tagesmenü (n)	set menu of the day
tauchen	to dive
Thunfisch (m)	tuna
Tor (n)	goal
Torte (f)	gateau
Trainingsanzug (m)	tracksuit
Trainingsschuh (m)	trainer, sports shoe
treffen (sich mit jemandem)	to meet (someone)
Trinkgeld (n)	tip (in restaurant)
turnen	to do gymnastics
unterhalten (sich)	to chat
Unterhaltung (f)	entertainment
Vegetarier/in (m/f)	vegetarian
verlieren	to lose
Volksmusik (f)	folk music
vorschlagen	to suggest
Vorspeise (f)	starter
Vorstellung (f)	performance
wandern	to walk, hike
weich	soft
Weintraube (f)	grape
Werbung (f)	advertising
Wettbewerb (m)	competition
Wurst (f)	sausage
zahlen	to pay

Clothing items (illustrated):

Gürtel (m)	
Hemd (n)	
Hut (m)	
Bluse (f)	
Krawatte (f) / Schlips (m)	
Rock (m)	
Schal (m)	
Schuh (m)	
Socke (f)	

Zeichentrickfilm (m)	cartoon
Zeitschrift (f)	magazine
Zeitung (f)	newspaper
Zeug (n)	things, stuff
Zucker (m)	sugar
Zuschauer/in (m/f)	spectator
Zwiebel (f)	onion
aufnehmen	to record
aufregend	exciting
Bergsteigen (n)	mountaineering
Dirigent (m)	conductor
Ente (f)	duck
Ergebnis (n)	result
ermüdend	tiring
Flachbildschirm (m)	flat screen (TV)
Flimmerkiste (f)	'box' (TV)
Forelle (f)	trout
Gans (f)	goose
geräuchert	smoked
Halbfettmilch (f)	semi-skimmed milk
hausgemacht	home-made
Honig (m)	honey
Kalbfleisch (n)	veal
Knoblauch (m)	garlic
Lachs (m)	salmon
Lammfleisch (n)	lamb
Leichtathletik (f)	athletics
Magermilch (f)	skimmed milk
Mehl (n)	flour
mit Untertiteln	with subtitles
Rindfleisch (n)	beef
Rührei (n)	scrambled egg
schlittschuhlaufen	to go ice skating
schmackhaft	tasty
Schweinefleisch (n)	pork
Spiegelei (n)	fried egg
Sprudelwasser (n)	fizzy water
Truthahn (m)	turkey
Überraschung (f)	surprise
Verein (m)	club
Vergnügen (n)	enjoyment, pleasure
Vollmilch (f)	full-fat milk
würzig	spicy

Now try this

Think of all the clothes items on this page that you have worn during the past week. Make a list in English then try to write the German equivalents without looking at the page.

Check back to see how many you got right. Learn the ones you got wrong!

③ Local, national, international and global areas of interest

Home, town, neighbourhood and region

Ampel (f)	traffic light
Angebot (n)	offer
anprobieren	to try on
Apotheke (f)	chemist's
Apparat (m)	appliance, gadget
aufräumen	to tidy up
ausgeben	to spend
Ausverkauf (m)	sale
ausverkauft	sold out
Bäckerei (f)	baker's
Backofen (m)	oven
baden	to have a bath
Badewanne (f)	bath tub
Bauernhaus (n)	farmhouse
Bauernhof (m)	farm
Benzin (n)	petrol
Bild (n)	picture
Blume (f)	flower
Brücke (f)	bridge
Buchhandlung (f)	bookshop
Bürgersteig (m)	pavement
Dach (n)	roof
Dachboden (m)	attic, loft
Decke (f)	blanket; ceiling
Denkmal (n)	monument
Diele (f)	hall
Doppelhaus (n)	semi-detached house

Drogerie (f)	chemist's
Ecke (f)	corner
Einfamilienhaus (n)	detached house
einkaufen	to shop
Einkaufstasche (f)	shopping bag
Einkaufswagen (m)	shopping trolley
einpacken	to pack
Einwohner (m) / Einwohnerin (f)	inhabitant
Elektrogeschäft (n)	electrical shop
Erdgeschoss (n)	ground floor
Etage (f)	storey
Etagenbett (n)	bunk bed
Fahrkarte (f)	ticket
Feld (n)	field
flach	flat
Fleischerei (f)	butcher's
Flur (m)	hall, corridor
Fluss (m)	river
Friseursalon (m)	hairdresser's
Fußboden (m)	floor
Fußgängerzone (f)	pedestrian zone
Gabel (f)	fork
Gegend (f)	region
günstig	value for money
Hafen (m)	harbour
Haltestelle (f)	stop (bus, tram)
Hauptbahnhof (m)	main station
Hauptstadt (f)	capital city
Haushalt (m)	household
Hecke (f)	hedge

Heizung (f)	heating
Helm (m)	helmet
Herd (m)	oven
Hochhaus (n)	high-rise block
Hügel (m)	hill
Insel (f)	island
Juweliergeschäft (n)	jeweller's
kaputt	broken
Kasse (f)	till, cash register
Kaufhaus (n)	department store
Kirchturm (m)	church tower
Kleidergeschäft (n)	clothes shop
Kommode (f)	chest of drawers
Konditorei (f)	cake shop, patisserie
Kopfkissen (n)	pillow
Kreuzung (f)	crossroads
Kühlschrank (m)	fridge
Kunde (m)	customer
Kunstgalerie (f)	art gallery
Laden (m)	shop
Land (n)	country
Landschaft (f)	landscape
Lebensmittelgeschäft (m)	food store, grocer's shop
Licht (n)	light
liefern	to deliver
Löffel (m)	spoon
mähen	to mow
Mahlzeit (f)	meal
Marke (f)	brand, make
Marktplatz (m)	market place
Mauer (f)	wall (outside)

Auto (n)

Zug (m)

Boot (n)

Bus (m)

Fahrrad (n)

Flugzeug (n)

Lastwagen (m)

Mofa (n)

Motorrad (n)

Straßenbahn (f)

Now try this

Make a list of all the forms of transport you have used in the past year. Memorise the words, then test yourself on the German spellings.

③ Local, national, international and global areas of interest

Messer (n)	knife
Metzgerei (f)	butcher's
Miete (f)	rent
mieten	to rent
Mikrowelle (f)	microwave
Möbel (pl)	furniture
Nachbar (m) / Nachbarin (f)	neighbour
Nachteil (m)	disadvantage
Nachttisch (m)	bedside table
Notausgang (m)	emergency exit
Obst- und Gemüseladen (m)	greengrocer's
Ordnung (f)	rules, order
Parkplatz (m)	parking space
Pflanze (f)	plant
Plakat (n)	poster
Platz (m)	square
Preis (m)	price
putzen	to clean
Quittung (f)	receipt
Rasen (m)	lawn
Regal (n)	shelf
Reihenhaus (n)	terraced house
Reinigung (f)	dry cleaner's
Rolltreppe (f)	escalator
Sache (f)	thing
Schaufenster (n)	shop window
Schlange stehen	to queue
Schlüssel (m)	key
Schrank (m)	cupboard
Schreibwarengeschäft (n)	stationery shop
Schublade (f)	drawer
Sonderangebot (n)	special offer
Spiegel (m)	mirror
Stadtrand (m)	outskirts of town
tanken	to fill up with petrol
Tankstelle (f)	garage
Tasse (f)	cup
Teelöffel (m)	teaspoon
Teller (m)	plate
Teppich (m)	carpet
Tiefkühlschrank (m)	freezer
Tischdecke (f)	tablecloth
Topf (m)	pan
Treppe (f)	stairs
Turm (m)	tower
umgeben von	surrounded by
Umgebung (f)	surroundings

umziehen	to move (home)
Vorhang (m)	curtain
Vorort (m)	suburb
Vorteil (m)	advantage
Wald (m)	forest
Wand (f)	wall (inside)
Warenhaus (n)	warehouse
Waschbecken (n)	washbasin
Wiese (f)	meadow, field
Wohnblock (m)	block of flats
Zebrastreifen (m)	zebra crossing

Abstellraum (m)	store room
ausschalten	to switch off
Besteck (n)	cutlery
Brunnen (m)	fountain
Einbahnstraße (f)	one-way street
einschalten	to turn on
Essecke (f)	eating area (in kitchen)
Fahrschein (m)	ticket
Gerät (n)	appliance
geräumig	spacious, roomy
Geschirr (n)	crockery
gratis	free of charge
Grünanlage (f)	green space, park
Mehrfamilienhaus (n)	house for multiple families
Möbelstück (n)	piece of furniture
öffentliche Verkehrsmittel (pl)	public transport
pleite (sein)	(to be) skint
preiswert	value for money, cheap
Rabatt (m)	discount
Sackgasse (f)	cul-de-sac
Sparkasse (f)	savings bank
Stadtteil (m)	part of town
Stadtviertel (n)	district of town
Stockwerk (n)	storey
Strom (m)	electricity
Tiefkühltruhe (f)	chest freezer
Treppenhaus (n)	staircase
umsonst	free of charge; in vain

Umzug (m)	move (home)
Wolkenkratzer (m)	skyscraper

Social issues

abhängig sein von	to be addicted to, to be dependent on
abnehmen	to lose weight
Ader (f)	vein
Altenheim (n)	old people's home
aufgeben	to give up
aufhören	to stop
Ausländer/in (m/f)	foreigner
ausländisch	foreign
betrunken	drunk
Bewegung (f)	movement
bewusstlos	unconscious
Bewusstsein (n)	consciousness
Bio-	organic
Blut (n)	blood
brechen	to break; to be sick
Droge (f)	drug
Drogenhändler (m)	drug dealer
Drogensüchtige (m/f)	drug addict
Einwanderer (m)	immigrant
entspannen (sich)	to relax

Bücher (pl)

Dom (m)

Einkaufskorb (m)

Rathaus (n)

Spielplatz (m)

Now try this

Without looking at the book, think about all of the amenities in your local town or city and make a list of them in German. Then open the book and check your spelling.

Local, national, international and global areas of interest

Ernährung (f)	food, nutrition
Erste Hilfe	first aid
Fett (n)	fat
fettig	fatty
fettleibig	obese
Feuerwehr (f)	fire brigade
freiwillig	voluntary
Freiwillige (m/f)	volunteer
gesund	healthy
Gesundheit (f)	health
Gewicht (n)	weight
Gleichheit (f)	equality
Hautfarbe (f)	skin colour
Heim (n)	home, hostel
Herz (n)	heart
hilflos	helpless
in Form sein	to be in good shape
krank	ill
Krankenhaus (n)	hospital
Krankenwagen (m)	ambulance
Krankheit (f)	illness
Krebs (m)	cancer
Leber (f)	liver
Magen (m)	stomach
Medikament (n)	medicine
menschlich	human(e)
Rasse (f)	race
Rassismus (m)	racism
rassistisch	racist
Rat (m)	advice
rauchen	to smoke
Rote Kreuz (n)	Red Cross
Ruhe (f)	peace
schädlich	harmful
Schmerz (m)	pain
-schmerzen haben	to have -ache
Sorge (f)	worry
sorgen für	to look after, care for
spenden	to donate
Spritze (f)	syringe
spritzen	to inject
sterben	to die
Sucht (f)	addiction
süchtig	addicted
Tierheim (n)	animal shelter
tot	dead
übel (mir ist)	(I feel) ill
Unfall (m)	accident
Vene (f)	vein
Verkehrsunfall (m)	traffic accident

verletzen (sich)	to injure (yourself)
Verletzung (f)	injury
wehtun	to hurt
Wohltätigkeit (f)	charity
Wohltätigkeitsveranstaltung (f)	charity event
zunehmen	to put on weight

abstinent	teetotal
Atem (m)	breath
Atembeschwerden (pl)	breathing difficulties
Bedürftige (m/f)	person in need
begehen	to commit
benachteiligen	to disadvantage
bewegen (sich)	to move
Drogenberatungsstelle (f)	drugs advice centre
ehrenamtlich	voluntarily
ein Mittel gegen	a medicine for
einatmen	to breathe in
Eingliederung (f)	integration
Entziehungskur (f)	drug rehab programme
erbrechen (sich)	to vomit
fettarm	low in fat
Gehirn (n)	brain
lebendig	lively
magersüchtig	anorexic
Nahrung (f)	food, nourishment
Rassenvorurteile (pl)	racial prejudice
Rassist (m)	racist
Raucherhusten (m)	smoker's cough
Rauschgift (n)	drug
schaden	to damage
Straftat (f)	crime
Überdosis (f)	overdose
übergewichtig	overweight
vermeiden	to avoid

Global issues

Abfall (m)	rubbish, waste
Abfalleimer (m)	rubbish bin
Abgase (pl)	exhaust fumes
Achtung (f)	respect, esteem

alternative Energiequelle (f)	alternative source of energy
Altpapier (n)	waste paper
anbauen	to grow
arbeitslos	unemployed
arm	poor
Armut (f)	poverty
aussterben	to die out
bedrohen	to threaten
Benzin (n)	petrol
Bettler/in (m/f)	beggar
Bevölkerung (f)	population
biologisch	biological, organic
Biomüll (m)	organic waste
bleifrei	lead-free
Brennstoff (m)	fuel
chemisch	chemical
Dieb (m)	thief
Diskriminierung (f)	discrimination
einsam	lonely
entsorgen	to dispose of (waste)
erfrieren	to freeze to death
Fahrradweg (m)	cycle path
FCKWs	CFCs
fliehen	to flee
Flüchtling (m)	refugee
Gebrauch (m)	usage
gefährlich	dangerous
Gesellschaft (f)	society
Gewalt (f)	violence
gewalttätig	violent
heizen	to heat
Heizung (f)	heating
im Freien	outside
Kaugummi (m)	chewing gum
keinen festen Wohnsitz haben	to be of no fixed abode
Kohle (f)	coal
Kraftwerk (n)	power station
Krieg (m)	war
Kunststoff (m)	synthetic material

recyceln
to recycle

Now try this

Choose 10 words and make learning cards for them – English or a photo on one side, and German on the other.

③ Local, national, international and global areas of interest

Lärm (m)	noise
Leben (n)	life
Luft (f)	air
Luftverschmutzung (f)	air pollution
Müll (m)	rubbish
Mülltonne (f)	dustbin
Not (f)	need
obdachlos	homeless
öffentlich	public(ly)
Opfer (n)	victim
Ozonloch (n)	hole in the ozone layer
Ozonschicht (f)	ozone layer
Pfand (n)	deposit
reinigen	to clean
sauber	clean
Sauerstoff (m)	oxygen
saurer Regen (m)	acid rain
schaden	to damage, harm
Schaden (m)	damage
schädlich	harmful
Schale (f)	skin (fruit), shell (egg)
schmutzig	dirty
schützen	to protect
schwach	weak
Solarzelle (f)	solar panel
Sonnenenergie (f)	solar energy
Sozialhilfe (f)	income support
Sozialwohnung (f)	social housing flat
sparen	to save
Spraydose (f)	aerosol
stark	strong
stehlen	to steal
Suppenküche (f)	soup kitchen
Treibhauseffekt (m)	greenhouse effect
überbevölkert	overpopulated

ultraviolette Strahlen (pl)	ultraviolet rays
Umwelt (f)	environment
umweltfeindlich	environmentally unfriendly
umweltfreundlich	environmentally friendly
unterstützen	to support
Unterstützung (f)	support
Verbrauch (m)	consumption
Verbrechen (n)	crime
Verbrecher (m) / Verbrecherin (f)	criminal
Verkehr (m)	traffic
Verkehrsmittel (n)	mode of transport
Verpackung (f)	packaging
verschmutzen	to pollute
Verschmutzung (f)	pollution
verschwinden	to disappear
vertreiben	to drive out
Wasserkraft (f)	hydroelectric power
wegwerfen	to throw away
weltweit	worldwide
zerstören	to destroy
Zuhause (n)	home

Abholzung (f)	deforestation
Auspuffgase (pl)	exhaust fumes
bedürftig	needy
Düngemittel (n)	fertiliser
Einwegflasche (f)	non-returnable bottle
Hauptverkehrszeit (f)	rush hour
Müllentsorgung (f)	waste disposal
Not (f)	need
Obdachlosenheim (n)	homeless shelter
überschreiten	to exceed

verpesten	to pollute
verschwenden	to waste
verwenden	to use
wiederverwerten	to recycle

Travel and tourism

abfahren	to depart
abholen	to collect, pick up

Deutschland	
die Schweiz	
die Türkei	
die Vereinigten Staaten	
England	
Frankreich	
Großbritannien	
Irland	
Italien	
Österreich	
Schottland	
Spanien	
Wales	

Now try this

Match the German place names to their English equivalents.

(a)	die Ostsee		Vienna
(b)	der Ärmelkanal		Baltic Sea
(c)	der Bodensee		Geneva
(d)	die Mosel		Danube
(e)	der Rhein		Moselle
(f)	die Donau		Cologne
(g)	Genf		English Channel
(h)	Köln		Lake Constance
(i)	München		Munich
(j)	Wien		Rhine

③ Local, national, international and global areas of interest

ankommen	to arrive
Ausflug (m)	trip, excursion
ausfüllen	to fill in
Ausland (n)	abroad, foreign country
Aussicht (f)	view
aussteigen	to get off
Bahnsteig (m)	platform
beliebt	popular
besichtigen	to visit, sightsee
Briefkasten (m)	postbox
Briefmarke (f)	stamp
Burg (f)	castle
Campingplatz (m)	campsite
Doppelzimmer (n)	double room
einsteigen	to get in/on
Einzelzimmer (n)	single room
entwerten	to stamp (ticket)
Erinnerung (f)	memory
erleben	to experience
Ermäßigung (f)	reduction
Fähre (f)	ferry
Fahrkarte (f)	ticket
Fahrkartenautomat (m)	ticket machine
Fahrt (f)	journey
Flug (m)	flight
Flughafen (m)	airport
Fotoapparat (m)	camera
Führung (f)	guided tour
Gepäck (n)	luggage
Gleis (n)	platform; track
Halbpension (f)	half board
herumfahren	to travel around
Jugendherberge (f)	youth hostel
Koffer (m)	suitcase
Küste (f)	coast
Linie (f)	line, number (bus, tram)
Meer (n)	sea
Mittelmeer (n)	Mediterranean
Notausgang (m)	emergency exit
Öffnungszeiten (pl)	opening hours

örtlich	local
Panne (f)	breakdown
Passagier (m)	passenger
Pension (f)	small hotel
Polen	Poland
Reise (f)	journey, trip
Reisebüro (n)	travel agency
reisen	to travel
Reisende (m/f)	traveller
Reisetasche (f)	travel bag
Reiseziel (n)	destination
Richtung (f)	direction
Rundfahrt (f)	round trip
Russland	Russia
Schließfach (n)	locker
Schloss (n)	castle
See (f)	sea
See (m)	lake
seekrank	seasick
sehenswert	worth seeing
Sehenswürdigkeit (f)	tourist attraction
Sicherheitsgurt (m)	seatbelt
sonnen (sich)	to sunbathe
Sonnenbrand (m)	sunburn
Speisewagen (m)	dining car (train)
Stadtbummel (m)	stroll through town
Stadtrundfahrt (f)	city tour
Stau (m)	traffic jam
Strand (m)	beach
Straßenkarte (f)	street map
suchen	to look for
Überfahrt (f)	crossing (sea)
übernachten	to stay the night
Übernachtung (f)	overnight stay
überqueren	to cross (road)
umsteigen	to change (transport)
unterwegs	on the way
Urlaub (m)	holiday
verbringen	to spend (time)
verpassen	to miss
Verspätung (f)	delay
Vollpension (f)	full board
Wartesaal (m)	waiting room

Weg (m)	path, way
Wohnwagen (m)	caravan
Zelt (n)	tent
zelten	to camp
Zweibettzimmer (n)	twin room

Andenken (n)	souvenir
ansehen (sich etwas)	to look at something
Aufenthalt (m)	stay
Auskunft (f)	information
Autovermietung (f)	car hire
beeilen (sich)	to hurry
begleiten	to accompany
bestätigen	to confirm
Dampfer (m)	steam boat
Empfang (m)	reception
entdecken	to discover
erinnern (sich an)	to remember
Fahrradverleih (m)	bicycle hire
Gepäckaufbewahrung (f)	left luggage
Klimaanlage (f)	air conditioning
Prospekt (m)	brochure
Strandkorb (m)	wicker beach chair
Verbindung (f)	connection
Verkehrsamt (n)	tourist information office
wegen	closed for holiday
Betriebsferien (pl) geschlossen	
Zoll (m)	customs
Zuschlag (m)	surcharge

My studies

Direktor/in (m/f)	head teacher
Fach (n)	subject
Fremdsprache (f)	foreign language
klug	clever
lehren	to teach

Fitnessraum (m)
gym

Schlüssel (m)
key

mit Bad
with a bath

mit Blick auf
with a view of

mit Dusche
with a shower

Now try this

Highlight 10–15 words on this page which could be used to describe a recent holiday you have had. Write sentences in German using each of them.

④ Current and future study and employment

Schulleiter/in (m/f)	school head
Stunde (f)	lesson; hour
(un)gerecht	(un)fair
Werken (n)	DT

Life at school/college

1 = sehr gut	very good
2 = gut	good
3 = befriedigend	satisfactory
4 = ausreichend	sufficient
5 = mangelhaft	unsatisfactory, fail
6 = ungenügend	extremely poor, inadequate

Abschlusszeugnis (n)	school leaving certificate
Anspitzer (m)	pencil sharpener
Antwort (f)	answer
anziehen (sich)	to get dressed
aufpassen	to pay attention
aufstehen	to get up
aufwachen	to wake up
Aula (f)	hall (assembly)
Austausch (m)	exchange
Auswahl (f)	choice
ausziehen (sich)	to get undressed
bestehen	to pass (test, exam)
blau machen	to play truant
dauern	to last
Erfolg (m)	success
erfolgreich	successful
erklären	to explain
erzählen	to tell
faul	lazy
fehlen	to be missing, absent
Ferien (pl)	holidays
fleißig	hard-working
Frage (f)	question
Ganztagsschule (f)	all-day school
Gesamtschule (f)	comprehensive school

gründen	to found
Grundschule (f)	primary school
Gymnasium (n)	grammar school
Hauptschule (f)	secondary school
Hausmeister/in (m/f)	caretaker
Internat (n)	boarding school
Klassenarbeit (f)	class test
Klassenfahrt (f)	class trip
korrigieren	to correct
Kreide (f)	chalk
Labor (n)	laboratory
Lehrerzimmer (n)	staffroom
Lineal (n)	ruler
malen	to paint
Mittagspause (f)	lunch break
mündlich	oral(ly)
nachsitzen	to have a detention
Note (f)	grade, mark
Notendruck (m)	pressure to achieve good grades
Pause (f)	break
plaudern	to chat
Prüfung (f)	exam
rasieren (sich)	to shave
Raum (m)	room
Realschule (f)	secondary school
rechnen	to calculate, do sums
Regel (f)	rule
schaffen	to create, manage, cope
schminken (sich)	to put on make-up
schriftlich	written
Schüler/in (m/f)	pupil
Schulhof (m)	playground
schwatzen / schwätzen	to chatter

Seite (f)	page
Sekretariat (n)	school office
setzen (sich)	to sit down
sitzen bleiben	to repeat a year
Stundenplan (m)	timetable
Tafel (f)	board
Turnhalle (f)	sports hall, gym
üben	to practise
Übung (f)	activity
Umkleideraum (m)	changing room
umziehen (sich)	to get changed
Unterricht (m)	lessons
unterrichten	to teach
Versammlung (f)	assembly
waschen (sich)	to wash
wiederholen	to repeat
Wörterbuch (n)	dictionary
zeichnen	to draw
Zeugnis (n)	school report

abschreiben	to copy
abwesend	absent
anwesend	present
Aussprache (f)	pronunciation
durchfallen	to fail (test, exam)
eine Frage stellen	to ask a question
Ergebnis (n)	result
Gang (m)	corridor
Leistung (f)	achievement
Leistungsdruck (m)	pressure to achieve
Patrone (f)	cartridge (pen)
Schere (f)	scissors
schwänzen	to truant
Strafarbeit (f)	punishment, lines
versetzt werden	to move up a year

Mathe(matik) (f)   Biologie (f)   Chemie (f)   Physik (f)   Deutsch

Englisch   Französisch   Spanisch   Erdkunde (f)   Geschichte (f)   Religion (f)   Informatik (f)   Kunst (f)   Sport (m)

Now try this

What GCSEs are you and your friends taking? Check that you can say / write all the subjects in German. If you're thinking of taking A levels, can you name those subjects too?

④ Current and future study and employment

Education post-16

Abitur (n)	A-level equivalent
Abiturient/in (m/f)	Abitur student
Arbeitspraktikum (n)	work experience
Ausbildung (f)	education
Ausbildungsplatz (m)	trainee place
(Azubi) = Auszubildende (m/f)	apprentice
Berufsberater/in (m/f)	careers adviser
Berufsschule (f)	vocational school
(sich) bewerben (um)	to apply (for)
Bewerbung (f)	application
Brief (m)	letter
Chef/in (m/f)	boss
entscheiden (sich)	to decide
Erfahrung (f)	experience
fertig	ready
Führerschein (m)	driving licence
Gelegenheit (f)	opportunity
Kollege / Kollegin (m/f)	colleague

Kurs (m)	course
Lebenslauf (m)	CV
Lehre (f)	apprenticeship
Lohn (m)	wage
Mindestlohn (m)	minimum wage
Nebenjob (m)	part-time job
Oberstufe (f)	sixth form
Rat (m)	advice
Semester (n)	term
Studienplatz (m)	university place
Studium (n)	studies
theoretisch	theoretical(ly)
verdienen	to earn

einstellen	to employ
Fachschule (f)	technical college
Hauswirtschaftslehre (f) home economics	
Pflichtfach (n)	compulsory subject
Sozialkunde (f)	social studies
Wahlfach (n)	optional subject
Wirtschaftslehre (f)	economics

Jobs, career choices and ambitions

Angestellte (m/f)	employee
Apotheker/in (m/f)	pharmacist
Arbeitszeit (f)	work hours
Bäcker/in (m/f)	baker
Bauarbeiter/in (m/f)	builder
bauen	to build
Beamte / Beamtin (m/f)	civil servant
Beruf (m)	job
berufstätig	employed
beschäftigt	busy
beschließen	to decide
besitzen	to own
Besitzer/in (m/f)	owner
Bezahlung (f)	payment
Briefträger/in (m/f)	postman/-woman
Büro (n)	office
erfüllen	to fulfil
Feuerwehrmann/-frau (m)	fire fighter
Fleischer/in (m/f)	butcher

der Arzt   die Ärztin

die Krankenschwester
der Krankenpfleger

der Friseur   die Friseuse

der Polizist   die Polizistin

die Gärtnerin   der Gärtner

die Zahnärztin   der Zahnarzt

Now try this

To help you learn the jobs vocabulary, make a list of five jobs that you would like to do and five jobs that you would not like to do, and then memorise them.

4 Current and future study and employment

ganztags	all day
Gehalt (n)	salary
Halbtagsarbeit (f)	part-time work
Hausfrau (f)	housewife
Karriere (f)	career
Kassierer/in (m/f)	cashier
Klempner/in (m/f)	plumber
Koch (m) / Köchin (f)	chef, cook
LKW-Fahrer/in (m/f)	lorry driver
Maler/in (m/f)	painter, decorator
Metzger/in (m/f)	butcher
Pfarrer/in (m/f)	priest
Nebenjob (m)	part-time job
Polizei (f)	police
Postbote (m)/ Postbotin (f)	postman/-woman
Rentner/in (m/f)	pensioner
Schauspieler/in (m/f)	actor
Schichtarbeit (f)	shift work
suchen	to look for
Teilzeitjob (m)	part-time job
Termin (m)	appointment
Tischler/in (m/f)	carpenter
Verkäufer/in (m/f)	sales assistant
Vollzeitarbeit (f)	full-time work
Vorstellungsgespräch (n)	interview
Werkstatt (f)	garage
Wunsch (m)	wish

Arbeitgeber/in (m/f)	employer
Besprechung (f)	meeting
Betrieb (m)	concern, business
kündigen	to hand in your notice
vereinbaren	to agree, arrange

Now try this

Write your top ten verbs and adjectives on this page. Try to choose words that you can use across a variety of topic areas.

Verbs	Adjectives

ANSWERS

1. Physical descriptions

D, F, G

2. Character descriptions

1 annoying / sits on sofa *or* doesn't help at home
2 lively / makes lots of noise *or* chats loudly on phone
3 nice *or* kind / helps with homework *or* helps with problems at school

3. Childhood

Listen to the recording

Transcript:
- *Teacher:* Was für Probleme gibt es oft bei Kindern?
- *Student:* Heutzutage haben junge Kinder viele Probleme, weil sie in einer digitalen Welt aufwachsen. Als ich in die Grundschule ging, hatte ich weder Handy noch Tablet zu Hause, weil sie sehr teuer waren. Nach der Schule habe ich mit Freunden im Freien gespielt oder wir haben vielleicht eine Radtour gemacht. Jetzt ist das Leben viel komplizierter, denn jeder muss das neueste Gerät haben, sogar wenn das Kind erst sechs Jahre alt ist! Andererseits langweilt man sich nicht, wenn man heute Kind ist. Es gibt so viele Sendungen, die man im Fernsehen sehen kann, dass das Leben sicher viel besser ist.
- *Teacher:* Was hat dir an deiner Grundschule besonders gut gefallen?
- *Student:* Als ich in die Grundschule ging, war Mittwoch mein Lieblingstag, weil wir uns dann immer einen Film im Klassenzimmer angesehen haben. Mir haben besonders die amerikanischen Filme gefallen, weil sie so cool waren. An einem Mittwoch haben wir ein Fest organisiert, wo wir uns alle als amerikanische Schauspieler angezogen haben. Wir haben Kekse gebacken und der Klassenlehrer hat Eis mit Schokoladensoße serviert. Das hat so viel Spaß gemacht und ich sehe mir heute noch gern die Fotos von diesem Tag an.
- *Teacher:* Wie könnte man deine Grundschule verbessern?
- *Student:* Meine Grundschule war sehr altmodisch und schlecht ausgestattet, also würde ich sie gern renovieren. Als Erstes würde es einen größeren Schulhof hinter der Schule geben, wo man in den Pausen spielen oder mit Freunden plaudern könnte. Die Schule würde auch neue Klassenzimmer bekommen, damit man besser lernen könnte. Ich finde es wichtig, dass man sich an der Schule wohlfühlt, also sollte das Schulgebäude bunt und hell aussehen, um die Laune der Schüler zu verbessern. Als Letztes würde ich die Schuluniform ändern, weil sie wirklich sehr hässlich ist!
- *Teacher:* Was werden die Kinder im Foto in Zukunft machen, meinst du?
- *Student:* Meiner Meinung nach werden diese Kinder in Zukunft noch miteinander befreundet sein, weil sie alle sehr sympathisch aussehen. Das Mädchen links mit den lockigen Haaren wird vielleicht um die Welt reisen und viele Abenteuer haben, weil sie unternehmungslustig aussieht. Vielleicht werden diese Kinder entweder Ärzte oder Lehrer werden, weil beide Berufe beliebte Karrieren sind. Es ist möglich, dass die Kinder in Zukunft nicht in derselben Gegend wohnen werden, aber durch Technologie werden sie immer in Kontakt bleiben können. Hoffentlich wird die Gruppe erfolgreich im Leben sein und ihre Träume erfüllen.

5. Friends

Sample answer:
1 Meine Freundin Carol ist klug/intelligent und sehr lustig.
2 Ich sehe meine Freunde/Freundinnen nach der Schule.
3 Mein Bruder hat keine Freunde.
4 Meine beste Freundin wohnt mit ihrer Familie in Spanien.
5 Letzte Woche hat mein Freund Golf gespielt.

6. Peer group

Sample answer:
- Seit letztem Trimester habe ich ein Problem an der Schule, weil ein Mitschüler mich dauernd mobbt. Ein Junge in der Klasse mag mich gar nicht, weil ich immer bessere Noten bekomme als er. Ich finde es schade, dass wir uns streiten, aber so was kann manchmal passieren, wenn jemand niedisch oder selbstsüchtig ist. Leider ist dieser Jugendliche noch zu jung, um nicht egoistisch zu sein, und daher ist dieses Problem entstanden.
- Wenn man einen festen Freundschaftskreis hat, ist das super, weil man sich dann immer gut unterhalten kann. Zum Beispiel kann man am Wochenende zusammen ins Kino gehen oder Computerspiele spielen und man muss nie einsam und traurig zu Hause sitzen. In der Familie ist es aber etwas anders und wenn man sich mit den Geschwistern oder den Eltern streitet, ist es nicht so schlimm. Mit der Familie kann man das Problem normalerweise schnell lösen – bis zum nächsten Krach!

7. Marriage

1 F, 2 NT, 3 T, 4 NT, 5 F

8. Partnerships

1 C, 2 A, 3 B

9. Social media

D and E

11. Online activities

1 mit ihren Eltern
2 spricht mit Schulkameraden
3 lädt Fotos hoch

13. Everyday life

1 technical/necessary skills
2 independence
3 one of: less personal contact with each other / life spent in front of a screen

14. Hobbies

1 A, 2 B

15. Interests

Sample answer:
He particularly likes listening to music. He goes swimming three times a week. Most of all he likes cycling. At the weekend he always goes to the cinema with his girlfriend. Last week they saw an exciting film.

17. Films

Sample answer:

- Ich möchte euch über ein Filmfest bei mir informieren, das unsere Gemeinde jeden Sommer in meiner Heimatstadt organisiert. Dieses Jahr heißt das Fest „Kino lebt" und es wird in der Woche vom 12. bis zum 19. Mai stattfinden. Das Fest ist bei allen Besuchern sehr beliebt, denn es gibt immer eine ausgezeichnete Auswahl an Filmen. Insbesondere gibt es zum ersten Mal dieses Jahr einige Fremdsprachenfilme, die mich besonders interessieren.

- Ein Filmfest ist viel spannender als ein normaler Kinobesuch, finde ich. Letztes Jahr war das Fest ein riesiger Erfolg und viele Leute haben dem Film-Team dazu gratuliert. Ich denke, es ist ihm gelungen, genau die richtige Mischung von Filmarten innerhalb einer Woche zu zeigen. Zum ersten Mal haben die Restaurants in der Stadt auch mitgemacht, indem sie Erfrischungen und Getränke auf dem Stadtplatz angeboten haben. Glücklicherweise war das Wetter sehr schön und viele Leute sind draußen gegessen und haben sich gut unterhalten. Die Stimmung in der Stadt war wunderschön!

18. Television

1 documentaries
2 three years
3 an American series / 30 episodes

19. Sport

Transcript:

Teacher: Welche Sportarten treibst du gern?
Student: Ich treibe gern viele Sportarten, aber seit der Kindheit ist mein Lieblingssport Fußball. Ich bin Mitglied der Schulmannschaft. Das macht immer viel Spaß, obwohl wir oft die Spiele verlieren.
Teacher: Wie viel Sport hast du letzte Woche gemacht?
Student: Letzte Woche habe ich viermal Sport getrieben, und der Höhepunkt war Basketball. Ich habe am Wochenende an einem Basketballturnier teilgenommen und am Ende haben wir alle eine Medaille gewonnen.
Teacher: Was ist dein sportlicher Traum?
Student: In Zukunft möchte ich Profifußballspieler werden. Ich weiß aber, dass das nur ein unrealistischer Traum ist, den ich nie erreichen werde. Ich möchte aber trotzdem immer für eine lokale Mannschaft Fußball spielen.
Teacher: Ist Sport als Pflichtfach in der Schule wichtig?
Student: Ich meine, dass Sport sehr wichtig ist, um fit zu bleiben. Daher ist es richtig, dass Sport als Fach auf dem Stundenplan steht und jeder das machen muss. Sport an der Schule bietet auch die Gelegenheit, neue Sportarten auszuprobieren, und das ist ein großer Vorteil davon.

20. Food and drink

Sample answer:

- Ich esse um acht Uhr Frühstück, weil ich das sehr wichtig finde.
- Mein Lieblingsessen ist Nudeln mit Fleischsoße und Käse.
- Ich esse gern Bananen, aber Äpfel schmecken mir nicht.
- Zum Geburtstag esse ich am liebsten Hamburger mit Pommes.

21. Meals

Ines: present – bread / future – roast
Alvin: past – soup / present – chicken

22. Eating in a café

Sample answer:

He is called Kai. He lives with his son. He often orders a lemonade and some chips. In summer he likes eating strawberry gateau with cream. Yesterday he did not come into the café, but tomorrow he will come again.

23. Eating in a restaurant

1 ein Freund hat es empfohlen / wegen der Nachspeisen
2 any one of: tanzen / zum Club gehen

24. Food opinions

Helena's favourite drink now: fruit tea
Ralf's opinion: tastes awful

25. Shopping for clothes

Transcript:

Teacher: Sie sind in der Modeboutique. Sie sprechen mit dem Verkaufer / der Verkäuferin.
Teacher: Wie kann ich Ihnen helfen?
Student: Ich habe dieses Hemd hier gekauft.
Teacher: Oh, und gibt es ein Problem damit?
Student: Ja, es ist zu klein.
Teacher: Also, was möchten Sie dann kaufen?
Student: Ich möchte eine blaue Hose kaufen, bitte.
Teacher: Moment.
Teacher: Wie finden Sie dieses Stück?
Student: Das ist sehr schön, denke ich.
Teacher: Toll.
Student: Wie viel kostet das?
Teacher: 45 Euro.

26. Shopping

1 die vielen Straßenbahnen / zweistöckige Autobusse
2 any one of: die Schaufenster von den Läden / die sehr hohen Häuser

27. Customs

Transcript:

Teacher: Du kommst bei deiner Gastfamilie in Österreich an. Du sprichst mit deinem Freund / deiner Freundin.
Teacher: Herzlich willkommen. Wie geht's?
Student: Ich bin ein bisschen müde.
Teacher: Was möchtest du trinken?
Student: Ein Glas Mineralwasser, bitte.
Teacher: Wie findest du das Wetter bei uns?
Student: Es ist sehr schön und warm.
Teacher: Gut. Was meinst du von unserem Haus?
Student: Es ist sehr groß.
Teacher: Hast du eine Frage für mich?
Student: Ja, wann isst man bei dir zu Mittag?
Teacher: Sehr bald.

28. Greetings

1 Y, 2 F, 3 S

29. Celebrations

1 buys balloons   2 drinks a glass of champagne

30. Festivals

Sample answer:
Meine Familie bleibt lieber zu Hause. Letztes Jahr ist meine Klasse zum Feuerwerk gegangen, aber das Wetter war schrecklich. Dieses Jahr werde ich an Silvester in die Stadtmitte gehen und ich werde tanzen gehen. Ich möchte meinen Geburtstag mit Freunden feiern, aber wir haben kein Geld.

31. Home

Sample answer:
We live in a medium sized detached house on the edge of town. We have a sunny garden, where I often play badminton with my friends. My older sister moved into her own flat a few months ago. One day I would like to travel to the United States (in order) to live on the West Coast there.

32. Places to see

1 it is one of the most popular tourist destinations in Germany
2 it is a small town
3 it is one of the oldest buildings in the town
4 in the town centre

33. At the tourist office

Transcript:
Teacher: Sie suchen Informationen beim Verkehrsamt in einer deutschen Stadt. Sie sprechen mit dem/der Angestellten im Verkehrsamt.
Teacher: Guten Tag. Wie kann ich Ihnen helfen?
Student: Ich interessiere mich für einen Ausflug am Mittwoch.
Teacher: Warum wollen Sie das machen?
Student: Weil ich gern neue Orte besuche.
Teacher: Wie finden Sie unsere Stadt?
Student: Ich finde die alten Gebäude besonders schön.
Teacher: Was wollen Sie heute machen?
Student: Heute will ich ins Stadtmuseum gehen.
Teacher: Sehr schön.
Student: Wann ist das Rathaus geöffnet?
Teacher: Um zehn Uhr.

34. Describing a town

Sample answer:
1 Ich wohne in einem Dorf und es ist hübsch/schön.
2 Unsere Kirche ist sehr alt.
3 Es gibt kein Schloss hier.
4 Ich gehe lieber in der Stadt einkaufen.
5 Gestern bin ich ins Kino gegangen.

35. Describing a region

1 any one of: to go walking / because of the beautiful hills

36. Volunteering

Wie könnte man helfen? – any one of:
• an einem Aktionsprogramm für Arbeitslose teilnehmen
• arbeitslosen Eltern bei der Jobbewerbung helfen
Warum? – um die Lebensqualität von armen Familien zu verbessern

38. Social problems

C

39. Healthy and unhealthy living

Sample answer:
Ich muss Chips / Kartoffelchips aufgeben. Als ich in Urlaub / in den Urlaub gefahren bin, habe ich drei Kilo zugenommen. Nächste Woche werde ich jeden Tag zum Fitnessraum gehen, um fitter zu werden. Ich möchte nie fettleibig werden, also versuche ich jetzt, einen gesunden Lebensstil zu pflegen / gesund zu leben.

40. Healthy eating

1 P, 2 A, 3 K, 4 E, 5 P

41. Feeling ill

Transcript:
Teacher: Sie sind im Skiurlaub in Österreich. Sie haben einen Unfall auf der Piste und sprechen mit dem Skilehrer / der Skilehrerin.
Teacher: Kann ich Ihnen helfen?
Student: Mein linkes Bein tut schrecklich weh.
Teacher: Oh je. Was ist passiert?
Student: Ich bin auf der Piste hingefallen.
Teacher: Das war Pech.
Student: Ja, ich muss sofort ins Krankenhaus fahren, glaube ich.
Teacher: Oh. Wo kann ich Ihre Eltern finden?
Student: Sie sind unten im Dorf in einem großen Hotel.
Teacher: OK. Haben Sie eine Frage?
Student: Wann kommt der Krankenwagen, um mich abzuholen?
Teacher: Bald.

42. Health issues

1 any one of: it has become a bad habit / he is addicted / unable to refuse if someone offers him a cigarette
2 C
3 any one of: his girlfriend will break up with him / his relationship will end

43. Weather

1 B, 2 A

44. Being green

Sample answer:
Positive aspects
Any two of: everything on computer so no need for paper, exercise or text books / can recycle everything / little rubbish on premises

45. Protecting the environment

1 Klimawandel zu vermeiden (NOT: seinen Effekt zu begrenzen / Strategien zu entwickeln)
2 wir müssen uns daran anpassen / uns an den Klimawandel anpassen (NOT: seinen Effekt begrenzen / Strategien entwickeln)
3 Menschen / Leute haben eine große Rolle dabei gespielt (NOT: negative Folgen)
4 extremes Wetter (NOT: any of the individual weather types)
5 die Alpen / Alpenregionen

46. Natural resources

Sample answer:
I am very interested in environmental protection. On our school roof we have solar panels, which I find great. The supermarkets should import less fruit and vegetables from faraway countries, because that is damaging to the environment. In the future I would like to work for an environmental organisation in order to help our planet.

47. Poverty

B, E

48. Global problems

1 any one of: equality / education
2 any one of: sent to war / injured in war
3 any one of: support families / raise awareness of issue and money in Europe

49. Travel

1 it's a shame / she regrets it
2 sufficient public transport
3 more investment / money for local buses / trains
4 proud

50. Countries

Sample answer:
• Wegen des schlechten Wetters hier in England hatten meine Eltern letztes Jahr eine Pauschalreise nach Griechenland für die ganze Familie gebucht. Ich habe mich von Anfang an sehr darauf gefreut, weil ich nie vorher geflogen war. Am ersten Tag des Urlaubs sind wir früh mit dem Flugzeug am Zielort angekommen und das Hotel war wunderbar. Ich bin sofort mit meiner Schwester zum Freibad gelaufen, wo wir dann den ganzen Tag bis zum Sonnenuntergang geblieben sind.
• Ich finde, der größte Vorteil von einem Urlaub im Ausland im Vergleich zu Urlaub hier in Großbritannien ist das gute Wetter, und unser griechischer Urlaub war ein echter Erfolg. Wenn man ins Ausland fährt, ist das Wetter garantiert schön. Das finde ich super, weil es bei uns zu Hause oft tagelang regnerisch und kalt ist. Natürlich kann Urlaub im Ausland ziemlich teuer werden, aber ich denke, es lohnt sich. Zum Beispiel habe ich in Griechenland einmalige Erfahrungen gesammelt und neue Städte kennengelernt.

51. Transport

Sample answer:
• Wenn ich samstags mit meinen Freunden in die Stadt fahre, nehmen wir immer die U-Bahn. Ich finde, dass die U-Bahn zuverlässiger als der Bus ist.
• Zur Schule muss ich mit dem Bus fahren, weil das am praktischsten ist. Ich würde lieber mit dem Rad fahren, aber ohne Fahrradwege wäre das zu gefährlich.
• Letztes Jahr sind wir mit dem Auto in den Urlaub gefahren, aber zuerst hatten wir eine Panne auf der Autobahn und dann war mein Bruder reisekrank.
• Am Samstag werde ich mit dem Zug nach Brighton fahren. Hoffentlich werden wir Fahrräder mieten und eine Radtour machen.

52. Directions

1 the cinema
2 left at the traffic lights
3 signs to the castle

53. Tourism

Transcript:
Teacher: Findest du Skifahren gut oder nicht?
Student: Meiner Meinung nach ist Skifahren teuer und nicht gut für die Umwelt. Die Berge finde ich sehr schön und ich gehe gern wandern. Ich interessiere mich nicht für Skifahren, weil man das nur im Winter machen kann. Ich finde andere Sportarten wie Federball und Hockey besser.
Teacher: Was hast du in den letzten Schulferien gemacht?
Student: In den Schulferien habe ich einen Tagesausflug nach Cambridge gemacht, um die Sehenswürdigkeiten zu besichtigen. Wir sind um neun Uhr früh in der Stadtmitte angekommen, aber es waren schon sehr viele Touristen unterwegs. Ich meine, dass Cambridge sehr schön ist, aber die Touristen zerstören diese kleine Stadt.
Teacher: Wohin fährst du in den Urlaub? … Warum?
Student: Wenn ich in den Urlaub fahre, versuche ich immer umweltfreundlich zu reisen. Zum Beispiel fliege ich nie mit dem Flugzeug, weil das schrecklich ist. In den langen Sommerferien arbeite ich gern freiwillig bei einer Tierschutzorganisation auf dem Land. Das finde ich besser als ein Luxushotel am Strand.
Teacher: Wie findest du Pauschalreisen?
Student: Ich habe nie an einer Pauschalreise im Ausland teilgenommen. Eine organisierte Reise interessiert mich gar nicht. Ich bin einmal mit der Bahn nach Frankreich gefahren, aber ehrlich gesagt, war das kein großer Erfolg.

54. Holiday preferences

Sample answer:
• In den Sommerferien fahre ich sehr gern ans Meer, da ich ein ziemlich großer Wassersportfan bin. Ich windsurfe äußerst gern.
• Letzten Sommer bin ich mit meiner Familie nach Spanien geflogen. Wir haben eine Woche in einem Hotel verbracht.
• Die Woche war wunderbar, weil wir in einem tollen Hotel gewohnt haben, wo es drei Freibäder gab. Wir sind jeden Tag schwimmen gegangen.
• Nächsten Sommer werde ich mit zwei Freundinnen nach München fahren, um zum Musikfest dort zu gehen. Ich freue mich sehr darauf, obwohl ich noch nie auf dem Musikfest war.

55. Hotels

1 in einem Hotel
2 schwimmen
3 Ninas Bruder
4 wieder in diesem Hotel bleiben / dieselben Zimmer reservieren

56. Campsites

1 tents
2 advisable / recommended
3 four
4 cold
5 in (at the start of) summer

57. Accommodation

Transcript:
Teacher: Übernachtest du lieber weg von zu Hause oder zu Hause? Warum?
Student: Ich übernachte gern weg von zu Hause, weil mir das ein schönes Freiheitsgefühl gibt. Ich finde es wichtig, ab und zu weg von zu Hause zu reisen, um neue Leute und Orte kennenzulernen. Wenn man immer zu Hause bleibt, wird das Leben mit der Zeit etwas langweilig.
Teacher: Was war deine beste Übernachtung weg von zu Hause?
Student: Die beste Übernachtung meines Lebens war letztes Jahr, als ich Urlaub auf dem Bauernhof meines Onkels gemacht habe. Das hat mir besonders gut gefallen, weil ich mich sehr für Tiere interessiere. Letztes Jahr durften wir zum ersten Mal in der neuen Hütte auf einem der Felder übernachten. Das liegt ziemlich weit vom Bauernhof entfernt, und wir durften dort viel Lärm machen, ohne dabei die Erwachsenen oder die Tiere zu stören.
Teacher: Wo willst du in Zukunft übernachten?
Student: In Zukunft will ich viel reisen, aber ich denke, es ist am besten, wenn man wegen der Arbeit reist. Ich werde daher eine Stelle im Ausland suchen, sobald ich mit dem Studium fertig bin. Auf diese Weise werde ich die Welt entdecken und auch Geld verdienen.

58. Holiday destinations

Sample answer:
As a family we go every year to the Baltic Sea, where we always spend our first day in the biggest nature park in Europe. I would also recommend a day trip to the picturesque villages, in order to visit the wonderful markets and buy lots of good-value souvenirs. Before we discovered this holiday location, we had always spent our summer holiday in a historic capital city.

59. Holiday experiences

1 P, 2 N, 3 P+N

60. Holiday activities

1 dogs can't run free
2 dogs can't go into the minimarket
3 no cycling in the playground
4 children under 8 can't use the open air pool alone
5 no mobile phone use after 9 p.m.

61. Holiday plans

Sample answer:
Ich reise gern und besuche gern neue Orte. Als ich in München war, habe ich ein paar / einige echt nette Leute kennengelernt. Wir werden uns im Mai wieder treffen, um einen Tagesausflug an den See zu machen. Ich möchte danach Urlaub mit Freunden machen, weil das so viel Spaß macht.

62. Holiday problems

Transcript:
Teacher: Sie sind an der Hotelrezeption. Sie beschweren sich über ein Problem.
Teacher: Guten Tag. Wie kann ich Ihnen helfen?
Student: Der Fernseher ist kaputt.
Teacher: OK. Wir werden mal schauen. Was ist Ihre Zimmernummer?
Student: Ich bin im Zimmer Nummer dreihundertacht.

Teacher: Wie lange bleiben Sie bei uns?
Student: Ich bleibe zwei Wochen.
Teacher: Was machen Sie gern im Urlaub?
Student: Ich besuche gern die Sehenswürdigkeiten.
Teacher: Toll.
Student: Was kann man hier am Abend machen?
Teacher: Gute Frage ...

63. School subjects

freiwillig arbeiten

64. Opinions about school

Transcript:
Teacher: Wie findest du die Schulfächer?
Student: Mein Lieblingsfach ist Geschichte, weil ich es ein sehr interessantes Fach finde, obwohl meine Freunde es echt schwierig finden. In Zukunft möchte ich vielleicht Geschichte und Wirtschaftslehre an der Uni studieren.
Teacher: Was war der beste Tag an der Schule letztes Jahr?
Student: Letztes Jahr habe ich an einem regionalen Mathewettbewerb teilgenommen. Unsere Mannschaft hatte dabei viel Erfolg und wir sind alle mit einer Medaille zurückgekommen, obwohl wir nicht auf den ersten Platz gekommen sind. Ja, dieser Tag war ein tolles Erlebnis ...
Teacher: Findest du die Schule stressig?
Student: Ich finde die Schule nicht stressig, weil ich fleißig lerne und die meisten Fächer gefallen mir gut. Die Prüfungen sind immer sehr stressig, weil es sehr wichtig ist, dass man jedes Mal eine gute Note bekommt.

65. Types of schools

Sample answer:
- Ich besuche eine Gesamtschule mit etwa tausend Schülern. Als ich zum ersten Mal in diese Schule gegangen bin, war ich erstaunt, weil das Schulgebäude einfach so viel größer war als meine Grundschule und es war sehr imposant.
- Mein Lieblingsfach ist Kunst, aber ich finde Naturwissenschaften sehr schwierig und bekomme meistens schlechte Noten, obwohl ich immer fleißig lerne.
- Letztes Jahr bin ich mit der Klasse in die Schweiz auf Klassenfahrt gegangen und das hat echt viel Spaß gemacht.
- Nach der Schule hoffe ich, an die Fachhochschule zu kommen, um dort Kunst zu studieren. / Nach der Schule hoffe ich, dass ich an die Fachhochschule komme, um dort Kunst zu studieren.

66. Primary school

1 any one of: frech / nicht brav / hat sich schlecht benommen
2 die Lehrer

68. School exchange

Transcript:
Teacher: Du sprichst mit deinem Austauschpartner / deiner Austauschpartnerin in der Mittagspause in der deutschen Schule.
Teacher: Hallo, wie findest du es hier in der Schule?
Student: Es gefällt mir hier gut.

Teacher: Wie findest du die Lehrer?
Student: Sie sind meistens nett.
Teacher: Wie findest du den Schultag bei uns?
Student: Die Schule beginnt zu früh, denke ich.
Teacher: Was willst du heute Abend nach der Schule machen?
Student: Ich will ins Kino gehen.
Teacher: Willst du etwas wissen?
Student: Wann ist die Schule heute aus?
Teacher: Um halb drei.

69. School events

1 five
2 spoke / said a word
3 talented / gifted
4 loudest

70. School day

1 behind some doors / classrooms
2 they are familiar / she likes one voice
3 it / the teacher is dictating to pupils
4 C

71. School facilities

Transcript:
Teacher: Wie helfen moderne Schulen beim Lernen?
Student: Ich besuche eine moderne Schule, die am Stadtrand von Hull liegt. Die Schule ist sehr gut ausgestattet, weil sie erst zwei Jahre alt ist. Als Schüler müssen wir die Gebäude respektieren, und unsere Schulordnung ist daher irrsinnig streng, aber das finde ich gerecht. Wenn man ein schönes Schulgebäude hat, muss man gut darauf aufpassen, und die Schüler lernen dabei besser.
Teacher: Was war deine beste Schulstunde?
Student: Gestern im Theaterunterricht haben wir an einem ausgezeichneten Kurs teilgenommen. Die Schauspieler vom Stadttheater haben uns besucht und sie haben uns in der Aula unterrichtet. Das hat so viel Spaß gemacht, dass ich jetzt denke, ich möchte in Zukunft Schauspieler werden!
Teacher: Wie ist ein guter Lehrer oder eine gute Lehrerin? Warum?
Student: Meiner Meinung nach ist ein guter Lehrer jemand, der immer interessante Stunden unterrichtet und auch fair ist. Ich mag es nicht, wenn ein Lehrer immer sauer ist und dauernd Strafarbeiten gibt.
Teacher: Wie willst du deine Schule verbessern?
Student: Obwohl unsere Schule modern ist, mag ich es nicht, dass wir eine Uniform tragen müssen. Wenn ich Direktorin wäre, gäbe es weder Krawatten noch Schulschuhe, weil sie unbequem und unmodisch sind. Es würde mir am besten gefallen, wenn wir unsere eigene Kleidung zur Schule tragen könnten.

72. School rules

Sample answer:
It really annoys me that we are not allowed to wear trainers to school. Last term a pupil/student smoked in the playground, because he thought that was cool. But the head teacher was very angry and sent the boy straight home. I would never smoke or drink alcohol at school, because I wouldn't want to get lines/be punished.

73. Pressures at school

Sample answer:
Die Schule gefällt mir sehr gut. Obwohl man oft Klassenarbeiten schreiben muss, kann man sich immer noch auf die Klassenfahrten freuen. Letztes Jahr habe ich fleißig gelernt, um gute Noten zu bekommen, und meine Eltern haben sich sehr darüber gefreut. Ich möchte auf/an die Universität gehen, weil ich Tierarzt / Tierärztin werden will.

74. Future study

Transcript:
Teacher: Warum sind Pläne dir wichtig oder nicht wichtig?
Student: Im Großen und Ganzen sind mir Pläne nicht so wichtig, weil ich lieber für den heutigen Tag lebe. Ich bin noch zu jung, um genau zu wissen, was ich in Zukunft machen werde, und es ist mir wichtiger, dass ich mich auf die Gegenwart konzentriere.
Teacher: Welche Pläne hattest du in der Grundschule?
Student: Als ich in der Grundschule war, wollte ich unbedingt Pilotin werden, weil mir das so aufregend und exotisch vorgekommen ist. Ich wollte in ferne Länder reisen und mehrere Sprachen sprechen. Sprachen lernen finde ich noch gut, aber ich möchte nicht mehr Pilotin werden, weil ich Angst vor dem Fliegen habe!
Teacher: Warum können sich Pläne oft ändern?
Student: Ich finde, als Teenager hat man so viele Ideen im Kopf, dass sich die Pläne oft ändern. Daher finde ich es besser, keine Pläne zu machen, weil man dann nie enttäuscht werden kann!

75. Training

Transcript:
Teacher: Willst du ein Arbeitspraktikum machen? … Warum oder warum nicht?
Student: Letztes Jahr habe ich ein Arbeitspraktikum an einer Grundschule gemacht, weil meine Mutter an der Schule arbeitet. Das Praktikum war ein gutes Erlebnis, weil ich herausgefunden habe, was man als Lehrer machen muss. Auf der anderen Seite war es nicht so gut, weil der Tag anstrengend war.
Teacher: Welche Arbeit hast du schon gemacht?
Student: Seit einem Jahr arbeite ich samstags als Schiedsrichter. Ich musste zuerst einen Kurs besuchen, und danach durfte ich Fußballspielen leiten. Ich finde das sehr gut, weil ich Geld dabei verdiene, aber die jungen Fußballer sind oft sehr nervig, weil sie immer gewinnen wollen!
Teacher: Was würdest du nicht gern bei einem Arbeitspraktikum machen?
Student: Ich würde nie ein Arbeitspraktikum in einem Büro machen, weil ich mich nicht so sehr für Büroarbeit interessiere. Ich würde weder gern Akten abheften noch Telefonanrufe machen, weil mir das als Zeitverschwendung vorkommt.
Teacher: Was findest du besser, trainieren oder studieren?
Student: Meiner Meinung nach ist es am Wichtigsten, sich nach dem Schulabschluss weiterzubilden. Wenn man auf die Uni geht, hat man später bessere Arbeitschancen, weil man gut qualifiziert ist. Ich persönlich würde gern Medienkunde an der Uni studieren, weil ich neulich beschlossen habe, dass ich Karriere als Journalist machen möchte.

76. CV

Sample answer:
• Ich bin freundlich, aber ich bin nicht sehr geduldig.
• Im Moment besuche ich eine Gesamtschule in der Stadtmitte.
• Ich treibe gern Sport, weil das entspannend ist.
• Ich arbeite als Kellner in der Stadt, und das gefällt mir gut.

77. Jobs

1 any one of: Saturday job / cashier / in a shoe shop
2 any one of: works long hours / exhausted after work (not: she's a doctor)
3 any two of: works in a hut in the garden / collects original ties (not: he is funny / collects originals)

78. Professions

Sample answer:
Her boss is called Angelika. She is forty years old and very nice. My mother likes her job, but she finds the long hours tiring. In the evenings we like to watch television together. But last week she worked nights.

79. Job ambitions

1 B
2 nette Kollegen / ein gutes Team

80. Opinions about jobs

1 P+N, 2 N, 3 P+N, 4 P, 5 N, 6 P, 7 P+N, 8 P+N, 9 N, 10 P

81. Job adverts

Sample answer:
1 Ich will Lehrer(in) werden.
2 Meine Tante verdient fünfzehn Euro pro Stunde.
3 Sie arbeitet in einem Büro in der Stadtmitte.
4 Ich brauche einen Job, weil ich kein Geld habe.
5 Letztes Jahr habe ich als Kellner gearbeitet.

82. Applying for a job

1 F, 2 R, 3 R, 4 NT, 5 R, 6 F, 7 NT, 8 F

83. Job interview

Listen to the recording

Transcript:
Teacher: Sie bewerben sich am Telefon für einen Job als Kellner / Kellnerin in der Schweiz.
Teacher: Wie kann ich Ihnen helfen?
Student: Ich telefoniere wegen des Jobs als Kellner in Ihrem Restaurant.
Teacher: Haben Sie schon Arbeitserfahrung?
Student: Ja, ich habe im Café in der Stadt gearbeitet.
Teacher: Warum wollen Sie bei uns arbeiten?
Student: Ich möchte meine Deutschkenntnisse verbessern.
Teacher: Was für Charaktereigenschaften haben Sie?
Student: Ich bin sehr fleißig und freundlich.
Teacher: Toll.
Student: Darf ich fragen, was die Arbeitsstunden sein werden?
Teacher: Sie müssen von acht Uhr bis vierzehn Uhr arbeiten.

84. Part-time jobs

Sample answer:
• Samstags arbeite ich jetzt seit zwei Monaten als Assistent im Sportverein und ich finde den Job abwechslungsreich und sehr interessant. Ich lerne viele neue Fähigkeiten, und die Erfahrung ist sehr nützlich, denke ich. Ich verdiene nicht viel Geld, aber das ist mir nicht so wichtig, weil die Erfahrung wichtiger für die Zukunft ist.
• Letzten Sommer habe ich bei einem Sportcamp in der Nähe von Manchester gearbeitet. Das war ein tolles Erlebnis, weil ich viele nette Leute kennengelernt habe. Ich konnte auch meine Sprachkenntnisse benutzen, denn manche Kinder waren aus Europa und konnten kein Englisch sprechen. Ich habe die Arbeit anstrengend gefunden, weil man immer gut gelaunt sein musste. Ich musste auch Aktivitäten selbst organisieren, und das war ziemlich stressig. Ich würde so einen Job gern noch mal machen und nächstes Jahr werde ich mich um eine ähnliche Stelle in Amerika bewerben, weil das meine Traumstelle wäre!

Grammar

85. Gender and plurals

(a) die Anmeldung / die Anmeldungen
(b) der Fahrer / die Fahrer
(c) das Rührei / die Rühreier
(d) die Haltestelle / die Haltestellen
(e) der Fernseher / die Fernseher
(f) das Brötchen / die Brötchen

86. Cases and prepositions

(a) gegen die Mauer
(b) außer einem Kind
(c) trotz des Schnees
(d) nach einer Stunde
(e) zu den Geschäften
(f) ohne ein Wort
(g) während des Sommers
(h) beim Arzt

87. Prepositions with accusative or dative

(a) der
(b) den
(c) dem
(d) die
(e) der
(f) den
(g) den
(h) die

88. *Dieser / jeder, kein / mein*

(a) I don't want to go shopping.
(b) She spent all her pocket money on clothes.
(c) Such people quickly become impolite.
(d) I find my life boring.
(e) This time we are going by train.
(f) His parents are unemployed.
(g) I find such rules stupid.
(h) Which book are you reading?

89. Adjective endings

(a) ausgezeichnete
(b) warmes
(c) preisgünstiges
(d) zentrale
(e) beliebtes
(f) meistverkauften
(g) verkaufsoffenen
(h) persönlichen

90. Comparisons

(a) einfacher
(b) jünger
(c) besser
(d) nützlicher
(e) winzigste
(f) langweiligste
(g) beliebteste
(h) schlechtesten

91. Personal pronouns

(a) sie   (c) dir   (e) mir, ihm
(b) mir   (d) uns   (f) mir

92. Word order

Possible answers:
(a) Ich fahre gern ins Ausland.
(b) Man findet Informationen beim Verkehrsamt.
(c) Normalerweise esse ich gesund.
(d) Manchmal sehen wir im Jugendklub Filme.
(e) Im Juli möchte ich im Sportzentrum arbeiten.
(f) Letztes Jahr habe ich in einem Büro gearbeitet.
(g) Morgen werde ich mit meiner Mutter ins Kino gehen.

93. Conjunctions

(a) Ich habe bei meiner Großmutter gewohnt, während meine Mutter im Krankenhaus war.
(b) Ich bin ins Café gegangen, nachdem ich ein T-Shirt gekauft habe.
(c) Ich war in Spanien im Urlaub, als ich einen neuen Freund kennengelernt habe.
(d) Er ist sehr beliebt, obwohl er nicht sehr freundlich ist.
(e) Ich werde für eine neue Gitarre sparen, wenn ich einen Nebenjob finde.
(f) Ich bin froh, dass ich gute Noten in der Schule bekommen habe.
(g) Ich muss meine Eltern fragen, ob ich ins Konzert gehen darf.
(h) Er hat mir gesagt, dass er mit mir ins Kino gehen will.

94. More on word order

1 (a) Ich fahre nach Italien, um meine Verwandten zu besuchen.
  (b) Ich gehe zum Sportzentrum, um 5 Kilo abzunehmen.
2 (a) Ich versuche, anderen zu helfen.
  (b) Ich habe vor, auf die Uni zu gehen.
3 (a) Das ist das Geschäft, das tolle Kleidung verkauft.
  (b) Hier ist eine Kellnerin, die sehr unhöflich ist.

95. The present tense

(a) höre   (d) Isst   (g) Gibt
(b) schläft   (e) fahren   (h) bleibt
(c) geht   (f) machen

96. Separable and reflexive verbs

1 (a) Ich sehe fern. Ich habe ferngesehen.
  (b) Ich steige um sechs Uhr um. Ich bin um sechs Uhr umgestiegen.
  (c) Ich lade Musik herunter. Ich werde Musik herunterladen.
  (d) Ich bin eingestiegen. Ich muss einsteigen.
2 (a) mich   (b) uns   (c) euch   (d) sich

97. Commands

To pay attention to their darlings and not to use the green spaces and paths as a dog toilet.

98. Present tense modals

(a) Ich muss um einundzwanzig Uhr ins Bett gehen.
(b) In der Schule darf man nicht rauchen.
(c) Du sollst Energie sparen.
(d) Kannst du mir zu Hause helfen?
(e) Ich will in den Ferien Ski fahren.
(f) Ich möchte nicht fernsehen.
(g) Ich kann das Problem nicht lösen.

99. Imperfect modals

1 (a) Ich musste Hausaufgaben machen.
  (b) Sie konnten mir nicht helfen.
  (c) Er wollte eine neue Hose kaufen.
  (d) Wir sollten die Fotos hochladen.
  (e) In der Schule durfte man nie Kaugummi kauen.
  (f) Alle Schüler mussten bis sechzehn Uhr bleiben.
2 (a) Es könnte schwierig werden.
  (b) Ich möchte die gelbe Jacke umtauschen.

100. The perfect tense 1

(a) Ich habe eine Jacke gekauft.
(b) Wir sind nach Portugal geflogen.
(c) Ich habe meinen Freund gesehen.
(d) Lena und Hannah sind in die Stadt gegangen.
(e) Ich habe meine Tante besucht.
(f) Ich bin im Hotel geblieben.
(g) Was hast du zu Mittag gegessen?
(h) Am Samstag hat er Musik gehört.

101. The perfect tense 2

(a) Ich habe zu viele Kekse gegessen.
(b) Haben Sie gut geschlafen?
(c) Wir haben uns am Bahnhof getroffen.
(d) Ich war krank, weil ich den ganzen Tag gestanden habe.
(e) Ich weiß, dass du umgestiegen bist.
(f) Warum hast du die E-Mail geschrieben?
(g) Ich habe ihr empfohlen, dass sie nicht mitkommen sollte.
(h) Ich war traurig, als er gestorben ist.

102. The imperfect tense

(a) Sie hatte Angst.
(b) Es war hoffnungslos.
(c) Es gab Toiletten im Erdgeschoss.
(d) Hörtest du das?
(e) Plötzlich kam uns der Mann entgegen.
(f) Das war eine Überraschung, nicht?
(g) Es war niemand zu Hause.
(h) Sie spielten gern Tischtennis.

103. The future tense

(a) Ich werde das Spiel gewinnen.
(b) Wir werden in den Freizeitpark gehen.
(c) Sie werden eine große Wohnung mieten.
(d) Ihr werdet große Schwierigkeiten haben.
(e) Er wird die Prüfung bestehen.
(f) Nächste Woche werden wir umziehen.
(g) Werdet ihr euch später treffen?
(h) Ich werde mich um sechs Uhr anziehen.

104. The conditional

(a) Ich würde gern ins Theater gehen.
(b) Er würde nie zu spät ankommen.
(c) Wir würden nie Bier trinken.
(d) Würden Sie mir bitte helfen?
(e) Zum Geburtstag würde sie am liebsten Geld bekommen.
(f) Nächstes Jahr würden sie vielleicht heiraten.
(g) Wenn Latein Pflicht wäre, würde ich auf eine andere Schule gehen.
(h) Wenn ich das machen würde, gäbe es Krach mit meinen Eltern.

105. The pluperfect tense

(a) Ich hatte zu Mittag gegessen.

(b) Sie hatten als Stadtführer gearbeitet.

(c) Warst du schwimmen gegangen?

(d) Wir waren in Kontakt geblieben.

(e) Sie waren mit dem Rad in die Stadt gefahren.

(f) Ich hatte sie vor einigen Monaten besucht, aber damals war sie schon krank.

(g) Bevor ich ins Haus gegangen war, hatte ich ein Gesicht am Fenster gesehen.

(h) Obwohl ich kaum mit ihm gesprochen hatte, schien er sehr freundlich zu sein.

106. Questions

1 (a) Lesen Sie gern Science-Fiction-Bücher?

(b) Finden Sie Ihre Arbeit anstrengend?

(c) Möchten Sie nur Teilzeit arbeiten?

(d) Werden Sie nächsten Sommer nach Australien auswandern?

2 (a) Wer könnte mir helfen?

(b) Wann macht das Restaurant auf?

(c) Warum gibt es eine Tasche hier?

(d) Wie komme ich zum Dom?

(e) Was kann man abends machen?

107. Time markers

(a) Seit drei Jahren spiele ich Klavier.

(b) Letzte Woche hat er die Hausaufgaben nicht gemacht.

(c) Nächsten Sommer werden wir in den Bergen wandern gehen.

(d) Am Anfang wollten wir das Betriebspraktikum nicht machen.

(e) In Zukunft wird man alle Lebensmittel elektronisch kaufen.

(f) Ich hoffe, eines Tages Disneyland zu besuchen.

(g) Vorgestern hatte ich Halsschmerzen.

(h) Früher haben sie / Sie oft Tennis gespielt.

108. Numbers

(a) 14.–23. Mai

(b) 07:45

(c) €3,80

(d) 27. Januar 1756

(e) €185 Millionen

(f) 15% Ermäßigung

(g) 16:35

(h) 35 Grad

121. Vocabulary

(a) Baltic Sea

(b) English Channel

(c) Lake Constance

(d) Moselle

(e) Rhine

(f) Danube

(g) Geneva

(h) Cologne

(i) Munich

(j) Vienna

Published by Pearson Education Limited, 80 Strand, London, WC2R 0RL.

www.pearsonschoolsandfecolleges.co.uk

Text and illustrations © Pearson 2017
Typeset and illustrated by Kamae Design
Produced by Out of House Publishing Solutions Ltd

Cover illustration by Miriam Sturdee

The right of Harriette Lanzer to be identified as author of this work has been asserted by her in accordance with the Copyright, Designs and Patents Act 1988.

First published 2017

20

10 9 8 7 6 5

British Library Cataloguing in Publication Data
A catalogue record for this book is available from the British Library

ISBN 978 1 292 13143 6

Printed in Great Britain by Bell and Bain Ltd, Glasgow

We are grateful to the following for permission to reproduce copyright material:

Statistics
Statistic on page 9 http://www.jugendundmedien.ch/chancen-und-gefahren/soziale-netwerke.html, Jugend und Medien, Nationale Plattform zur Förderung von Medienkompetenzen, Bundesamt für Sozialversicherungen

Text
Extract on page 7 from Thomas Sünder: *Wer Ja sagt, darf auch Tante Inge ausladen. Tipps vom Profi für die perfekte Hochzeitsfeier*

© 2013 Blanvalet Taschenbuch Verlag, München, in der Verlagsgruppe Random House GmbH; Extract on page 45 adapted from *50 einfache Dinge, die Sie tun können, um die Welt zu retten. Und wie Sie dabei Geld sparen.* Heyne (Schlumberger A. 2015); Extract on page 70 adapted from Christine Nöstlinger, *Stundenplan* © 1975, 1992 Beltz & Gelberg in der Verlagsgruppe Beltz · Weinheim Basel; Extract on page 26 from *Emil und die Detektive*, Dressler (Kästner E. 2011), © Atrium Verlag, Zürich 1935; Extract on page 82 adapted from *Der Marder mit den Katzenpfoten und andere Geschichten*, BoD – Books on Demand (Lapp K. 2013)

Photographs

(Key: b-bottom; c-centre; l-left; r-right; t-top)

123RF.com: Dmitriy Shironosov 55, Graham Oliver 56, HONGQI ZHANG 10, photopips 79bc, pressmaster 20, wavebreakmediamicro 79bl, weerapat wattanapichayakul 14bl (b); **Alamy Images:** Agencja Fotograficzna Caro 34, Blend Images 23, Cultura Creative (RF) 107, Jim West 47, OJO Images Ltd 28; **Fotolia.com:** Artem Merzlenko 77t, belahoche 37b, davit85 67, Funny Studio 59, John Smith 29, kristina rütten 51, Monkey Business 38, monticelllo 14l, Phase4Photography 81, slonme 14br (b), Studio Gi 71t, Svyatoslav Lypynskyy 14br (a), Syda Productions 100, TEMISTOCLE LUCARELLI 77b, V&P Photo Studio 80, WavebreakMediaMicro 98, YakobchukOlena 39; **Getty Images:** Anadolu Agency 48, Siri Stafford 65; **Imagestate Media:** John Foxx Collection 53; **Pearson Education Ltd:** Sophie Bluy 73, 104l, 104r; **PhotoDisc:** 70; **Shutterstock.com:** Alexander Raths 78, Alexandr Vlassyuk 14c, Andre Blais 95, dotshock 19, Ersler Dmitry 14r, Goodluz 71b, gosphotodesign 79cl, infografick 26, Joshua Haviv 61, Maksym Gorpenyuk 57, Martin Valigursky 58, Masson 2, Mikadun 32, Monkey Business Images 3, Nata-Lia 14c (b), oliveromg 79cr, racorn 76, RoxyFer 16, runzelkorn 75, S-F 14c (a), Singkham 79br, SpeedKingz 84, Vicki L. Miller 36, wavebreakmedia 37tr, You can more 14bl (a); **www.imagesource.com:** 60, 79c

All other images © Pearson Education

Note from the publisher
Pearson has robust editorial processes, including answer and fact checks, to ensure the accuracy of the content in this publication, and every effort is made to ensure this publication is free of errors. We are, however, only human, and occasionally errors do occur. Pearson is not liable for any misunderstandings that arise as a result of errors in this publication, but it is our priority to ensure that the content is accurate. If you spot an error, please do contact us at resourcescorrections@pearson.com so we can make sure it is corrected.